LANCASTER COUNTY, VIRGINIA

DEED BOOK ABSTRACTS

1701-1706

Ruth and Sam Sparacio

The Antient Press Collection
from

Colonial Roots
Millsboro, Delaware
2016

Colonial Roots

Helping You Grow Your Family Tree

ISBN 978-1-68034-334-2

p.
1
THIS INDENTURE made ye Eleventh day of March in the fourteenth year of ye reigne of or: Sovereigne Lord William by the grace of God of England, Scottland, France & Ireland, King, Defender of the faith &c., Betweene RICHARD FLINT of ye Pish: of St. Marys Wt. Chapple in ye County of Lancaster of ye one part and JOHN LAWRIE of ye aforesd. Pish: & County of the other part; (Witnesseth) that the said RICHD: FLINT for & in consideracon of ye sume of Thirty pounds lawfull money of England to him in hand paid or secured to be paid by the said JOHN LAWRIE att & before the sealing & delivery of the sd. presents, the receipt whereof he doth hereby acknowledge and for divese good causes & consideracons in the Law, him thereunto moveing, hath granted sold & confirmed and by these presents doth grant and confirme unto ye said JOHN LAWRIE all ye messuage peice or p:cell of land situate & being in ye Parrish aforesd. Beginning att a marked white Oake, corner tree standing on a point tree unto Mr. THOMAS MARSHALLs Dwelling House on ye Northward side of a Creek called MARSHALLS CREEK, & River, the severall courses thereof to a marked corner white Oake of JOHN BERRIES standing on ye Westward side of a Cove called WINSMOORES COVE, neer unto ye mouth thereof, thence by and along JNO: BERRIES line of marked trees 326 pole to a corner red Oake standing neer unto Mr. THO: MARSHALLs Tobbo. Ground upon ye Hill, thence along Mr. THO: MARSHALLs line of marked trees N. E. 74 pole to a marked corner Dogwood standing on ye Northward side of a Branch or Swamp that makes ye head of MARSHALLS CREEK just by ye Path yt: leads from ye COURT HOUSE to ye said MARSHALLs, thence down ye said Swamp & Creek E. 1/2 point S. 60 pole to ye corner white Oake where it first began, the said land being part of a tract of land formerly taken up by Capt. THO: HACKETT as may more at large appear by Pattent dated ye 9th of June 1652, and late in ye tenor & occupacon of JOHN SHARP and by him sold to the said RICHD: FLINT containing by estimacon Sixty acres more or less and all houses out houses barns stables tobbo. houses in & upon the said Sixty acres of land & all orchards gardens pastures fences woods timber & timber trees ways waters priviledges comodities & appurtenances whatsoever to ye said messuage p:cell of land belonging; and ye reversions & remainders rents issues & profitts of all & singular ye said premisses and all ye Estate right benefitt & demand whatsoever of ye said RICHD: FLINT of & to ye same or any part thereof, together with all escripts minumts. & writeings which he now hath in his custody or yt: he can come by

p.
2
To have and to hold the sd. messuage or tenemts. of Land & premisses aforesd. unto ye said JOHN LAWRIE his heires & assignes forever to ye only proper use of ye said JOHN LAWRIE is heires & assignes for evermore; To be helden of the Cheife Lord or Lords of the fee or fees of ye premisses by the rents & services for ye same due and of right accustomed to be paid, And the said RICHD: FLINT for himselfe his heires agree to and with ye said JOHN LAWRIE that he att ye time of ye enfealing & delivery of these premisses hath in himselfe good right and full & absolute authoritye to sell & confirme the said p:cell of land & premisses & every parcell thereof & every of their appurtenanes unto ye said JOHN LAWRIE his heires & assignes free & clear & freely acquitted from all manner of former & other gifts sales dowers

& Titles of Dower Judgments & execucons and from all other charges & incumbrances whatsoever had made & supposed to be done by the said RICHD: FLINT his heires or assignes or any other p:sons claiming under him and that he ye said RICHD: FLINT his heires & assignes upon ye reasonable request of ye sd. JNO: LAWRIE his heires att ye next Court held for this County or at any other Court held acknowledge these presents and shall & will at any time within ten yeares next after ye date hereof att ye reasonable request and proper charges & cost in ye Law of ye said JNO: LAWRIE his heires and assignes acknowledge & execute all & every such devices in ye Law for the more better asureing & conveying of said tract of land & premises aforesd. unto ye said JOHN LAWRIE as by the said JOHN LAWRIE his heires or assignes

p. 3 are advised or required. In Wittness whereof the parties first above named hath hereunto sett his hand & seale the day & year first above written
Sealed & delivered in presence of
(no witnesses recorded)   RICHD. FLINT   Seale
   Recognitr: in Cur Com Lancaster uno decimo March 1701/2 p RICHD. FLINT et Uxor. et Record p Idem
                     Test JOS: TAYLOE, Cl

   KNOW ALL MEN by these presents that I RICHD: FLINT of ye Pish: of St. Marys White Chapple in the County of Lancaster am holden unto JNO: LAWRIE of ye said Pish & County his heires in ye full sume of Sixty pounds lawfull money of England to ye true paymt. whereof well & truely to be made I bind my selfe my heires firmly by these presents. Sealed with my seale this 11th day of March 1701/2
   THE CONDITION of ye above obligacon is such that as RICHD: FLINT hath this day sold unto JOHN LAWRIE one tract of land Now if RICHD. FLINT shall at ye next Court held for this County cause ye said Land to be acknowledged and finally that ye said RICHD: FLINT shall fully keep all clauses of ye said Sale, That then this present obligacon to be void or else to abide in full power force & virtue
Sealed & delivered in presence of
(no witnesses recorded)   RICHD. FLINT
   Recognitr. in Cur Com Lanc. 11th March 1701/2 p RICHD. FLINT & Recordt.
                     JOS: TAYLOE, Cl.

p. 4 KNOW ALL MEN by these presents tht I JOHN PURVIS of LONDON, Merchant, Administr: of ye Will annext of MOTTROM WRIGHT, late of MILE END in the Parrish of St. Dunstans Stepney als. STEVONHEATH in the County of Middx., Mercht., deced., dureing the infancy of MOTTROM WRIGHT, Son of the said MOTTROM WRIGHT, deced., have for sundry good causes appointed my Trusty & well beloved Friend, EDWIN THACKER in the Co. of Middx. in Virginia Gemnt. to be my true & lawfull Attorney (as Administratr. of the said MOTTROM WRIGHT, deced., during the infancy of his said Son, MOTTROM WRIGHT) into all those houses orchards plantations and hereditaments with the appurtenances to enter to give and deliver possession thereof and of the sd. premises unto the sd. JOHN PURVIS or the said MOTTROM WRIGHT as he shall be required and directed. And I do hereby further grant unto my sd. Attorney (during the infancy of the sd. MORTON WRIGHT) full power to implead and condemn all p:sons as are debtors to the said Estate and discharges

to deliver and to execute and finish all and everything wch: may be necessary
of the said Estate in such manner as I the said JOHN PURVIS in my owne p:son
might or would do confirmeing and alloweing the same to be done giveing my
said Attorney power to make more Attorneys under him if he shall think fitt.
In Wittness whereof I have hereunto sett my hand and seale this 10th day of
November Anno Dm. 1701 and in the 13 year of the reigne of or: Sovereigne
Lord William the Third by the grace of God, King of England, Scottland, France
& Ireland, Defendr. of the faith, &c.
Sealed & delivered in ye presence of
    THO: GRAVES,   JOHN PURVIS
    SAMLL. GOSLIN,
    THO: MERRALL
   Probat: uno decimo die March 1701/02 p sacramt. THO: GRAVES & SAMLL.
GOSLIN. Jurat in Cur.
               Test JOS: TAYLOE, Cl.

   I JAMES PUCKLE Notary and Tabellion Publick dwelling in LONDON by Royall
Authority admitted and sworne, do hereby certifye and attest that Mr. JNO:
PURVIS, Merchant, in the aforegoing Letter of Attorney mentioned, did signe
seale and as his act and deed deliver the said Letter of

p.   Attorney done in LONDON aforesaid the tenth day of Novembr: Anno
5   Dom. 1701
      JABUS PUCKLE   Notarius   Publick
   Record   23d March 1701/2.   JOS: TAYLOE, Cl.

   KNOW ALL MEN by these presents that I JAMES MacCLUER, Merchant of the
Ship, "WILLIAM of BELFAST" in the Kingdome of Ireland and now in Virginia
do hereby appoint my trusty Friend, THO: CARTER, of the County of Lancaster
in Virginia my lawfull Attorney to receive all debts from all p:sons whatsoever and do impower him to sue any persons that will not pay and appoint one
or more Attorneys under him as occasions shall require and further I do hereby reatify whatsoever my Attorney shall lawfully doe as just and faire as if I
my selfe were p:sonally present. Wittness my hand and seale this 23d day of
Febry. 1701
Signed Sealed and delivered in presence of
    HEN: CARTER,   JAMES McCLUER
    WILLIAM MORE
   Proate County of Lancaster 11th March 1701/2
         Test   JOS: TAYLOE, Cl.

   KNOW ALL MEN by these presents that we NICHOLAS GEORGE of Xt.
Church Parish in the County of Lancaster, Planter, and MARY GEORGE, Wife
unto the said NICHOLAS GEORGE, are bound unto WILLIAM MITCHELL of St.
Marys Wt. Chappell in the aforesd. County in the sume of Twenty thousand
pounds of good legall Tobo. and caske convenient to water in the abovesd.
County upon demand to be well and truely made and done we bind our selves
our heires by these presents. Sealed with our seales dated this 11th day of
March 1701/2
   THE CONDICON of this Obligacon is such that whereas NICHOLAS GEORGE sup-
posing himselfe to have a right to a p:cell of land formerly belonging to his
Grandfather, NICHOLAS GEORGE (deced), being in COROTOMAN in Lancr. County

and by him, sd. NICHOLAS GEORE as aforesd. (deced), in and by his Last Will & Testament did bequeath and give unto his Daughter, GRACE GEORGE, the now Wife of THOMAS SAMPSON of the aforesaid County and before the intermarriage was relict and widow of JOHN ARNOLD (deced), who in his life time did occupy and possess and enjoy the said Lands, WILLIAM MITCHELL by the free license and consent of him the said ARNOLD pt. of the aforesaid land hath ever since occupied and enjoyed the other part him the said SAMPSON by virtue of his Wife doth possess for and dureing her life, after whose dec: the said

p. 6   NICHOLAS GEORGE aforesaid conceiveing himselfe to be heire unto the said land for the value of 2000 lbs. of Tobo. in hand paid, the rect.
whereof he doth acknowledge to be fully satisfyed and hath sold unto WILLIAM MITCHELL of the aforesaid County all his right wch: he hath after her the said GRACE SAMPSON (deced) which sd. land is on the North West side of COROTOMAN RIVER joyning upon the land of JOHN EDWARDS, upon the line of marked trees before NICHOLAS HEALs last Survey, he the said NICHOLAS GEORGE doth for himselfe his heires from hence forth and forever after the death of her the said GRACE, Daughter of the said NICHOLAS GEORGE, SENR., (deced), as aforesd. quitt claims to the said land and the said MARY GEORGE, Wife unto him the said NICHOLAS GEORGE, from her Thirds of Dower doth give her full assent to the sale thereof and the same to save harmless to the only proper use of him the sd. WM. MITCHELL from him the said NICHOLAS GEORGE and MARY his Wife their heires and assignes for ever att all times fully p:forme and keep; the said MARY shall her own part as in right of Dower shall acknowledge at the next Court held for this County that then this obligacon to be void and of none effect or else to be and remaine in full power and vertue Signed Sealed & delivered in the presence of us

     THO: MARTIN.   NICHOLAS GEORGE
     JOHN CARNEGIE   MARY GEORGE
     & recorded in Lancaster County Court 13 March 1701/02
          Jos: TAYLOE, Cl

p. 7   KNOW ALL MEN by these presents that I RICHARD WISE of the County of ST. MARYES in the Province of MARYLND, Husbandman, hath made and appointed my trusty and well beloved Friend, MATTHIAS GILES to be my lawfull Attorney to receive from all persons whatsoever all sumes of money bills bonds or accots., granting my said Attorney authority to sue arrest and out of prison to deliver & make sufficient discharges in my name and generally to p:secute every thing in the Law whatsoever as my said Attorney shall think needful to be done, ratifying all my said Attorney shall doe or cause to be done about the p:misses. In Wittness whereof the said RICHARD WISE have hereunto sett my hand and seale this eight day of December being in the year 1701
Signed Sealed and delvd. in presence of us

     MATTHIAS ROSE,   RICHARD WISE
     JOSEPH HOLLAND
     Recorded 11th day March 1701/02
          JOS: TAYLOE, Clk

THIS INDENTURE made this eighth day of Aprill in ye yeare of our Lord God 1702 & in ye 15th yeare of ye raigne of our Sovereigne Lord William ye 3d by ye grace of God of England, Scotland, France & Ireland, King, Defendr. of ye faith &c., Betweene FRANCIS WEEKES, SENR. of ye County of MIDDLESEX in Virginia, Gent., and ELIZTH: his Wife of the one part and ANDREW JACKSON of ye County of Lancastr: in Virginia of ye other part;   Wittnesseth

p.   that ye sd. FRANCIS WEEKES & ELIZTH: his Wife for ye sume of 270
8   pounds of good lawfull money of England, hath granted & confirmed
        unto the said ANDREW JACKSON his heires & assignes for ever, 350 acres
of land be ye same or less together with ye plantacon comonly called or known
by ye name of FAIR WETHERS NECK, scituate on ye North side of RAPPAH:
RIVER on FAIR NECKS CREEK in ye County of Lancastr. aforesd., & lately purchased of Mr. RAWLEIGH TRAVERS by the abovesd. FRANCIS WEEKES as by a
Deed of Sale bearing date ye 31th day of May 1687 may more at large appeare &
recorded in Lancastr: Court Records, together with all profitts & apurtenances
belonging with all houses orchards gardens feedings woods ways to ye sd. land
belonging and allsoe all ye Estate right interest whatsoever of them ye sd. FR:
WEEKES & ELIZTH: his Wife, together with all Deeds, Evidences, Writeings concerneing ye land;   To have and to hold unto ye said ANDREW JACKSON his
heires & assignes subject unto ye quit rents which shall grow due unto his
Majties. his heires & Successors and the said FRANCIS WEEKES for the consideracon aforesd. doth agree att all times defend ye sd. Sale and every part
thereof unto ye sd. ANDREW JACKSON his heires & assignes

p.   and shall att all times occupy ye land & pr:misses without trouble or
9   molestation of them ye said FRANCIS WEEKES & ELIZTH: their heires &c.
        and that freely acquitted and kept harmless by sd. FRANCIS WEEKES &
ELIZA: his Wife their heires from all former ba rgains & conveyances and
shall within ye time hereby limited acknowledge this Deed of Sale att ye Court
to be held for the sd. County of Lancastr: In Wittness whereof to ye true intent of this present Indenture FRANCIS WEEKES & ELIZTH: his Wife have hereunto sett their hands and seales the day & yeare first above written
Signed Sealed & dd. in presence of us
        JOHN CARNEGIE,   FRANCIS WEEKES
        ALEXR: SWAN,   ELIZTH: WEEKES
        JOS: BELFIELD
     Recorded 8th Apr: 1702 p. JOS: TAYLOE, Clk.

p.   KNOW ALL MEN by these presents that I FRANCIS WEEKES, SENR., of
10   County of MIDDLESEX in Virginia stand indebted unto ANDREW JACKSON
        of ye County of Lancastr. in Virginia, Clerk, in ye penall sume of two
hundred seventy pounds of good lawfull money of England for which paymt. I
bind myselfe my heires by these presents this eighth day of Aprill Anno Dom:
1702
     THE CONDICON of this obligacon is such that if FRANCIS WEEKES his heires
&c. doe well & truely observe all ye covenants which ought to be observed
comprised in an Indenture of Sale bearing date with these presents, that then
this obligacon to be void & of none effect or else to stand in full force & virtue
Signed Sealed & dd. in presence of
        JOHN CARNEGIE,   FRANCIS WEEKES
        ALEXR. SWAN, JOS: BELFIELD
     Apr. 8th 1702. Recorded p JOS: TAYLOE, Cl

TO ALL TO WHOME these presents shall come, I SAMLL. MATHEWS, Esqr., Governr: & Capt. Genll. of Virga: send Greeting in or: Lord God ever lasting; Whereas by the Articles dated att JAMES CITTY ye 12th of March 1651 concluded & signed by the Commissionrs: appointed by authority of Parliamt., for ye reduceing settling & governing of Virginia, it was provided that ye priviledge of fivety acres of land for every person transported into this Collony should be continued as formerlie granted and whereas by Act of a Grand Assembly made ye 26th of Aprill 1652, it was provided that all Patents hereafter should be signed by ye Govrnrs: hand with ye Secretaries & shall be accompted authentique & valid in Law untill a Collony Seale shall be provided & appointed; Now Know yee that I yee said SAMLL. MATHEWS, Esqr., doe with the consent of ye Councill of State accordinglie give unto VINCENT STANFORD Six hundred acres of land lying & being in ye County of Lancastr: on ye East side of a dividend of land of WM: CLAPHAMs, now in the possession of THOMAS CARTER, & upon ye North side of a dividend of EPAHRADITUS LAWSON (deced), now in ye possession of WM: CLAPHAM, JUNR., the said Land being to him the

p. said VINCENT STANFORD by & for ye transportacon of 12 p:sons into this
11 Collony whose names are in Records menconed under this Patent. To
    have and to hold the sd. Land with all rights belonging to him ye sd.
VINCT. STANFORD in as large & ample purposes as is expressed in a Charter of Orders from ye late Treasurer & Company dated ye 18th day of Novr. 1618 or by conveyance may be justly collected paying unto ye Rent Gatherers thereunto appointed for every fivety acres of land hereinby granted att ye Feast of St. Michael ye Archangell the fee rent of one shilling which paymt. is to be made seven yeares after seating thereof and not before provided the said VINCENT STANFORD doe not seat or cause to be planted or seated upon ye sd. land w:thin three yeares next ensueing that then it may & shall be lawfull for any Adventurer or Planter to seat thereupon. Given undr. or: hands ye 1st day of June 1657

SAMLL: MATHEWS
W. CLAYBOURNE

Recorded 20th Apr: 1702
p JOS: TAYLOE, Clk
p. ROBERT POLLARD, Secretary

TO ALL TO WHOME these presents shall come, I WM: BERKLEY, Knt., Governr: & Capt. Genll. of Virga. send Greeting. Whereas by instructions from ye Kins most excellent Majesty directed to me & ye Councill of State, his Majesties was most graciously pleased to authorize me ye sd. Governr., to grant Pattent & to assigne such proportions of Land to Adventurers & Planters as have bin usuall here to fore in ye like cases either for Adventurers of Mony or transportation of people into ye sd. Collony according to the Charter of Ordr: from ye late Treasurer & Company, and that ye same proportion of fivety acres be assigned for every person transported hither since midsummer 1625, and that ye same couse be continued untill it shall be otherwise determined by his Majtie., Now Know yee that I ye sd. Sr. WM. BERKLEY, Knt., Governr., &c. doe with ye consent of ye Councill of State give unto VINCENT STANFORD 1000 acres

p. in the County of Lancastr: upon the North side of RAPPH: RIVER in
12 Virga., begining att a marked Spanish Oake standing on ye Northward
    side of a Branch of a small Creeke that runneth up & devideth ye Mountaine & runneth for length by the head of a devidend of land formerly sur-

veyed for Capt. DANIELL GOOKINS by the side of ye Mountain N. and by W. Northerly 767 poles, thence East & by North 253 poles, thence by a line parallel with ye first course to a Northwest Branch of COROTOMAN RIVER, thence West & by South to ye place first specified, the sd. land being formerly granted to ye sd. STANFORD by Pattent ye first of June 1657 and now renued in his Majties name by Ordr. of ye Quarter Court; To have and to hold with all rights paying for every 50 acres of land yearely at ye Feast of St. Michael ye Archangell the fee rent of one shill:, provided yt: if ye sd. VINCENT STANFORD doe not seate or plant upon ye sd. land w:thin 3 yeares, then it shall be lawfull for any Adventurer and Planter to make choice & seat thereon. Given att JAMES CITTY undr. my hand & ye seale of ye Colony this 18th da of March 1662, in ye 15th yeare of ye reigne of our Lord King Charles the Second &c.

Mr. VINCENT STANFORDs Patent for 1000 acres   WILLIAM BERKLEY
                                                      THO: LUDWELL, Secry.

Test FRA: KIRKMAN
Record PHIL: LUDWELL, Cl.
Recordr. 20th Apr. 1702, p. JOS: TAYLOE, Clk.
                    p. ROBT. POLLARD

28th March 1702. Received for HUGH BRENT one pied Heifer, two yeares old marked with a crop on bouth eares & staple in one & a slitt in the other
                    p JOS: TAYLOE

p.   BY THIS PUBLICK INSTRUMT. of PROCURACON be it manifest unto all
13   people that on this day being the 14th day of 8br: 1701, before me,
        THOMAS COOKE, Notary Publick, being in ye Citty of DUBLIN in Ireland, personally appeared ROBERT McKERELL, JAMES KING & GEORGE FORBES of the Citty of Dublin, Merchts., and that they doe make appoint BENJAMIN YOUNG of ye sd. Citty, Mercht., to be their lawfull Attorney to claim whatsoever belonging to them from the hands or custody of MARK GENDRON, Mercht. in Virginia. In Wittness whereof ye sd. Consituents have hereunto put their hands & seales ye day month & yeare above written
Sealed & delivered in ye presence of us
        SAMLL. TRAVERS,   ROBERT McKERELL
        JNO: HIND,   JAMES KING
        JNO: BLACKWELL   GEO: FORBES
    Recorded att ye instance of Mr. BENJA: YOUNG, att ye Court for ye County of Lancastr: ye 13th May 1702
                    JOS: TAYLOE, Clk.

p.   DUBLIN, October ye 14th 1701
14   BENJAMIN YOUNG
        Sr. You are to repair on board ye Good Ship called ye, "AMERICA of LONDON," JOHN HEAD, Comdr., for Virginia wth: whome wee have agreed & paid for yor: passage & victualing and other accomodations for you for yt: voyage & when it pleases God yt: you arrive there and he puts you on shoar in any place that stands best for yor: conveniency, you are imediately to endeavour to make ye best of yor: way direct for ye River of RAPPAHANOCK and repaire unto Mr. MARK GENDRON which att present remaines there in our Imploy and deliver him our Lettr. of Attr., in yor: custody a settlemt. of all our Accots. our former power given him for acting in or: affaires there with all papers, bookes lists of

debts relateing thereto.

2dly. Likewise you are to receive from him all such goods now in said GEN-
DRONs cutody wth: account sale of what he may have disposed of wch: com-
pare wth: ye original invoyces of each p:ticular copies of wch: you have allong
wth: you and see whats different or wanting of our effects, only what Rum and
Sugar he has purchased there from time to time and disposed of for our
accompt, sale of which you must likewise demand & see how it corresponds
wth: his drafts on us paid p JAMES FOULER in LONDON, all which you have an
accot. of and make an end wth: him and receive our tobbo. and unsold goods
from him. You must endeavour to dispose thereof for ready pay in tobbos. and
not to contract any debts but imediately on yor: haveing our effects in yor:
custody as aforesd, purchase what tobbos. you can gett in what debts outstan-
ding, the which you are to ship on board or: Ship, "PROVIDENCE," WM. LIGGATT
Comdr. and now in Virga, and to use ye best of yor: endeavours to sell & dispose
of all. drawing or: affaires there into as small a compress as possible leaveing
as little of or: effects unshipt as you can gett in or by any means you can recover al which you are to ship on board or: sd Ship, 'PROVIDENCE," together
with what you may receive from sd. GENDRON for or: accot.

3dly. If any thing more then may load or: sd. Ship, gett it shipt off on
freight for LIVERPOOLE or WHITEHAVEN, that noe tobbo. may be left behind as
aforesd., but if what or: said effects be not sufficient to give ye Ship her full
freight, wee hereby ordr: to draw on us for what may be defficient payable att
ye House of WM: BROWN in LONDON, but wee hope there may be noe occasion;
Yor: draft must be provided yt: good leafe tobbo. be from nine to ten shills p.
1/2 hundred not to exceed yt.

p.   4thly. After yor: stateing & settleing accompts wth: sd. GENDRON, if
15   you find him faire in ye matter and desirous for our interrest you may
        att yor: departure leave our concerne in his hands but in case you doe
not find sd. GENDRON not propr to intrust him on yt: occasione, leave all in ye
custody of Coll. ROBT. CARTER, Esqr., wth: power to receive all such debts as
may remaine; however, for yor: own good & or: interrests keep as faire a correspondency wth: sd. GENDRON as possible, allwayes treating him civily by
reason he is att home there and you a Stranger being allwayes aforehim as
wise as a Serpent & as Inocent as a Dove, he being of a cunning crafty consti-
tution and in regard to his engagemts., be allwayes prepared for such persons
and be thoughtfull and mindfull of yor: businesse proposeing & endeavouring
what you can for our interrest for you are not unsensable of or: sufferings all
ready by bad managemt. in Virga.

5thly. WM: LIGGATT, Comdr. of or: sd. Ship, "PROVIDENCE," may be aiding
and assisting to you. Wee have wrote him to endeavour what he can to dispatch businesse allwayes consult him & take his advice in any that he may
have more knowledge of then ye and that your may think may be for or: interrests endeavour to keep a faire correspondency wth: him. You know ye
necessity of Mastrs. & Merchants agreeing together severall designes have
been over thrown by their liveing att variance one with ye other

6thly. Use all endeavours possible to dispatch businesse to be in a readyness
to port: when a Convoy offers as aforesd. and come directly to BEWMAURICE to
enter yor: tobbos. but if you should put into another place of this Kindgdom
neglect not to advise us thereof and if any conveniency offer from thence to
RAPPH: shall sent you some provisions for which reason you may omit pro-
videing yor: selfe wth: any for yor: homeward voyage untill ye last extremity

And yt: you and or: sd. Ship be in a readyness to part att which time if you find none comes you must see & provide yor: selfe for provisions and things necessary

    7thly. But for any utensills yt: you may want for the Ships use, you may purchase them there and draw on us payable in LONDON as aforesd., You have receipts for three yeares wages paid to said GENDRON att settlemt. of accots.

p.   You are to pay him for what time he has been more then the three
16   yeares haveing regard to ye date of sd. receipt his time commenced and
        what is due to him. Keep all wages seperate from ye Ship, "PROVI-
DENCE," and "HOPEWELLs" effects and lett them be distinguished by different marks. Likewise what of ye outsanding debts you gett in p:ticularize therein according to ye nature of their purchase whether of CROMWELLs Contraction or otherwise not forgetting to demand of sd. GENDRON what accompts he has of ye sale of the Ship, "PROVIDENCE," Servants. Keep as faire a correspondency for fear they should leave you and those that is most assisting to you promise them a gratification which they shall be sure to have att their return and apply yor:selfe to Coll. ROBERT CARTER, Esqr., on occasion endeavouring to make or: service acceptable, for he being a leading man & one knowing ye Law may be very usefull in recovering ye debts and likewise apply yor:selfe to Mr. FRAN: MOORE if in yt: place for advice. Now we shall conclude wth: prayers for your health comitting you into ye protection of allmighty God, wee remaine
                Sr. Yor: affectionr: Freinds,
                  ROBERT McKERELL
                  JAMES KING
                  GEO: FORBES

    If the Ship, "PROVIDENCE," be come away then you may stay in ye Country untill ye returne of ye "HOPEWELL," or some other which shall be sent for or: effects. Loose noe time in sale of ye goods and calling in tobbo. & omit noe opertunity of writeing to your Loveing Freinds;
                  ROBERT McKERELL
                  JAMES KING
                  GEO: FORBES
    Recorded att ye instance of Mr. BENJ: YOUNG att a Court held for ye County of Lancastr: ye 13th day of May 1702.
            Test   JOS: TAYLOE, Clk.

p.   Received of WM: ROBERTSON ye 7th of June 1701, a Note on RICHARD
17   BURGIS of BRISTOLL for five pounds ye effects of wch: if I can gett I
        promise to return according to his ordr: bearing date ye same day
abovesd., but on ye sd. ROBERTSON's Risque but if by any accident I should loose ye Bill, I am noe wayes responsible as Wittness my hand ye day abovesd.
    JAMES BALL   JAMES COMELINE
    Record ye 4th July 1702 att ye request of Mr. ROBINSON
            Test   JOS: TAYLOE, Clk.

    By this Publicke Instrumt: of Procuration, bee it known unto all those who shall heare ye same that on ye 14th day of Novr., 1701, in ye thirteenth yeare of ye reigne of or: Soveraigne Lord William ye Third &c., before me JAMES PUCKLE, Notarie Publick dwelling in LONDON, personally appeared Captaine GEORGE PURVIS of LONDON, Marrinr:, who declared to have made Collo. JOSEPH BALL of Lancastr. County, RAPPH: RIVER in Virga., his true &

lawfull Attorney granting lawfull authority for him to his use to recover & receive from all p:sons whom it shall or may concerne inhabiting in Virga. aforesd., perticulerly & more especially from Mr. JOSEPH TAYLOE of Lancastr: County aforesd. his heires all such sumes whatsoever wch: ye sd. JOSEPH TAY-LOE his heires now doe or shall stand indebted to him ye sd. Constituant due or in any wise apertaining to adjust all accounts thereof

p.   and generally in & concerneing ye premisses and affaires of me ye sd.
18   Constituant to act & execute all & whatsoever shall be requisite as he ye
        sd. Constituant might doe if personally present. This done and passed in
LONDON as aforesd. in ye p:sence of Capt. THO: GRAVES & THOMAS MORRALL, wittnesses herein required
Sealed & delivered in ye p:sence of
        THO: GRAVES,   GEO: PURVIS
        THO: MORRALL,   SAMLL. GOSTLIN
                In p:sence of JACOBUS PUCKLE
        Recorded in Lancaster County Court 20th May 1702
                JOS: TAYLOE, Clk.

        KNOW ALL MEN by these presents that I ROBERT POLLARD of ye Pish: of St. Marys White Chaple in ye County of Lancaster for a valuable consideracon in hand paid by JAMES BALL of ye sd. Pish: & County, Gent.,

p.   have sold unto ye sd. JAMES BALL all that residue of ye wth:in Pattent
19   for Four hundred acres of land unto ye sd. JAMES BALL his heires &c.,
        for ever in manner & form following (viz.) The sd. JAMES BALL being
now actually possest of 200 acres of land part of ye p:misses formerly sold by ye sd. ROBERT unto HENRY BRADLEY and by him ye sd. HENRY given unto ye sd. JAMES BALL by Deed of Gift acknowledged in ye County Court of Lancastr. And 200 acres more the residue of the p:misses hereby sold unto ye sd. JAMES BALL alwayes provided yt: ye sd. ROBERT doth reserve to himselfe a certaine p:cell of land part of ye sd. 200 hereby sold being betweene ye line of marked trees belonging to ye sd. JAMES by virtue of ye sd. Deed of Gift and ye lands of ROBERT POLLARD part of another Pattent of 600 acres of land, and all ye rest of ye said 200 acres part of ye sd. Pattent to be hereby sold. To have and to hold unto ye sd. JAMES BALL his heires or assignes forever; And I ye sd. ROBERT POLLARD doe hereby further promise with ye sd. JAMES BALL that I will with MARTHA my Wife acknowledge these p:misses at ye next Court to be held for this County of Lancastr: In Wittness whereunto I have sett my hand & seale this 18th of Apr: 1702
Signed sealed & delivered in presence of
        JOSEPH TAYLOE,   ROBERT POLLARD
        NICHS: GEORGE
        Recorded 13th May 1702   p. JOS: TAYLOE, Clk.

p.   TO ALL TO WHOM these presents shall come, I RICHARD BENNET, Esqr.
20   Capt. Genll. of Virga., send Greeting. Whereas by Articles dated in
        JAMES CITTY ye 12th of March 1651, signed by the Commissionrs: appointed by authority of Parliament for seating of Virga., it was provided that 50 acres of land for every person transfered into this Collony should be granted; And whereas by Act of Grand Assembly made ye 26th of Apr. 1652, it

was provided Pattents should hereafter be signed by ye Governrs: hand wth: ye Secretary and shalbe accounted authenticke untill a Collony Seale shalbe provided. Now Know ye that I RICHD. BENNETT, Esqr., doe in ye name of ye Keepers of ye Liberties of England by the authority of Parliament wth: ye consent of ye Councill of State give unto JNO: PHILLIPS 400 acres of land scituate in ye County of Lancastr: on ye North side of RAPPH: RIVER begining att a marked Spanish Oake standing on ye Northward side of a Branch of a small Creeke yt: runeth up & devideth ye Mountaines, and runing for length by the head of a devidend of land formerly surveyed p Capt. DANIELL GOOKINS by ye side of ye Mountaines North by West 300 poles to a marked Hickory standing on ye head of a small Valley, from thence East by North 213 poles, thence by a line parralel to ye first course 300 poles to a North West Branch of COROTOMAN RIVER and soe West by South to ye place where it begane, includeing ye sd. quantitie of land, ye sd. land being due unto ye sd. JNO: PHILLIPS by & for ye transportacon of eight persons into this Collony whose names are in Records mentioned undr: this Patent; To have and to hold to him ye sd. JOHN PHILLIPS his heires & assignes forever paying unto ye Rent Gatherers for every fivety acres of land yearely att ye Feast of St. Michael the Archangell the fee rent of one Shilling which paymt. is to be made seven yeares after ye first grant, provided if ye sd. JNO: PHILLIPS doe not plant or seate upon ye sd. land within three yeares ensueing that then it shall be lawfull for every

p.   Adventurer or Planter to make choice & seate thereupon.   Given undr.
21   or: hands this 13th of July 1653

                          RICHD: BENNETT
                          WM: CLAYBOURN, Secretary
     Recordr. 12th June 1656

   I MOORE FANTLEROY, ye Administrator of ye Estate of JOHN PHILLIPS (deced) doe hereby assigne over this Pattent unto VINCENT STANFORD his heires & assignes for ever. Wittness my hand this 2d day of Apr: 1656
Wittness RICHD: BLEWFORD p sig: M. FANTLEROY
     Recordr. 12 June 1656

   I MOORE FANTLEROY, Administr: of ye Estate of JNO: PHILLIPS, deced., doe by these presents sell unto VINCENT STANFORD one Pattent of Four hundred acres belonging to ye Estate of ye abovesd. JOHN PHILLIPS & one Cow and a yearling wth: their encrease for ever, which is upon Mr. COLEs att RAPPH: RIVER to him ye sd. STANFORD his heires for ever to enjoy. Wittness my hand March ye 19th 1655
Wittness RICHD: JAMES
     Record 12 June 1656   JOS: TAYLOE, Clk.

   Recognitr. in Court 13th die May 1702 p ROBERT POLLARD & MARTHA Uxoria JAMES BALL et recordr.
                          JOS: TAYLOE, Clk.

   THIS INDENTURE mad Mar: ye 2d in ye yeare of or: Lord 1701/2. Betweene WM: DRAPER of ye County of Lancaster, Blacksmith, of ye one part and SAMLL. FOX of ye same County of ye other part; (Wittnesseth) that ye sd. WM: DRAPER for ye sume of 1000 lbs. of good & legall tobacco to be pd. to him or his Ordr., att or suddenly after ye ensealing & delivery of these presents hath granted

p.   unto ye sd. SAMLL. FOX and his heires for ever all my right of a p:cell of
22   land scituating in ye County of Lancastr: lying on RAPPH: RIVER on ye
      South side of a Swamp Marsh Pond & Run, commonly called by ye name
of WASHINGTONS RIVER, & bounding on ye Land whereon ye sd. FOX now lives
with all & singular appurtenances thereunto belonging now or late in ye
tenor or occupacon of ye sd. WM. DRAPER; To have and to hold unto ye sd.
SAMUEL FOX his heires and assignes for ever and will warrant and for ever
defend by these presents and to that true intent & meaning doe hereunto sett
my hand & seale ye day & date
Signed saled in presence of us
     JNO: WELLS,   WM: DRAPER
     THO: MARTIN, JNO: ADAMS,
     JNO: CHILTON
    Recognitr: in Cur Com Lancastr: 13th die May 1702 et record
          p JOS: TAYLOE, Clk.

     THIS INDENTURE made ye 12th day of July in ye yeare of or: Lord 1699
Betweene JOHN HUTCHINS of ye Pish: of Christ Church in ye County of Lancastr
in ye Collony of Virginia of ye one part and WM. LISTER of ye sd. Pish in ye sd.
County of ye 2nd part;

p.   Wittnesseth that ye sd. JNO: HUTCHINS for a valuable consideracon paid
23   by ye sd. WM: LISTER hath granted unto him, ye sd. WM: LISTER, his
      heires or assignes a certaine p:cell of land lying in ye sd. Pish: & County
aforesd., and bounded as followeth; Beginning att the head of a small Branch
yt: runneth out of COROTOMAN nigh ye House of JNO: FLOYD (deced), att a white
Oake in a Valey neer WM: FLOYD and runing from thence South unto a marked
Gum and from ye sd. Gum South & by West by a line of marked trees neer ye
part yt: goes out of FLEETS BAY to ye sd. HUTCHINS House unto a corner red
Oake standing in GABRIELL THATCHERs line and runing due East to a corner
red Oak saplin and runing from thence by a line of marked trees South & by
West over ye Branch it first began & soe up ye South side of ye sd. Branch unto
ye white Oake where it first began; To have and to hold the sd. p:cell of land
with all profitts whatsoever unto ye sd. WM: LISTER his heires and assignes
forever and I JOHN HUTCHINS doe hereby agree to warrt: & for ever defend ye
sd. tract of land to ye sd. WM: LISTER against all manner of persons whatsoever & agree to & wth: ye sd. WM. LISTER to acknowledge this Conveyance in
Court according to Law and yt: ELLINR: my now Wife will likewise acknowledge and relinquish her right of Dower yt: she now hath or may hereafter
have to ye sd. Land. In Wittness whereof I have hereunto sett my hand & seale
ye day & yeare above
Signed sealed written & delivered in the presence of
     RICHD: BALL, GEO: CHILTON,   JOHN HUTCHINS
     JNO: MOTT ack. p his Wife
    Recognitr. in Cur Com Lancastr. 13th die 7bris 1699 et record 15th die
sequend   JOS: TAYLOE, Clk.

p.   KNOW ALL MEN by these presents that I WM. LISTER of ye County of
24   Lancastr: doe hereby assigne over all my right of ye within mentioned
      tract of land with appurtenances thereunto belonging unto JAMES

KIRKE him his heires & assignes and I doe hereby bind myselfe to acknowledge this unto ye sd. KIRKE ye next Court held for this County, Wittness my
hand & seale this 23d day of June 1702
Signed sealed & delivered in presence of
     JNO: TURBERVILL   W. LISTER
     JEREMY (? JAMES),
     CHRIST: KIRK
       Recognitr. in Cur Com Lancastr: 8th die July 1702 et record
             p   JOS: TAYLOE, Clk.

       KNOW ALL MEN by these presents that I JAMES WORTHINGTON of ye
Kingdom of England, Mercht., & now in Virginia, doe apoint my trusty Freind,
THO: CARTER of ye County of Lancastr: my true & lawfull Attorny to receive all
debts due unto me in Virginia, to arrest or sue any p:sons that will not pay, and
doe hereby ratifie & confirme whatsoever my Attorny shall lawfully doe in ye
sd. pr:misses as just & firme as if I my selfe were personally present, as
Wittness my hand this 2 day of June 1702
Sealed signed & dd. in presence of us
     PETER CARTER,   JAMES WORTHINGTON
     CHARLES KING
  Probata fait Lettr: Attor: in Cur Com Lancastr: 8th die July 1702 p sacramr.
PETER CARTER et CHARLES KING.
       Recordr. p JOS: TAYLOE, Clk.

       KNOW ALL MEN by these presents that I THO: COOPER of ye Citty of BRIS-
TOLL, Marrinr., have made and appointed THO: CARTER OF CORROTOM in ye
County of Lancastr: in ye Province of Virginia, Planter, my true & lawfull
Attorny for me to receive sue for and recover all sumes of money oweing unto
me ye sd. THO: COOPER from severall parties whose names are hereunto
subscribed to use and take all lawfull wayes in my name

p.   for recovery of ye same and in my name to do all other acts & things
25   whatsoeer as I myselfe could doe were I p:sonally present. In Wittness
      whereof I hereunto sett my hand and seale this 3d day of July in ye first
yeare of ye Raigne of Lady Ann first Queen over England &c. Ano. Dom: 1702
                            THO: COOPER
     JNO: STOTT, WM. CAMMELL, JNO: HILL
     JNO: BUSH, WILL: SMOOT, ANN CHEWNING, CHARLES BERTRAND;
     WILL: LAX, JOHN ROACH, JOHN WELLS, EDWD. TOMLIN
      JOHN THOMAS, PETER REYNOLDS, JOHN PHILLIPS, JOHN CORNEGIE
Wittness. HENRY CARTER,   THO: POPE
Probat: Lettr: Attor: in Cur Com. Lancastr: 8th die July 1702 p sacremt. HENRY
CARTER & THO: POPE
       Recordr. JOS: TAYLOE, Clk.

     Mr. HENRY DICKESON.   Bristoll ye 31th of May 1701
     We have shipt on ye "JNO: & SUSANA" a p:cell of goods as p Invoyce
hereto anexed amounting to L. 216...10...0. in which you are one 8th part concerned yor: selfe which when please God you arrive att PENSILVANIA & Virginia, wee would have you take to and dispose of for or: most advantage laying
ye proceeds in good sound tobacco & weighty noe hhds. if possible weighing
less then six hundr: of nett tobbo. or any thing elce you think will be there

to or: advantage shiping ye same on ye "JNO: & SUSANA" or any other Ship or Ships bound for this Port or LONDON consigning the same to our selves agreeing for freight as cheap as you can only on ye "JNO: & SUSANA" you are to ship twenty hhds. att six pounds p tun which have taken freight for heer provided you can lode them in ye same time yt: ship is loading. Wee have all we shipt on sd ship 26 Servants ye names & times of servitude being on ye other

p.   side, which when please God send you safe to PENSILVANIA you are to
26   dispose of soe many goods or Bills of Exchange payeable in England
       paying Capt. COOPER seven pounds p head in PENSILVANIA for their passage and the remaindr: invest in Negroes, Rum, Sugar, Mollasoes or anything elce you think will turn best to acct. in Virginia which when there you are to lay out and ship as above directed. You know wee have been att great expence att cloathing ye Servts., therefore would have a p:ticular care taken about their cloathes & beding tht what they doe not use or is left after their disposall may be sold for ye most advantage. If any thing of a markett offers in PENSILVANIA for Servts. wee think it not best to carry any to Virginia p reason of those you carry there you must pay a thousand pounds of tobbo. a head for their passage. Be sure you bring a Certificate of ROBERT SMITHs Landing in PENSILVANIA or Virginia. ye hand of two Justices of ye Peace. In case of mortality (which God forbid) or: ordr: is that Capt. THO: COOPER may take care of or: concerne or in case of his, then to Mr. NICHO: SMITH in RAPPH: RIVER, who is to follow ye directions aforesd. Be carefull of ye concerne and lett us heer from you by all opertunitys. Wee wish you a good voyage and safe return to yor: Loveing Freinds

You are to have 10 p cent of lott	SUSANA DUDLESTON
att Home for all you ship for yor:	JNO: BEACHER
Commission	JEREMIAH DEVERALL
	HENRY DICKESON

     Recordr. ye 9th of May 1702,
          p. JOS: TAYLOE, Clk.

     THIS INDENTURE made ye 12th day of Octobr: in the first yeare of the Raigne of or: Soveraigne Lady Ann by the grace of God of England, Scotland, France & Ireland, Queen, Defendr. of the faith, 1702, Betweene NICHOLAS WREN of the Pish: of Christ Church in the County of Lancastr: of the one part and RICHARD CHICHESTER of the Pish: & County aforesd., Esqr., of ye other part; Wittnesseth tht ye sd. NICHO: WREN for the sume of 12000 lbs. of good tobbo & casque & 40 Shills., Sterling money of England to him in hand paid

p.   hath granted unto the said RICHARD CHICHESTER and to his heires &
27   assignes for ever the tract of land whereon NICHOLAS WREN late of
      this County formerly lived and now in the actuall possession of the said RICHARD CHICHESTER, together with all and every part & p:cell of land being in the County aforesd. that ye sd. NICHO: WRENN now hath or for ever hereafter shall have as heire to his Father, NICHO: WREN (deced), according to their bounds and courses within their severall grants with all rights of him the sd. NICHO: WRENN to ye same, together with all writeings he now hath in his custody; To have and to hold unto the sd. RICHRD CHICHESTER his heires & assignes for ever

p.
28   and I the said NICHO: WREN will att all times for ever defend ye sd. RICHARD CHICHESTER his heires & assignes against any claime of any p:son whatsoever;   In Wittness whereof the parties first above named hath hereunto sett his hand and seale the day & yeare first above written Sealed & delivered in presence of
    ROBERT SCHOLFEILD,   NICHO: WREN p sig.
    ROBERT GIBSON, JOHN ROBERTSON
    Recognitr. in Cur Com Lancastr: 14th day Octobr: 1702 p. NICHO. WREN & recordr. p   JOS: TAYLOE, Clk.

THIS INDENTURE made this 19th day of August 1699 & in the 11th yeare of the Raigne of or: Soveraigne Lord King William of England, Scotland, France & Ireland &c., Betweene WILLIAM MORE & HANAH his Wife of the one party & JOSEPH DUKESSHALL of the sd. County of the other party;   (Wittnesseth) that ye sd. WM: MORE in consideracon of 1000 lbs. of tobacco by Bill made for ye same from JOSEPH DUKESHALL payable to WILLIAM MORE his heires &c. bearing equall date with the tenor of this date; Therefore I WILLIAM MORE have sold unto ye sd. JOSEPH DUKESHALL all that tract of land being the one moiety or 1/2 part of a certaine tract or parcell of land formerly bought by JOHNATHAN GUESS of JOHN BAILEY (deced), containing 35 acres & bounding betweene the lines of STEPHEN TOMLYN & FRANCIS FRIZELL comonly called or known by the name of TYLERS NECK, ye moyetie whereof being seventeene acres & a half more or less with all houses and profitts whatsoever thereunto belonging

p.
29   p:tent of ye sd. Land & by the rents therein contained;   To have and to hold to him ye sd. JOSEPH DUKESHALL his heires & assignes for ever and the sd. WM: MORE and HANAH his Wife further agree that he hath good right to ye sd. Land without any encumbrances from or: undr: us or: heires;   In Wittness whereof, wee have hereunto sett or: hands & seales the day and yeare first above written
Signed Sealed & delivered in ye presence of us
    FRAN: FRIZELL,   WM: MORE
    WM: BALEY   HANAH MORE
    Recognitr. in Cur Com Lancastr: 14th die Octobr: 1702 et record
        p. JOS: TAYLOE, Clk.

Cor: RAPPA.   Virginia   15th June 1700
Goods on board the Shallope called "YE VINE of RAPPA." TERENCE WEBB Mastr.   vizt.
4 pds. Linceo, 2 doz. stays, 2 hunting sadles, 1 dozn 1/2 snaffle bridles in horse halters, 1 end tick, 2 pr. bird eyd curtains, 2 pr. desk drab kersey, 16 woolen hosse girts, 2 dozn. woms. yarne hose, 2 prs. of dark colld. furstian, 26000 pinns, 6 shoe makers knives, 7 gss. coat chubs, 7 gss. silk Gimps, 12 paper colld. tape, 11 paper colld. ditto, 2 prs. Manchester Binding, 2 payrs. white cape, 1 pack sheet, 2 large ruggs, 1 pr. dark colld. Spannish broad cloth, 5 prs. Irish Line, It. 187 1/2 yds. 4 gross mohair buttons, 2 lbs 1/2 colld. thred, 6 pr. woms. stays, 6 pr tow cards, 6 pr. woole do., 1 pr. Lincey, 7 pr. spurs, 1 gross mettle buttons, 2 pr. womans slipers, 4 pr. girles shoes, 2 pr. woms. ditto in 2 chests No. 4-5, LV for wch. he hath produced Cocquets of theire legall importation undr. ye hand of RALPH WORMELEY & GAWIN CORBIN, Esqrs., Collectr. and late Navll. Officer of ye Port,

These are therefore to Licence and p:mitt the sd. TERENCE WEBB, Master as aforesd., to saile out of this Port and Collony wth: his sd. Shallope & goods bound for PENSILVANIA. Given undr. my hand & seale of ye Office ye day and yeare above

p.   Written to whome these may concerne. RICHD, CHICHESTER
30   Recordr. att ye instance of Mr. EDWD. (? AGBRINBY)
                    Test   JOS: TAYLOE, Clk.

        Sr.   October ye 13th 1702
        Desire you to Record a mark for my Son, RUBEN ROSS.
        The mark is a crop & undr: keele on ye right eare and a crop on ye left, noe more from yor: Freiend & Servt. to comd.
To Mr. JOSEPH TAYLOE, Clk. of Lancastr. Court
        7br: 20th 1703. Order sent by his Wife to informe yt: it is a Heifer ye above mark belongs to, wch: is to be had with all female encrease
                            FRANCES WALLER

        WM: LAX records for ROBERT PRITCHARD one mare fillee branded with R. P., This 10th die Decembris 1702
                    Test   JOS: TAYLOE, Clk.

        Decr. ye 15th 1702
        MATHIAS GILES records his mark as followes (vizt); a crop & slitt & undr: bitt on ye right eare and a crop & hole & undr: bitt on ye left eare
                    Test   JOS: TAYLOE, Clk.

        KNOW ALL MEN by these presents that I THO: BUCKLEY of the County of Lancastr: and Parish of Christ Church, Planter, doe and stand firmely bound unto THOMAS MARTIN of the County aforesd. and Parish of St. Marys Whtie Chapple, Gent., and RICHARD FLINT of the said County and Pish:, Taylor, and every of them their heires &c. in the sume of twenty eight thousand, eight hundred fifty and eighty pounds of tobacco, to the true payment to be made I do for my selfe my heires bind and make over unto the said THOMAS and RICHARDto them their heires &c., all the lands houses orchards fences timber woods and other appurtenances belonging being within the said County of Lancastr: and now in the occupacon of him the said THO: BUCKLEY with war- ranty from him the said THOMAS his heires or from any claimeing undr: him them or either of them for ever. Sealed wth: my seale and dated the 11 day of Janry. 1702/3.
        THE CONDITION of this obligation is such that whereas a Commission of Ad- ministration upon the Estate of ROBERT HILL, late of this County,

p.   (deced) was granted unto the above bounden THO: BUCKLEY upon the
31   Ninth day of Febry. 1698/9, in case whereof the abovesd. THOMAS MAR-
        TIN and RICHARD FLINT became security for the said BUCKLEYs faith- full discharge of his Office of Admr. Now if the abovesaid THOS: BUCKLEY shall at all times hereafter save harmless the said THO: MARTIN and RICHARD FLINT their heires from all incumbrances or the like that may now or hereafter shall be levied upon the bodys of them or either of them or upon the Estates real & personall of them, that may now or hereafter shall arise by occasion of the pr:misses, That then this pr:sent obligation to be voyd and of noe effect

or else to remain in full strength & virtue.
Sealed and delivered in p:sence of
     JOS: TAYLOE   THOMAS BUCKLEY
     THO: CARTER, EDWIN CONWAY
   Record duo decimo die sequend p JOS: TAYLOE, Clk.   .

      THIS INDENTURE made this thirteenth day of January Ano. Dom. one thousand seven hundred and two & in ye first yeare of ye reigne of our Sovereigne Lady Ann of England Scotland France and Ireland, Queen, Defendr. of ye faith, &c., Betweene ROBT. SCHOFEILD of ye County of Lancastr:, Planter, of ye one part & MOTTROM WRIGHT, the Son of MOTTROM WRIGHT, late of ye sd. County of Lancastr:, deced., Gentleman, of the other part; Wittnesseth that the said ROBERT SCHOFEILD for ye valuable sume of one hundred pounds Sterling money to him in hand paid, hath given unto ye said MOTTROM WRIGHT his heires & assignes for ever One hundred ninety one acres & a halfe of land scituate in ye County of Lancaster lying and being in RAPPA: FORREST, bounded as follows, vizt., Begining att a corner marked Hickory, corner tree of Mr. CHARLES LEE alias MADISON,

p.   and extending thence North West three hundred and sixty poles to a
32   Stake standing in Mr. LEE's line neare to a corner Hickory bearing
North East from ye sd. Stake from thence North East ninety five poles and a halfe to a corner marked Holly tree standing in a small. Branch in Mr. LEE's North East line, from thence along a line devideing from Mr. MOTTROM WRIGHT alias GREG's South forty nine degrees East two hundred twenty three poles & twenty links to a corner now devideing Mr. WRIGHT & Mr. LAWSON and this land, from thence to the begining Hickory along Mr. LAWSONs line, wch: said land was formerly granted to ye sd. ROBT SCHOLFEILD, JUNR. by WILL: FITCH HUGH and GEORGE BRENT by Deed registered in the Proprietors office dated ye 11th day of Novr: 1697, & also all proffitts & appertenances to the sd. one hundred ninety one acres and a halfe of land belonging, ye sd. MOTTROM WRIGHT paying ye Quitt Rents wch: from henceforth to grow due to be paid and further I the sd. ROBT. SCHOLFEILD doth hereby authorize JOS: TAYLOE and DANIEL McCARTY or either of them to appeare att Lancastr: County Court and acknowledge these presents in open Court to the end the same be entred upon ye Records of ye sd. County; In Wittness whereof the said ROBT: SCHOLFEILD hath here unto sett his hand and seale the day and yeare first abovesd.
Written sealed and delivered in the pr:sents of
     GEORGE HARWARD,   ROBERT SCHOLFEILD
     JNO: HUTCHINGS, THO: WALLTER
   Recorded in Cur Com Lancastr: 13th day Janry. 1702/3
          JOS: TAYLOE, Clk.

p.   TO ALL WHOME these presents come, Know ye yt: wee JNO: MULLIS and
33   ELIZTH: MULLIS, Wife of the said JNO: MULLIS, out of the naturall love &
affection we have & bare to our foure Sons, vizt., STEPHEN MULLIS, JNO. MULLIS, RICHD: MULLIS and GEORGE MULLIS doe give and devise to them all that Land being ye quantity of Three hundred acres in maner and forme hereafter exprest (vizt), to us the sd. JNO: & ELIZ: MULLIS dureing our or either of our naturall lifes to hold occupie & freely enjoy all and singular ye lands aforesd., and ye reversion att ye decease of ye sd. JNO: & ELIZTH: MULLIS to them ye sd. STEPHEN, JNO., RICHD., & GEORGE MULLIS according to the fol-

lowing derections. First wee ye sd. JNO: & ELIZTH: MULLIS doe give unto the sd. STEPHEN MULLIS ye just quantity of ninty acres of land wth: ye Plantation he hath now newly seated included lying on & adjoyning to the lands of Coll. ST. LEGER CODD, and soe runing his course along that line soe farr as shall reach the aforesaid quantity of ninty acres and for want of length to make out ye said quantity upon the sd. line to be made up out of ye residue of ye sd. Three hundred acres as conveniently as can be contrived to the said Plantacon aforesd. whom the sd. STEPHEN MULLIS and his heires male of his body lawfully begotten and wee the sd. JNO: & ELIZTH: MULLIS doe likewise give and grant unto ye sd. JNO: & RICHD: MULLIS all the rest residue and remaindr: of the sd. land wch: is now in ye actuall possession of us, ye sd. JNO: & ELIZTH: MULLIS, excepting ye lands before given unto STEPHEN & the Plantacon whereon wee now live with as much land as will make out the quantity of Seventy acres unto GEORGE MULLIS the quantity before given to each of them or: sd. Sons, RICHD: and JNO: MULLIS, being in all the quantity of Three hundred acres before menconed; To have & to hold the sd. land given to them ye sd. STEPHEN, JNO: RICHD. & GEORGE MULLIS and to the severall male heires of their bodys lawfully begotten, alwayes p:vided notwithstanding ye pr:misses and it is the true meaning of us the sd. JNO: & ELIZTH: MULLIS that if ye sd. STEPHEN shall dye without male issue as aforesd. that then his pt. of ye sd. land to goe to ye next by succession and ye male heires of theire bodys lawfully begotten & finally there may be noe dispute hereafter arise or grow betweene them, ye sd. STEPHEN, JNO:, RICHD., and GEORGE MULLIS, it is our will & pleasure that if either of ye sd. devisees dyes wth:out male issue, yt: his pt. decends to the next heire & soe successively as ye Law p:scribes in such cases and in case that all my said Sons dye without male issue as aforesd., yt: then the whole three hundred acres of land be equally devided among my three Daughters in coparcenership (to witt) ELIZTH:, MARY & ABIGALL MULLIS to them and theire heires male as aforesd. for ever, furthermore wee do apoint that ye lands given unto JNO: & RICHD: MULLIS be equally devided in quantity and quality between them as neer conveniently may be & if it be left to ye choice of either of them ye sd. JNO: & RICHD., to buy or sell ye disproportion of ye quantity & theire quality as it shall be adjudged by indifferent men betweene them. In Wittness whereof wee the partys above menconed have hereunto sett our hands

p,   and seales this 7th day of November 1702
34   Sealed & delivered in p:sence of
        JOS: TAYLOE,   JOHN MULLIS
        ANN 5 WMS.   ELIZTH: X MULLIS
        Recognitr in Cur Com Lancastr: decimo die Febry. 1702/3 & record
                JOS: TAYLOE, Clk.

        Virga: Apr: ye 13th 1702.
        KNOW ALL MEN by these presents that I BRYON GROVE of ye Pish: of Christ Church & County of Lancastr: doe appoint & ordaine my loveing Brother WM: CHILTON, of ye sd. Pish: my true & lawfull Attorney to sue for & receive, to prison & out of prison THOMAS THOMPSON of the sd. Pish: for a yearely rent due by Lease to ye sd. BRYAN GROVE bearing date ye 26th of March 1698; As Wittness my hand the day & yeare above written
Test   ISAAC ROWDEN,   BRYAN GROVE
        JNO: DUGGAN

Probat fait Lettr. Attor. in Cur Com Lancastr. 13th Janry. et recordr.
JOS: TAYLOE, Clk.

WHEREAS the LADY MARGTT. CULPEPER, THOMAS LORD FAIRFAX &
KATHARINE his Wife, Proprietors of the Northern Neck of Virginia by a Power
of Attorney bearing date (blank) proved before the Genll. Court in Octobr: last
appointed in ye roome & stead of Coll. WM. FITZHUGH & Capt. GEORGE BRENT
their Lts., Agents & Attorneys, me ROBERT CARTER, Esqr. of Lancastr. County in
the sd. Northern Neck to be their sd. Attor: in as full & ample manner as were
the sd. WM: FITZHUGH & GEORGE BRENT as by the sd. Lettr: of Attorny doth more
fully appeare,   Now Therefore, Know All Men by these presents that I ye sd.
ROBERT CARTER have appointed THOMAS WALTER in ye County of Lancastr: in
sd. Northern Neck aforesd. to be my true & lawfull Attorny & Collectr: for ye sd.
County of STAFFORD giveing unto my sd. Attor: full & ample power to receive
all debts rents that are due from all p:sons tenants or landholdrs: in ye said
County unto ye sd. Proprietors as aforesd. unto ye daye of the date of these
presents and if any of the sd. Tenants within ye sd. County of STAFFORD shall
refuse or deny paymt., of any of their sd. debts rents or arrears of rents unto
my sd. Attorney

p.   I doe hereby further impower my sd. Attorney to sue imprison & im-
35   plead him or them soe refuseing and to levie distress for ye sd. rents and
       arreares and use all other lawfull wayes for ye recovery of ye sd. debts
& doe all things relateing to oye pr:misses as I my selfe might doe and I doe
ratifie whatsoever my sd. Attorney shall doe or cause to e done by these presents;   Wittness my hand & seale this Eleventh day of Febry. in ye first yeare of
ye Reigne of or: Sovereigne Lady Queen Ann 1702/3
Signed sealed & delivered in presence of
     ROBT: JONES,   ROBERT CARTER
     JOHN (? BARR)
     Recognitr in Cur Com Lancastr: 11th die Febry. 1702/3 et recordr.
               JOS: TAYLOE, Clk
     Att a Court held for Lancastr: County ye 11th Febry. 1702/3
Came into Court (in properia p:son) the within menconed ROBERT CARTER &
acknowledged ye within Lettr. of Attorney to be his act & deed and delivered
the same unto ye sd. THOMAS for ye uses therein menconed
               Test   JOS: TAYLOE, Clk.

THIS INDENTURE made the thirteenth day of October seventeen hundred
and two and in the first yeare of the reigne of our Soveraigne Lady Ann of
England, Scotland, France and Ireland, Queen, Defendr. of the faith, &c;, Betweene THOMAS PETTY of Sittenburne Parish in County of RICHMOND, Planter,
of the one part and SAMUELL STEELE of St. Maryes White Chappell Parish in
the County of Lancastr:, Planter, of the other part;   (Wittnesseth) that the sd.
THO: PETTY for good consideracons him thereunto moveing hath farm lett unto
the said SAMLL. STEELE all that tract of land bounded as followeth;   Begining at
a red Oake joyning on the line of ABRAHAM BUSH and THO. (? COTTEN) and
from thence down a Branch joyning on ROBT. CHRISTOPHER, then up the
Branch to the red Oake where it first began, being by computacon sixty five
acres;   To have and to hold the said land for and dureing

p.   the full time of ninety nine yeares from the date hereof unto the said

SAMLL. STEELE his heires and assignes from thence to enjoy with all houses woods thereunto belonging to be enjoyed without trouble or molestation of Law paying yearely one eare of Indian Corne at the Feast of St. Symon and Jude being the 28 of October only if the same be demanded, & I sd. THO: PETTY doe oblige my selfe to warrant the said Land from any p:sons whatsoever in the sume of ten thousand pounds of tobacco to be paid unto said SAMLL. STEELE if every article herein contained is not truely p:formed according to the meaning hereof;   In Wittness whereof I have hereunto sett my hand and fixed my seale the day and yeare above menconed
Signed sealed & delivered in presence of us
    JAMES   PHILLIPS,   THOMAS ⟍ PETTY
    THO: ⟋⟍CARPENTER
    Recognitr. in Cur Com Lancastr: 14th die April 1703 et recordr.
               p JOS: TAYLOE, Clk.

    KNOW ALL MEN by these presents that I KATHARINE PETTY of the County of RICHMOND doe by these presents appoint Mr. THOMAS CARPENTER of Lancastr: County my true and lawfull Attorny for to acknowledge a parcell of land unto SAMLL. STEELE that my Husband, THO: PETTY, hath sold him and doe acknowledge that it shall stand in vertue as if I were there present, as Wittness my hand this 12th of Janry. 1702/3
Test   JNO: KELLY,   KATHARINE   PETTY
    AMY (sig.) KELLY
    Recognitr in Cur Com Lancastr: 14th die April 1703 et recordr.
               p. JOS: TAYLOE, Clk.

p.   KNOW ALL MEN by these presents that I THOMAS LOE of Lancaster
37   County stand bound and indebted unto Mr. JOSEPH HARRISON of the same
       County, Gent., in the penall sume of Sixty pounds of lawfull money of England and twelve hundred pounds of good merchantable tobacco & casque to the wch: paymt. to be made I bind my selfe my heires togehter all and singular my Estate of what kind so ever (vizt) household goods, cattle, chattles and all other moveables as also a Plantacon and two hundred and six acres of land lately bought of JOHN PINKARD lyeing and being in the County of Lancaster aforesd., unto the abovesd. JOSEPH HARRISON his heires or assignes firmly by these presents dated this 10th day of March 1696/7 and in the 38th yeare of his Majesties Reigne
    THE CONDICON of this obligacon is such that if the above bound THOMAS LOE doe truely hereafter keep harmless the above menconed JOS: HARRISON his heires from all manner of troubles that may happen and accrue to him by reason of is being joyntly & severally bound and obliged in a Bond payable to his Majesties Justices of the Peace of the said County of Lancastr: for all the p:sonall Estate of JOHN BERRY, late of this County, deced., as by appraisement amounts to Thirty pounds Sterling money & six hundred pounds of good merchantable tobacco wch: was reposed and intrusted and putt into the hands of said THOMAS LOE for the use of SARAH BERRY, Daughter and heire of sd. JOHN BERRY, late deced., to be paid to her when she shall attaine to full age and then fully discharge the said JOSEPH HARRISON his heires &c., without fraud or coven that then this pr:sent obligacon to be voyd or else to stand in full effect
Signed sealed and delivered in pr:sence of us
    JOHN LAWNE,   THO: LOE
    THO: BARKER

Recordr. 14 die Apr. 1703, p JOS: TAYLOE, Clk.

From my MILL.   Febry. 27th 1702
Sr. PHILLIP STONE hath now settled his business wth: me. I desire you therefore to deliver up to him his Bond and the accon. I shall noe farther prosecute.
To Mr. JOS: TAYLOE   Yr. Freind.
                                                ROBERT CARTER

Recorded p ordr: of PHILLIP STONE,
            p. JOS: TAYLOE, Clk.

p.   KNOW ALL MEN by these presents that I ROBT: GIBSON of Christ
38   Church Parrish in Lancastr: County am held and firmly bound unto
        Capt. ALEXDR. SWAN, Capt. HENRY FLEET, Mr. GEO: HARWOOD and Dr.
JOSEPH BELFEILD in ye sum of one thousand pounds Sterling money to be paid
to ye sd. Capt. ALEXDR. SWAN, Capt. HENRY FLEET, Mr. GEO: HARWOOD and Dr.
JOS: BELFEILD or to either of ym. or either of their certain assignes, to ye true
p:formance of which I bind my selfe my Execrs. firmly by these presents.
Signed with my hand and seale ye eleventh day of Decembr: 1701
THE CONDITION of ye above obligation is such yt: whereas there is a marriage intended betweene ye above bound ROBT: GIBSON and MRS. RUTH WRIGHT,
Wid. & Relict of Mr. MOTTROM WRIGHT, late of Virginia, (deced). If therefore
the above bound ROBT. GIBSON shall give unto ye above mentioned RUTH
WRIGHT full power and authority by Will or Deed of Gift to dispose off, bequeath or give away as shall best please ye above mentioned RUTH WRIGHT
thirty pounds Sterling mony of England & one fourth pt: of all ye Estate yt:
shall bee obtained by her, ye sd. RUTH WRIGHT, by virtue of her marriage wth:
ye abovesd. MOTTROM WRIGHT, and shall from time to time give and make any
other Deed or Deeds grant or conveyance as shall be desired by ye abovesd.
RUTH WRIGHT for ye firm secureing and conveying ye above mentioned sum
of mony and estate, to wch: use ye abovesd. RUTH WRIGHT shall devise then
this abovesd. obligation to be void & of noe effect, otherwise to bee and
remaine in full force power & virtue
Signed seal'd & delover'd in ye pr:sence of
        JNO: COOKE,   ROBT. GIBSON
        GEO: WALE,   ELIZA: COOKE p sig.
    Recordr. p ordr. of ye Court 14 Apr. 1703.
                    JOS: TAYLOE, Clk.

KNOW ALL MEN by these presents yt: I NATHLL. DAVIS late of LONDON-
DERRY now in BELFAST for severall good reasons doe appoint my well beloved
Freind, ye Revern'd Mr. FRANCIS MAKENIE in POTOMACK in Virginia to be my
lawfull Attorney for me to demand and receive all debts to me by Mr. PHILIP
SHAPLEIGH in LITTLE WICOCOMOCO in Virginia, either by Bill or tobacco or
otherwise; in case of non payment to arrest and imprison ye sd. PHILLIP
SHAPLEIGH

p.   To acct. for my acco. as he shall think fitt, he or they holding me acct.
39   I doe ratifie and confirme as if I were there personally p:sent. as Witt-
        ness my hand and seale att BELFAST Janry. 8th 1702.
    Wittness present. (turn over).   The wch: in Lettr. of Attorney signed sealed
and delivered in presence of us.

ARCHIBALD MILLING, GEO: TOBY
JNO: MAIN, WILL: DUNN
     Probatum Lettr. Attor: in Cur Com Lancastr: due decimo die May 1703 p
sacramt. ARCH: MILLING, JOHAN MAIN et WILL: DUNN JUNR., in Cur et Recordr
                         p JOS: TAYLOE, Clk.

     KNOW ALL MEN by these presents that I MOTTR: WRIGHT, SENR. doth by
these presents give & deliver these eight Negroes as being foure men & foure
women bought by me, ye sd. WRIGHT, for my Son, MOTTR: WRIGHT before these
present persons as shall here wittness ye same Instrumt. of Writeing, and for
my sd. Son, MOTTR: WRIGHTs use with their increase for ever without any
mollestacon what ever as Wittness my hand and seale this ye 11th day of
Octobr: 1695
Signed sealed & delivered in ye presence of
     ROWLAND LAWSON, SENR.,   MOTTR: WRIGHT
     EDWD. GIBSON p. sig.
     JOHN GWYE, CHARLES HIGGINSON
     Negro Frank, Negro Nora & her encrease, Negro Betty & her encrease,
Negro Peter, Negro Dido & her encrease
     Att a Court held for Lancastr: County ye 10th day of Febry. 1702
EDWD. GIBSON made Oath ytt: he see the sd. WRIGHT signe seale & deliver ye
above Instrumt. to the uses therein exprest
                    Test   JOS: TAYLOE, Clk.

p.   KNOW ALL MEN by these presents that I JAMES HALTRIDGE of ye
40   Kingdom of Ireland doe hereby constitute and appoint THOMAS CARTER
        in ye River of RAPPH: in Collony of Virga., as my lawfull Attorney for
mee to receive all such sums as to me is due in sd. Collony by any p:sons inhabiting, hereby ratifying whatsoever my sd. Attorney shall lawfully doe and
allsoe all such receipts & discharges as sd. Attorney in my name shall make.
Given under my hand & seale this 19th day of Xbr: 1702
Signed sealed & delivered in presence of
     GABRIELL CRAIG,   JAMES HALTRIDGE
     PATRICK MOORE, JAMES McCLUER
     Probatr. Lettr. Attor: in Cur Com Lancastr: 12th die May 1702 p sacramt.
GABRIELL CRAIGG et JAMES McCLUER, JUNR., in Cur et record
                    JOS: TAYLOE, Clk.

     KNOW ALL MEN by these presents that I WILLIAM ROBINSON of BELFAST
in ye Kingdome of IRELAND, Mercht., have appointed my trusty & well beloved
Freinds, Mr. THO: CARTER & Mr. HENRY CARTER, them or either of them both of
COROTOMAN on RAPPH: RIVER & Lancastr: County in ye Provice of Virginia my
true & lawfull Attornys for me to receive all sumes either of tobacco or money
due to me from any p:sons in ye Province of Virga., either by Bill or any other
manner or way and to do all other acts in ye Law as fully as I my selfe might
doe were I personally present, ratifying all yt: my sd. Attornys shall legally
doe in ye premisses, as Wittness my hand & seale dated att BELFAST ye 17 day of
9br 1702
Signed sealed & delivered in presence of
     GABRIELL CRAIG, JAMES McCLUER,   WM: ROBINSON
     HUGH SCOT, JOHN CRAWFORD
     Probatr. Lettr. Attor. in Cur Com Lancastr. 12th die May 1703 p sacremt.

GABRI: CRAIG & JAMES McCLUER, Jur in Cur et record
Test   JOS: TAYLOE, Clk.

p.   THIS INDENTURE made ye 12th day of Octobr: in ye first yeare of ye
41   reigne of or: Soveraigne Lady Ann &c., Anoq: Dom: 1702, Betweene
        ROBERT SCHOLFEILD of the Parish of Christ Church in ye County of
Lancastr: of ye one part and ROBERT GIBSON of ye aforesd. Pish: & County of ye
other part; (Wittnesseth) that ye sd. ROBERT SCHOLFEILD for sume of Ninety
pounds Sterling money of England by good Bills of Exchange and foure thousand pounds of good merchantale tobbo. (vizt) two thousand of sweet sented
tobacco and two thousand pounds more ye other moyetie thereof in good
arronocoe tobbo., to be paid by ye sd. ROBERT GIBSON and for divers good causes
hath granted unto ye sd. ROBERT GIBSON all that tract of land in ye Pish: &
County aforesd. containing One hundred acres bounding as followeth (vizt).
Begining att a corner marked Chesnutt standing in ye sd. GRIGGS line half a
mile from ye River, thence runing alonge ye sd. GRIGGS line of marked trees
North East 160 poles to a markt. corner wt: Oake standing on ye North East side
of ye mouth of a small Creeke which issueth out of SLAUGHTERS CREEKE on ye
South East side thereof, from ye white Oake runing by marked trees South East
100 poles to a corner white Oake standing on ye South West side of a Branch
which issueth out of SLAUGHTERS CREEKE and neer unto a Path which runs
from ye sd. GRIGGS Plantacon to his Quarters att ye head of ye Creeke, thence
runing by marked trees South West crossing ye Branch of a Creeke to a small
corner Pine standing on ye side of a Valley on ye South side of ye Main Creeke
neer unto ye sd. Creeke which sd. Creeke issueth from RAPPAH: RIVER between Mr. THOMAS MEDSTAIDs Old Plantacon and the Plantacon whereon LAW-
RENCE MOULD formerly lived and from ye sd. Pine North West by marked trees
crossing ye Main Creeke 100 poles to ye corner tree where it first began, and is
part & pr:cell of a devidend of land containing 1000 acres formerly taken up &
patented by one EPAPHRODITUS LAWSON as by the Pattent thereof bearing date
ye 22th day of May in ye yeare of or: Lord 1650 doth appeare, which said Pattent was assigned over unto one THOMAS MEDSTAID by one ROBERT DAVIS &
ELIZABETH his Wife, Daughter & heire unto ye sd. EPAPHRODITUS LAWSON as
by the Records of Lancastr: Court bearing date ye 11th day of Septembr: 1666
may appeare & since by ye sd. MEDSTAID renewed in his own name as by the
Pattent thereof bearing date ye 26th day of Aprill Anoq: Dom: 1668, relacon
being thereunto had may appeare and by him, ye said MEDSTAID, to ELIZA-
BETH, his Daughter, the now Wife of Mr.

p.   CHARLES LEE, late of NORTHUMBERLD. County, Gent. (deced), and by
42   them, ye sd. CHARLES LEE & ELIZABETH his Wife, sold unto Mr. MICHALL
        GRIGGS as by their Deed of Sale indented bearing date ye first day of De-
cembr: 1684 may appeare and by him, ye sd. MICHALL GRIGGS given by his
Last Will & Testamt. unto his Wife, ANN, ye Daughter of ROBERT & ELINR:
SCHOLFEILD, late of this County, (deced), and in case of her mortality to ROBERT
SCHOLFEILD, the Father of ye sd. ANN, whereby she, ye sd. ANN, dyeing the sd.
ROBERT, ye Father of ye said ANN, came by his right to ye sd. Land & was thereof possest as lawfully he might by ordr: of ye Genll. Court; And by him, ye sd.
ROBERT, willed unto ye above sd. ROBERT, party to these presents, and all
houses buildings tobbo houses in & uppon ye sd. One hundred acres of land and
all orchards woods advanges & appurtenances whatsoever, To have and to
hold ye sd. pr:cell of land hereby granted unto ye sd. ROBERT GIBSON his heires

& assignes for ever to be holden to the Cheife Lords of ye fees of the premisses without   incumbrances

p.   done by the sd. ROBERT SCHOLFEILD or any other p:sons claiming under
43   him and by sd. ROBERT SCHOLFEILD and JUDITH his Wife will acknow-
        ledge these presents;   In Wittness whereof the sd. ROBERT SCHOLFEILD
hath sett his and & seale ye day & yeare first above written
Sealed & delivered in presence of
        DANLL. McCARTEY, JOS: BELFIELD,   ROBERT SCHOLFEILD
        PHILLIP STONE, RICHD: GARRETT
    Recognitr. in Cur Com Lancastr: 12 die May 1703 p ROBERT SCHOLFEILD et
JUDITH Uxor. et Record
                    JOS: TAYLOE, Clk.

    THIS INDENTURE made ye 12th day of Apr: Ano. Dom: 1703 & in ye 2d
yeare of ye reigne of or: Soveraigne Lady Ann &c., Betweene BRYON STOTT,
SENR. of ye Pish: of St. Marys White Chaple in ye County of Lancastr:, Gent., of
ye one part and JOHN WILLCOX of ye Pish: & County aforesd. of ye other part;
Wittnesseth that ye sd. BRYON STOTT for ye full sume of eight thousand pounds
of good sound & merchantable tobbo wth: casque part thereof allready paid to
ye sd. BRYON STOTT and ye remaindr: to be paid by ye sd. JOHN WILLCOX by he
last of Decembr: which shall be in the yeare of or: Lord God 1704 by these presents have sold unto the said JOHN WILLCOCKS his heires & assignes Seventy
acres of land being in ye Pish & County aforesd. and bounded as

p.   followeth (vizt) Begining att a Stake standing in ye line which parts
44   this land from Mr. TOMLINs land, the sd. Stake being att ye South most
        corner of Mr. BRYON STOTT, JUNR., his land surveyed by EDWIN CON-
WAY in March last & from ye sd. Stake runing allonge ye sd. STOTT, JUNR. his
line North 33 degrees West 101 p;ches to a red Oake, thence N. N. W. 34 p;ches to
a Dogwood tree, thence S: 47: degrees West 116 p;ches to ye WATTERY SWAMP,
thence allonge ye sd. Swamp South 40 degrees East fivety p;ches & South 21
degrees East 44 p;ches to a red Oake sapling standing in ye aforesd. line which
devides this & Mr. TOMLINs land, thence allonge ye sd. line 110 p;ches to ye
first mentioned station (the place wherein it began) the sd. Seventy acres of
land (by ye aforemenconed bounds courses & distances included) the sd.
BRYON STOTT doth by these presents confirme unto ye sd. JOHN WILLCOCKS his
heires & assignes;   To have and to hold from henceforth forever subject
nevertheless unto ye Quitt Rents wch: shall grow due;   In Wittness whereof the
sd. BRYON STOTT, SENR. to this present Indenture hath sett his hand & seale the
day & yeare above written
In presence of JOHN STOTT,   BRYON STOTT
        JAMES HILL p sig.

p.   Recognitr in Cur Com Lancastr. decimo die May Ano: Dom: 1703 p
45   STEPH: TOMLIN, ye Attor: BRYON STOTT et recordr.
                    JOS: TAYLOE, Clk.

    KNOW ALL MEN by these presents that I THOMAS HINDE of LIVERPOOLE
in ye County of Lancastr: & Kingdome of England, Merchat., have appointed
my trustly & well beloved Freind, JOHN LANCASTR: of LIVERPOOLE in ye County
aforesd., Marrinr:, Comandr: of ye good Ship called the (?"PLANER of LIVER-

POOLE," aforesd. my trusty lawfull Attorney to demand from Mr. JNO: BER-
TRANDs Exors. or Admrs. or whom else it may concerne in RAPPH. within
Virga: in America all sumes of money by him received on acct. of any Bills left
in his hands and to settle & adjust all accots. depending with ye sd. JNO: BER-
TRAND touching or relateing to ye same & receive all such sumes due unto me
from any persons in Virginia;   In Wittness whereof I have hereto put my hand
& seale ye 2d day of Janry. Ano: Dom: Ann Anglia &c. 1702
                                   T. HINDE
     Att a Court held for Lancastr: County ye 14 day of July 1703
Att ye motion of Mr. JNO: LANCASTR: the within Lettr. of Attorney being
ordered to be admitted to Record, I doe hereby certify ye same yt: pr:suant to ye
sd. Ordr. ye same is recorded in Lancastr: County
          p   JOS: TAYLOE, Clk.
   (In margin: Signed Sealed & delivered on double strength paper by the within
THOMAS HINDE in presence of JOHN COCKSHUTT, Mayor of LIVERPOOLE
                    RA: PETERS

p.   KNOW ALL MEN by these presents that I BRYAN STOTT, SENR. of the
46   County of Lancastr: have made my loveing Brother, STEPH: TOMLIN, my
         true & lawfull Attorney to acknowledge Seventy acres of land laid out by
Mr. EDWIN CONWAY unto JOHN WILLCOCKS of ye same County to him & his
heires for ever.
Signed sealed & delivered in ye presence of
     JOHN STOTT,   BRIAN STOTT
     JAMES HILL p sig.
     Probatr. in Cur Com Lancastr. duo decimo die May 1703 et record
               JOS: TAYLOE, Clk.

     THIS INDENTURE made ye 6th day of Febry. in ye yeare of or: Lord 1702/3
Betweene WM: DRAPER of ye County of RICHMD. of ye one pte. and NICHOLAS
BUTTLER of ye County of Lancastr: of ye other part;   Wittnesseth that ye sd.
WM: DRAPER for five thousand four hundred pounds of tobacco to be pd. by the
sd. BUTTLER, ye sd.WM: DRAPER doth demise & mortgage unto the said NICHO:
BUTTLER & his heirs a certaine Plantacon lying in Lancastr: County whereon
ye sd. WM: DRAPER formerly lived and now in his tenur & possession, bounded,
(vizt.) Begining upon the River upon the mouth of WASHINGTONS RIVER,
runing alonge ye Pond & Marsh till it meets wth: ye line of Capt. SAMLL. FOX,
thence alonge his line to ye line of Mr. ROBERT POLLARD and thence to ye line
of JAMES GATES and alonge the sd. GATES his line to ye River, which bounds
include ye qt. of 100 acres of land with all woods minerals mines &c., together
with ye Plantacon;   To have and to hold for ye full space & terme of time of
ninety nine yeares fully to be compleat & ended unto ye sd. NICHO: BUTTLER &
his heires from ye day of ye date of these presents, he paying ye Quitt Rents
that shall be due for ye sd. Land and ye sd. WM: DRAPER doth covenant with ye
sd. NICHO: BUTTLER to defend ye sd. land soe mortgaged against all p:sons
whatsoever.   In Wittness whereof the partys abovesd. have sett their hands &
seales the day & yeare above written
Signed sealed & delivered in presence of us
     WM. HANKS p sig, SENR.   WM: DRAPER

p.   ZACHARIAH NICHOLS,
47   EDWARD JEFFREY

Memod.   That this Covenant endorsed on ye back side of this present Deed of Mortgage made by and betweene ye within bounden WM: DRAPER of ye one pte: and the within menconed NICHO: BUTTLER of ye other pte: was by agreemt. before the ensealing & delivery of these words (vizt.)

And the sd. WM: DRAPER doth Covenant to & with ye sd. NICHO: BUTTLER that he ye sd. WM: DRAPER & his heires shall at all times hereafter acknowledge any Deed or other writing unto ye sd. NICHO: BUTTLER as his learned Council in ye Law shall reasonably devise;   As Wittness my hand & seale this 5th day of Febry. in ye first yere of or: Sovereigne Lady Queen Ann by the grace of God of England, Scottland France & Ireland, Defendr. of ye faith, Annoque Dom: 1702/3

      WM: HANKS, SENR. p sig.   WM: DRAPER
      ZACHARIAH NICHOLS
      EDWD. JEFFREY

Recognitr in Cur Com Lancastr: 12th die May 1703 p EDWARD JEFFREY, Atto: of WILLM. DRAPER et recordr.
      JOS: TAYLOE, Clk.

KNOW ALL MEN by these presents that I WILLIAM DRAPER of the County of RICHMD. doe make my good Freind, EDWARD JEFFREY, of ye sd. County of RICHMOND my lawfull Attorny for me to acknowledge a Mortgage made by me of ye one pte. and NICHO: BUTTLER of the County of Lancastr: of ye other pte., and this shall be his warrt. for ye same,   As Wittness my hand this 6th day of Febry. 1702/3.

Testes WM: HANKES, SENR. p sig.   WM: DRAPER
      ZACHARIAH NICHOLS

Probatr. Lettr: Atto: Cur Com Lancastr. 12th die May 1703 et record
      JOS; TAYLOE, Clk.

p.   KNOW ALL MEN by these presents that I WM: DRAPER of ye County of
48   RICHMD. am indebted unto NICHO: BUTTLER of ye County of Lancaster in
      ye sume of ten thousand eight hundred pounds of tobbo. & caske to be paid unto ye sd. NICHO: BUTTLER to ye which paymt. I binde my selfe my heires Sealed with my seale dated this 6th day of Febry. 1702/3

THE CONDICON of ye above bounden obligacon is such that if WM: DRAPER doe at all times observe all articles in a Deed of Mortgage betweene ye above bounden WM: DRAPER and NICHO: BUTTLER, that then this obligacon to be void or else be in full force

Sealed signed & delivered in ye presence of
      WM: HANKS, SENR.   WM: DRAPER
      ZACHARIAH NICHOLS,   EDWD. JEFFREY

Recognitr. in Cur Com Lancastr: 12th May 1703 et record
      Test   p   JOS: TAYLOE, Clk

Virga. ss. TO ALL CHRISTIAN PEOPLE to whom this present writeing shall come, I THOMAS PHILLIPS, late of Lancastr: County, now of PRINCESS ANN County send Greeting in or: Lord God. Know yee yt: I the sd. THOMAS PHILLIPS for many valuable consideracons & especially for two thousand eight hundred pounds of good merchantable tobacco & caske allready receaved have made over unto THOMAS CHETTWOOD of Lancastr: County in White Chaple Pish., and to his heires one devidend of land conteigning sixty three acres being in Lancastr: County aforesd. and bounded as followeth (vizt) from ye head of a Creek

called (? MACIH: POINT CREEK) and runing from ye head of ye said Creek into
ye woods to a marked white Oake which parts this land and the land of WM:
MERRYMAN and was formerly bought of ROBERT NEASUM of Lancastr: County
abovesd. by THOMAS WILDGOOSE as by Deed of Sale dated ye 3d of July 1684 may
more at large appeare, and by the said THOMAS WILDGOOSE conveyed unto THO-
MAS PHILLIPS, Father of sd. THOMAS PHILLIPS as by Deed of Sale dated ye 29th
day of September 1688 may allsoe appeare; To have and to hold the said Devidend of land with houses meadows swamps waters profitts

p.   to him ye sd. THOMAS CHETTWOOD & his heires for ever; In Wittness
49   whereof I the said THOMAS PHILLIPS have hereunto sett my hand &
        fixed my seale this 5th day of March 1700/1
Signed selaed & acknowledged in presence of
        THOMAS MASON,   THO: PHILLIPS
        FRANCIS MORSE
    Recognitr in Cur Com Lancastr: 14th die May 1701 p GEO: CHILTON, Attor. et
rcord 16th die sequend
                p.   JOS: TAYLOE, Clk.
    Recognitr in Cur Com Lancastr: 12th die May 1703 p THOM: CHITTWOOD &
record   p   JOS: TAYLOE, Clk

    Virginia ss. KNOW ALL MEN by these presents that I THOMAS PHILLIPS of
PRINCESS ANN County doe owe & am indebted unto THOMAS CHETTWOOD of Lancastr: County or to his heires in ye full sume of five thousand six hundred
pounds of very good sound & merchantable tobacco & casque

p.   in paymt. thereof I doe binde my selfe my heires. In Wittness whereof
50   I have sett my hand & seale this 5th day of March 1700/1
    THE CONDICON of the above obligacon is such that I THOMAS PHILLIPS
hath sold unto THOMAS CHITTWOOD Sixty three acres of land in ye Pish: of
White Chaple bounded as is exprest by his Deed for ye same. If I the sd. THO-
MAS PHILLIPS his heires att all times hereafter keep harmless the abovesd.
THOMAS CHETTWOOD his heires from all trouble of any p:sons whatsoever, Then
this present obligacon to be void or otherwise to remaine in full power
Signed sealed & delivered in p:sence of us
        THO: MASON,   THO: PHILLIPS
        FRANCIS MORSE
    Recognitr in Cur Com Lancastr: 14th die May 1701 et record 16th die.
                JOS: TAYLOE, Clk.
    Recognitr in Cur Com Lancastr: 12th die May 1703 p THO: CHITTWOOD et
recordr.   JOS: TAYLOE, Clk

    KNOW ALL MEN by these presents that I EDWARD CARTER of Pish: of
Christ Church in ye County of Lancastr: Gent., am firmly bound unto THOMAS
CARTER, HENERY CARTER & JOHN CARTER & every of them their heires jointly
& severally in ye sume of Five hundred pounds Sterling money of England.
Sealed with my seale & dated this 24th day of June 1703
    THE CONDICON of ye above obligacon is such that whereas THOMAS CARTER,
late of this County, Gent. (deced), did by his Last Will & Testamt. bearing date ye
16th day of Augt: 1700 give &

p.   bequeath unto his Sons, THO: CARTER, HENERY CARTER & JOHN CARTER,

50.   three hundred acres of land to them & their heires for ever to be
equally devided betweene them within six months from and after ye decease of ye sd. THOMAS CARTER, ye donor of ye pr:misses; And forasmuch as ye
above bounden EDWD. CARTER hath been privy & consenting to ye Will of ye
sd. THOMAS, now (deced), and allsoe to ye division of ye sd. lands before given,
Now if ye sd. EDWARD CARTER shall for himselfe his heires at all times hereafter truely keep indemnified ye sd. THOMAS CARTER, HENERY CARTER & JOHN
CARTER & every of them their heires in their lands aforesd., according to ye
meaning of ye sd. Last Will of ye sd. (deced), and according to ye allotments laid
out & devided by a line or lines of markt trees by Mr. EDWIN CONWAY, Surveyor, and shall likewise keep indemnified the aforesd. THOMAS CARTER,
HENERY CARTER & JOHN CARTER from all incumbrances concerning ye sd.
EDWD. CARTER his heires, That then this obligacon shall be void or else to remaine in full force
Sealed & delivered in pr:sence of
          THOMAS SAMPSON,   EDWARD CARTER
          JOHN DAVIS
     Recorded att ye instance of Mr. THOMAS CARTER
               p. JOS: TAYLOE, Clk.

     KNOW ALL MEN by these presents yt. wee THOMAS CARTER, HENERY
CARTER & JOHN CARTER all of ye Pish: of Christ Church in ye County of Lan-
castr:, Gent., are joyntly holden & indebted to EDWARD CARTER of ye sd. Pish: &
County, Gent., in ye sume of One hundred pounds Sterling money.   Sealed wth:
my seale & dated ye 24th day of June 1703
     THE CONDICON of this obligacon is that whereas Majr. EDWD. DALE, late of this
County (deced) in his lifetime did make & acknowledge one Deed of Gift for dis-
posing of one Negroe boy named James and one Molattoe boy named Robin to
Mr. THOMAS CARTER and CATHERINE his Wife, late of this County (deced), and
after their decease the said Mollatoe boy, Robin, to EDWARD CARTER as by the
said Deed with Certificate of acknowledgement thereon bearing date ye 7th day
of Octobr: 1687

p.   Now if ye sd. THOMAS CARTER, HENERY CARTER & JOHN CARTER and
52   every of their heires shall hereafter save & defend the sd. EDWARD
        CARTER his heires full & quiet possession of the sd. Molattoe Robin now
in his actuall possession by vertue of a Deed of Gift that then this obligacon
shall be void or else to remaine in full force
Sealed & delivered in presence of
          THO: SAMPSON   THO: CARTER
          JOHN DAVIS   HENR: CARTER
     Recorded   att ye instance of Mr. THO: CARTER
               p. JOS: TAYLOE Clk.

     THIS INDENTURE wittnesseth that EDWD. FLIN of his free & voluntary
will hath put himselfe Apprentice to JOHN LAWRIE of ye County of Lancastr:
SHIP CARPENTER, his heires or assignes to learn the trade & calleing of a Ship
Carpenter which he ye sd. LAWRIE now useth to be taught and with him after
ye manner of an Apprentice to dwell & serve the sd. LAWRIE from ye day of ye
date hereof unto ye full terme of eight yeares fully to be compleated, all which
terme the sd. Apprentice to ye sd. JOHN LAWRIE well & truely shall serve; his
secretts shall keep close; his commandmts. lawfull & honest he shall gladly doe

harm to his Master he shall not doe or suffer to be done but shall imediately
admonish his sd. Mastr. thereof; the goods of his sd. Master he shall not in-
ordinately wast nor them to any body lend; att dice or any other unlawfull
game he shall not play. shall not absent himselfe but in all things as a good &
faithfull Apprentice shall behave himself dureing ye terme aforesd. And the
sd. JOHN LAWRIE doth oblidge himselfe to his sd. Apprentice the trade &
calleing he shall teach and allsoe to learn him to write & ciffer and dureing
the sd. terme of eight yeares provide him with clothing & dyett and other
necessarys and at ye expiration of ye sd. terme to give unto ye sd. EDWD: FLIN
one whole sett of Carpenters tooles fitt for one of his trade & one suit of good
aparrell; In Wittness whereof the partys above named have interchangably
putt their hands & seales this 3d day of May 1703
Signed sealed in ye presence of
      THO: CARTER,   EDWD: FLIN
      WM: HEWARD
    Att a Court held for Lancastr: County ye 12th day of May 1703
Att ye instance of Mr. JOHN LAWRIE, the above Indenture ws ordered to be
transmitted to Record and is recorded
           p. JOS; TAYLOE, Clk.

p.   (The above Indenture is repeated and signed by JOHN LAWRIE)
53   Att a Court held for Lancastr: County ye 12th of May 1703
    Att ye instance of Mr. JOHN LAWRIE, the above Indenture was ordered
to be transmitted to Record and is recorded
           p. JOS: TAYLOE, Clk.

p.   20th die Septembr: 1703.
54   Recorded for SARAH LAWRENCE a yearling Heifer marked with a
    Crop & two over keeles with all her encrease p ordr: of MARY LAW-
RENCE, Widdow
      Test p JOS: TAYLOE, Clk.

    JOSEPH TAYLOE records for his Daughter, ELIZTH: TAYLOE, one Heifer of
two yeares old called Cherry of a red couler marked with a crop and two slitts &
overkeele on ye left eare & slit & overkeele on ye right eare
    7br. ye 20th 1703. Test JOS: TAYLOE, Clk.

    ELIZBTH: MULLIS records for her Son, JOHN MULLIS, his marke of Cattle
& hoggs being two crops & two slitts. 8br. 19th 1703.
      Test JOS: TAYLOE, Clk.

    MARYLAND ss. KNOW ALL MEN by these presents yt: I ST. LEGER CODD of
KENT County in the Province of MARYLAND aforesd., Gent., am held & firmly
bound unto WILLIAM TAYLOE of RICHMOND County of the Collony of Virginia
his heires in the full sume of two hundred and thirty pounds Sterling money.
Sealed with my seale and dated this Twelfth day of August 1693
    THE CONDICION of the above obligacon is that if the sd ST. LEGER CODD att or
upon the third day of October next ensueing the date hereof shall meet att St.
Marys in MARYLAND or within three dayes of the time aforesd. and yt: there
the sd. ST. LEGER CODD shall make a sufficient conveyance of all his rights
from him and all claims under him unto the said WILLIAM TAYLOE his heires
or assignes of a seate of land late in occupacon of the abovesd. CODD & lying att

the head of COROTOMAN RIVER in Lancastr: County in the Collony of Virginia by estimacon two thousand three hundred acres according to the bounds men- coned in a Pattent granted to EDWYN CONWAY, that then this obligacon to be voyd or else to remaine in full force
Signed sealed & delivered in the presence of
     RICH: LEE,   ST. LEGER CODD
     ROBERT BURMAN
  Record p JOS: TAYLOE, Clk.   10th 9br. 1703.

p.   THIS INDENTURE made the sixth day of Octoer in the yeare of or: Lord
55   one thousand six hundred ninety and three Betweene ST. LEGER CODD of
      KENT County in the Province of Maryland of the one part and WILLIAM
TAYLOE of RICHMOND County in he Collony of Virginia, Gent., of the other part; Wittnesseth that said ST. LEGER CODD for the sume of One hundred and fifteen pounds of currant money of England to him paid, hath sold unto the sd. WM: TAYLOE a parcell of land formerly in the tenor and occupacon of the sd. ST. LEGER CODD and by him purchased from SAMUEL PENSAX of LONDON, Mariner, scituate in the County of Lancaster in the sd. Collony and on the South East side of the head of CORROTOMAN RIVER, begining att the mouth of a Creek called CONAWAYS CREEK and so runing North Easterly along the said River six hun- dred twenty five poles to a white Oake standing att the side of a Mill by a Great Swap side being marked on four sides, thence South East by marked trees to an other corner marked white Oake standing nere a Run and Swamp which runs towards JO: MEREDITHs, thence runing by marked trees South West six hun- dred and twenty five poles to a marked Pockicory and from thence North West by marked trees to the mouth of CONAWAYS CREEK six hundred & forty poles to the place where it first began, containing two thousand three hundred acres of land which said tract of land was formerly purchased by the said SAMLL. PENSAX of EDWYN CONWAY, deced., together with all houses &c., appurte-nanes except and allwayes reserved out of this present Indenture unto WILLIAM GOURDOUNE his heires & assignes two hundred acres of land sould by the said CONWAY to the said GOURDOUNE

p.   adjoyning unto the land of JO: JONES bought of JO: MEREDITH and for-
56   merly Patented in the name of ELYAS EDMONDS, begining att a marked
      white Oake or nigh unto the said Oake being a corner tree, and runing
for breadth by the said JONES Land and for length into the woods towards the head of the North West Branch of CORROTOMAN RIVER; To have and to hold the sd. two thousand five hundred acres of land (except as before excepted) unto the said WILLIAM TAYLOE his heires and assignes for ever against all persons that may hereafter claim any part of the pr:misses under the said ST. LEGER CODD or his heires. In Wittness whereof the above named have sett their hands & seales the day & yeare above written
Sealed and delivered in presence of
     NICHOLAS SEWALL,   ST. LEGER CODD
     CHA: CARROLL, E. CHILTON

p.   Recognitr in Curia Com Lancastr: decimo die 9bris 1703 per WILLIAM
57   ALLERTON, Attor. de ST. LEGER CODD, Gent., et recordr.
          p. JOS: TAYLOE, Clk

     KNOW ALL MEN by these presents that we ST. LEGER CODD & ANNA the

Wife of the said ST. LEGER CODD both of KENT County and Province of MARY-
LAND have made our well beloved Freinds, Coll. RICHARD LEE, Collo. ISAACK
ALLERTON & Mr. WILLOUGHBY ALLERTON of WESTMORELAND County in Virginia our true and lawfll Attorneys to acknowledge in Lancaster County or any
other Court in Virginia our right of a parcell of land lying att the head of
CURRATOMAN RIVER formerly bought of SAMUELL PENSAX containing two
thousand three hundred acres unto Mr. WILLIAM TAYLOE of RICHMOND County
in the Collony of Virginia.   In Wittness whereof we have hereunto sett our
hands & seales this 30 day of Sept. 1693
Signed sealed & delivered in the presence of
        E. CHILTON,   WILLIAM TOMLINSON,   by the above named
        BERKELEY CODD,   JOHN LEWIS   ST. LEGER CODD
                                                      ANNA CODD

      Recordr. decimo die 9bris 1703.
                    p. JOS: TAYLOE, Clk.

      Record for GEO: CHEWNING one Cow & her encrease marked with a slitt &
uper keele on ye right eare & a crop on ye left eare
1703 9br. ye 7th.   p. JOS: TAYLOE, Clk

p.   KNOW ALL MEN by these presents yt: I JOHN BUXSTON of ye County of
58   Lancaster in Virginia doe give & bequeath all my right of a certaine
        parcell of land it being in ye County of Lancaster unto JOHN BUSH of ye
aforesd. County his heires for ever, the bland bounded as followeth, Begining
at a corner white Oak standing in ye Main Branch betweene ye VINE NECK and
GRIMLEYs Old Field, from thence runing South by a long line of marked trees
to a Branch of HOGGS HEDD NECK from thence down ye sd. Swamp to a marked
Beach, from thence up ye Main Branch to ye white Oake where it first began;
To have and to hold with all ye pertinences thereto belonging as warrant from
me ye sd. JNO: BUXSTON my heires unto ye sd. JNO: BUSH his heires for ever; In
Wittness hereof I have sett my hand and seale ye 12th day of July 1703
Test   BENJ: BROWNE,   JNO: ⊥ BUXSTON
       NACE BUSH
      Recognitr in Cur Com Lancastr: 13 die July p. JNO: BUXSTON & MERCY Uxor et
record   p. JOS: TAYLOE, Clk.

      KNOW ALL MEN by these presents yt: I JOHN BUSH of ye County of Lan-
caster in Virginia doe give all my right of a certaine p:cell of land it being
scituate in ye County of Lancaster unto JOHN BUXSTON of ye aforesd. County his
heires for ever, ye sd. land bounded as followeth, Begining at a Pear tree standing on ye sd. JNO: BUXSTONs line, from thence runing down to a Branch on
NEW PLANTACON NECK, then up ye Branch to ye sd. JNO: BUSHes head line, from
thence Westerly to a corner white Oake of ye sd. JOHN BUXSTONs, ye sd. land ye
sd. JNO: BUXSTON to have and to hold together with ye pertenances thereto belonging wth: warrant from ye sd. JOHN BUSH his heirs for ever, unto JOHN
BUXSTON his heires and assignes for ever; In Wittness hereof I have sett my
hand & seale ye 12 day of July 1703
Test   BENJ. BROWNE   JNO: BUSH
       NACE BUSH, | his mark   MARGARETT ℋ BUSH

p.   TO ALL TO WHOME these shall come Greeting. Know yee yt: I NACE BUSH
59   of ye County of Lancaster in Virginia do by these presents sell unto

JOHN BUSH of ye aforesd. County a certaine p:cell of land scituated in ye County of Lancaster bounded as followeth, Beginning at a forked Popular standing in ye Main Swamp of MORRATTICO, from thence due South to a corner Pear tree, from thence running Westerly to a Branch wch: divideth this from ye land of SMLL. STELE, from thence up ye Main Swamp to ye Popular where it first began, ye sd. land ye sd. JNO. BUSH to have and to hold together with all priviledges thereto belonging wth: warrant from me ye sd. NACE BUSH my heires dureing ye whole terme & time of Ninety nine yeares ensueing ye date hereof I ye said NACE BUSH haveing allready reced. a valuable consideracon in hand; In Wittness my hand and seale this 12th day of July 1703
Test   BENJ: BROWNE,   NACE ⊥ BUSH
        JNO: BUXSTON
        Recognitr in Cur Com Lancastr: 14th die July 1703 p NACE BUSH & record
                p. JOS: TAYLOE, Clk

        KNOW ALL MEN by these presents that I ANN LADNER, ye Wife of HUGH LADNER, of ye Pish. of St. Marys White Chappell in Lancastr: County for sundry consideracons have made and appointed my trusty & well beloved Friend, Mr. THO: BARKER, JUNR., my true and lawfull Attorney for me to ye only proper use & behoofe of Capt. RICHD: BALL his heirs to acknowledge my free and voluntary consent to ye sale of ye MILL now held by my sd. Husband, HUGH LADNR, to ye sd. RICHARD BALL his heires & assignes, together with all ye right I now have by right of Dower or otherwise, wch: sd. Deed of Sale for ye sd. MILL and pr:misses beares even date with these presents; In Wittness whereunto I have hereunto sett my hand & seale this 14th day of July 1703
Sealed & published in presence of us
        WM: BALL   ANN A LADNER
        JAMES COMMELINE,
        ANN ⊥ CHEWNING
        Recognitr in Cur Com Lancastr: 14 die July 1703 et record
                p. JOS: TAYLOE, Clk

p.   THIS INDENTURE made ye 14th day of July in ye yeare of or: Lord God
60   1703 and in ye Second yeare of ye reigne of or: Sovereigne Lady Ann by
        ye grace of God of England, Scotland France & Ireland, Queen, Defender
of ye faith &c., Betweene HUGH LADNER of ye Pish: of St. Marys White Chappell in ye County of Lancaster, Gent., of ye one pte. and RICHARD BALL of ye afsd. Pish & County of ye other pte., Wittnesseth that ye sd. HUGH LADNER for one hundred pds. of good & lawfull money of Engld. to him pd. hath confirmed unto sd. RICHD. BALL his heires & assignes all yt: his WATER MILL scituate & being upon ye head of COROTOMAN RIVER & is comonly caleld by name of FOXES MILL & late in ye tenure & ocupacon of MRS. ELIZABETH WILKS, Widd. of Mr. THOMAS WILKES, late of this County, deced., & by her ye sd. ELIZABETH held and enjoyed dureing ye naturall life of Mr. GEORGE SPENCERwth: whome ye sd. ELIZABETH intermarried after ye decease of ye sd. THOMAS WILKS, and afterwards solde by her, the sd. ELIZABETH, & WM. MAN, her then Husband, to WM: DRAPER of ye sd. County & Pish:, Blacksmith, as by Deed bearing date ye 6th day of Septr. 1697 recorded in the Office of ye sd. County and by him, ye sd. WM: DRAPER, solde unto ye sd. HUGH LADNER, party to these presents, as by his Deed bearing date ye 28th day of Janry. 1698, both of which will more fully appeare together wth: ye Mill House, outhouses stones instruments & implements to ye same appertaining and all wayes waters stakes dammes troughs &c. to ye sd. Mill be-

longing as amply as he, ye sd. HUGH LADNER, held & enjoyed ye same with all
ye appertenaces thereunto belonging as allsoe every lands belonging thereunto as is provided by ye 3d. Act of Assembly made at JAMES CITTY ye 3d day of
Septr. 1667, entituled, "An Act for Encouragement of Erecting of Water Mills,"
To have and to hold to the proper use of him ye sd. RICHARD BALL his heires
clear from ye sd. HUGH LADNER his heires or any other person claiming

p.   of him forever, and ye sd. HUGH LADNER doth further agree in two
61   months from ye date hereof that he, ye sd. HUGH, in p:son and ANN his
        Wife in p:son or by their Lawyer shall acknowledge this pr:sent Inden-
ture;   In Wittness whereof I have hereunto sett my hand and seale ye day &
yeare   abovesd:
Signed sealed & delivered in ye presence of us
        WILLIAM BALL,   HUGH LADNER
        JAMES COMMELINE,
        THO: BARKER, JUNR.
        Recognitr in Cur Com Lancastr: 14 die July 1703 p HUGH LADNER & ANN,
Uxoris et record.   p JOS: TAYLOE, Clk.

p.   THIS INDENTURE made this 12 die July 1703 Betweene THOMAS WILL-
62   SON, late of Lancaster in ye Kingdome of England, Labourer, of ye one
        part and MATHIAS GILES of Lancaster County in ye Collony of Virginia
of ye other part;   Wittnesseth tht THOMAS WILLSON doth covenant & agree with
ye sd. MATHIAS GILES his Exrs. & assignes to serve him ye full terme of seven
yeares commencing from ye 25th day of May last past untill ye full end &
terme thereof fully to be ended in any such service or imployment as he, ye sd.
MATHIAS, shall imploy him according to ye custome of ye Country.   In Consideracon whereof ye sd. MATHIAS GILES doth covenant wth: ye sd. THOMAS
WILLSON to finde & allowe him sufficient dyet lodging washing & clothes
dureing his sd. terme & doe his uttermost endeavour to instruct him in ye
occupacon of a Smith, wth wch: consideracon ye parties both hereunto subscribed being well agreed have hereunto interchangeably sett their hands &
affixed their seales ye day & yeare above written
Sealed & delivered in ye presence of us
        JOS: TAYLOE,   THOMAS WILLSON
        JOHN ROBERTSON
        Recognitr in Cur Com Lancastr: 14 die July 1703 p THO: WILLSON & record
                 p   JOS: TAYLOE, Clk.

        (The above Indenture between THOMAS WILLSON and MATHIAS GILES is repeated
and signed by MATHIAS GILES.)

p.   KNOW ALL MEN by these presents yt: I ROBERT MOON of LIVERPOOLE,
63   Marrinr:, have made my trusty & well beloved Friend, Mr. THOMAS
        CARTER of COROTOMAN in ye County of Lancaster, Planter, my true &
lawfull Attorney from me to demand from Capt. WM: BALL & WM: MANN their
Exrs. & assignes or whome else may concerne in Virginia in America all such
sums of money, merchandize for & on accot. of any Bills, Accounts in their
hands belonging to me (or Owners) from any person or persons wt:soever in
Virginia.   In Wittness hereof I have hereto put my hand & seale the 12th dy of
July 1703
Test   ROBERT GOODRIAR   ROBT: MOONE

Recordr.14th die July 1703. p JOS: TAYLOE, Clk.

p.   (Same Power of Attorney) from ROBERT MOONE of LIVERPOOLE, Marriner,
64   to Mr. THOMAS CARTER of COROTOMAN dated the 21st day of July 1703
        Test   JNO: ✝ SHELLTON   ROBERT MOONE
        RICHD: R STEPHENS,
        EDWD. CARTER
     Recognitr in Cur Com Lancastr: 14 Aug 1703 & prob: p sacramt. EDWD. CAR-
TER & RICH: STEPHENS et record
                    p. JOS. TAYLOE, Clk.

     THIS INDENTURE made ye 10th day of May 1703 Betweene JOHN CALLI-
HAN of ye County of Lancaster of ye one pte. and THOMAS WHITE of RICHMOND
County of ye other pte., Wittnesseth yt. ye sd. JNO: CALLIHAN for ye considera-
con of Fifty pds. Sterl. in hand allready reced., hath sold unto

p.   ye sd. THOMAS WHITE his heires and assignes all yt: p:cell of land
65   scituate in ye Pish: of Wt. Chappell in ye County of Lancaster containing
        One hundred & fifty acres, being bounded as followeth (yt: is to say) Be-
ginning at a marked Pine tree standing by or near MORATICO CREEK on ye
South side of ye sd. Creek dividing this land from the land of Mr. BRYAN STOTT
& runing thence up ye sd. Creek its severall courses & being brought into a
streight line is ninety six perches to a Stake in ye Marsh at ye mouth of a small
Branch, thence runing South twenty seven degrees East forty perches to ye
head of a Gully, thence South fifteen degrees East one hundred perches &
South forty nine degrees East forty two perches and South eighty five degrees
East twenty two perches, and thence South South East to ye back line of ye land
wch: parts ye sd. JNO: CALLIHANs land from ye land of ye sd. STOTT, thence
along ye line North North West to ye first mentioned station, ye same being pt.
or p:cell of a great tract of land now in ye occupation of ye sd. JNO: CALLIHAN'
To have and to hold and singular ye houses orchards fences waters profitts and
any part thereof belonging to ye same to him ye sd. THOMAS WHITE his heires
or assignes for ever; free from ye sd. JNO: CALLIHAN his heires or assignes for
ever;

p.   In Wittness whereof ye sd. JNO: CALLIHAN hath hereunto set his hand &
66   seale the day & yeare first above written
        Sealed & delivered in ye presence of us
        JAMES PHILLIPS,   JNO: CALLIHAN
        JNO: STOTT,   JNO: PHILLIPS
     Recognitr. in Cur Com Lancastr: 14 die July 1703 & record
                    p. JOS: TAYLOE, Clk.

     TO ALL TO WHOM these presents shall come, Greeting in our Lord God
everlasting. Know yee yt: I ANN CHEWNING, Widd., of ye County of Lancastr: in
Virginia as well for ye naturall love & affection I bear to my Son, JOHN PYNES,
of ye County afsd., as allsoe for other good causes have given to ye sd. JOHN
PYNES one Negroe man named Tom; To have and to hold unto him ye sd. JNO:
PYNES his heires or assignes for ever (after my decease), absolutely wth:out
any manner of condicon wt:soever & further know ye yt: ye sd. ANN CHEW-
NING have put ye sd. JNO: PYNES in peaceable & quiet possession of ye abovesd.
Negro, Tom, In Wittness whereof, I have hereunto put my hand & seale this

14th day of August 1703

ANN ⟨mark⟩ CHEWNING

p.   Signed sealed and delivered & possest in and seizin of ye sd. Negroe in
67   ye sd. Deed of Gift menconed taken and delivered to ye sd. JNO: PYNES by
ye delivery of ye sd. Negroe in ye name of Seizin in ye presence of
WILLIAM BALL,
HANNAH BALL, ELIZA: BRYAN
    Recognitr in Cur Com Lancastr: 8 die Septr. 1703 et record
        p JOS: TAYLOE, Clk

    BE IT KNOWN to all men by these presents yt: I WM: MILLNER, late of ye
County of Lancaster for divers considerations have sold unto ISAAC ROBINSON
his heires a certaine tract of land now in ye possession of JNO: LUCKHAM wth:
all ye houseing fenceing & all other edificies containing about sixty or seventy acres more or less, ye sd. land wth: warranty thereof to be good from me my
heires without molestacon from any p:sons whatsoever; To have & to hold for
ever & I doe oblige my selfe to acknowledge this my Deed of Sale in ye Court of
Lancaster wth:in two months after ye date hereof; In Wittness hereof I have
sett my hand & seale this 7th day of xbr: 1698
Signed sealed & delivered in ye presence of
    JNO: MOTT, JUNR.   WM;   MILLNER
    WM: ⟨mark⟩ ROBINSON
    Recognitr. in Cur Com Lancastr: 10 9bris 1698 p WM: MILLNER et record 16
die.   Test   JOS: TAYLOE, Clk

    TO ALL TO WHOME these presents shall come, I ISAAC ROBINSON of ye
County of Lancaster for ye sume of two thousand pounds of good tobbo have
sold unto him ye sd. GILES ROBINSON his heires or assignes all ye right of me to
all ye lands & Plantacon thereunto belonging as exprest in ye wth:in Bill of
Sale & do warrt. ye same to him ye sd. GILES ROBINSON agst. me my heires and
yt: ELIZABETH my now Wife shall relinquish her right of Dower to ye same
wth:in ye limitted time; In Wittness whereof I have sett my hand & seale this
11 day of 8br: 1703.
Signed sealed & delivered in ye presence of
    JOS: TAYLOE,
    WM: ✕ GARTON   ISAAC ⟨mark⟩ ROBINSON
    Recognitr. in Cur Com Lancastr: 13 Octobr: 1703 et record
        p.   JOS: TAYLOE, Clk

p.   KNOW ALL MEN by these presents yt: I SAMLL. WRIGHT of ye County of
68   Lancastr: for divers good consideracons have impowered my trusty &
    well beloved Friend, CHRISTOPHER KIRK, JUNR., of ye aforesd. County
my true & lawfull Attorney to demand and receive all such debts as is due to me
in tobbaccoes moneys; & in case of non payment to sue & imprison, hereby
ratifying wt. my sd. Attorney shall do as if I were p:sonally pr:sent; In Wittness whereof I have hereunto sett my hand and seale this 25th of July 1703
Signed sealed & delivered in presents of
    CHRIST: KIRK,   SAMLL. WRIGHT
    THO: KIRK
    Recognitr. in Cur Com Lancastr: 13 die Octobr: 1703 et record
        p.   JOS: TAYLOE, Clk.

THIS INDENTURE made ye 10th day of 9br. 1703 Betweene JNO: STANLEY of this County & Pish: of St. Marys White Chappell of ye one part and OZWALE WHALEY of ye sd. County and Pish: of ye other pt., Wittnesseth yt: ye sd. JOHN doth covenant & agree wth: ye sd. OZWALE to serve him or his assignes ye full terme of eight yeares commencing from ye day of ye date hereof in any such service as he or they shall imploy him according to ye custome of ye Country in ye like kind. In consideracon whereof ye sd. OZWALE doth agree to allowe him good & sufficient diet washing lodging and clothes dureing ye sd. terme of eight yeares and at ye expiracon thereof to pay him one good suit of clothes and three barrells of Indian corne containing five bushells to ye barrell. In Wittness whereof ye sd. partys to this Indenture have hereunto sett their hands and affixed their seals the day and yeare above written
Sealed & delivered in ye presence of ye Court
Ye sd. boy judged 13 yeares of age   JOHN   STANLEY
                                              OZWALE   WHALEY
        Recognitr in Cur Com Lancastr: 10 die Novr. 1703 et record
                p   JOS: TAYLOE, Clk.

p.   THIS INDENTURE made ye 4th day of May in ye yeare 1700 by and be-
69   tweene JAMES HAYNES of ye Pish: of Christ Church in ye County of Lan-
       castr: and ye Collony of Virga. of ye one pty., and THO: BURROUGHS of ye
same Pish: & County & Colony of ye other pty., Wittnesseth yt. ye sd. JAMES HAYNES for a valuable consideracon have sold unto ye sd. BURROUGHS his heires & assignes a certain p:cell of land being in FLEETS BAY in Pish: & County aforesd. ye sd. Neck of land being purchased by ye sd. JAMES HAYNES of THOMAS COX & MARY his Wife as by their Bill of Sale bearing date ye 20th of July in ye yeare of or: Lord 1699 may appeare, ye sd. Neck being by estimacon Fifty acres of land; Begining at a corner Pine tree first spoken of in Mr. THO-MAS COXes Pattent, thence running up WM: GARTONs line to ye head of TAR-KILL COVE, thence down ye sd. Cove to NANTEPEYSON CREEK, thence down ye sd. Creek to ye aforesd. corner Pine, ye sd. Neck of land being comonly known by ye name of TORKILL NECK, To have and to hold ye afsd. Neck of Land unto ye sd. THOMAS BURROUGHS his heires or assignes and further I ye sd. JAMES HAYNES doe warrant ye sd. Land unto ye sd. THO: BURROUGHS his heires and assignes from me my heires and any other person, as Wittness my hand & seale ye day and yeare above written
Sealed & delivered in ye presence of us
        WM: HEARD,   JAMES HAYNES
        MARTHA HEARD
        Recognitr in Cur Com Lancastr: 8th May 1701 et record
                p   JOS: TAYLOE, Clk
On ye back side of ye above Deed was this following Indmt. unto JOHN TURBERVILLE his heires or assignes wth: warranty from me my heires & admrs. or any other claiming by from or undr. me as Wittness my hand this 10th day 9br: 1703
Test   WM: DARE,   THOMAS BURROUGHS
        JOHN HARRIS
        Recognitr in Cur Com Lancastr: 10 9br: 1703 et record
                p.   JOS: TAYLOE, Clk.

p.   THIS INDENTURE made this 29th day of 8br. in ye yeare of or: Lord 1703
70   betweene MARK GENDRON & MARY his Wife of ye Pish: of Christ Church

in ye County of Lancastr: in Virginia, Planter, of ye one pty., and JOHN GRAS-
SON of sd. Pish: of the other party; Wittnesseth that ye sd. MARK GENDRON &
MARY his Wife for consideracon of Fifty pds. of lawfull money of England
have sold unto ye sd. JOHN GRASSON and to his heires for ever a certain p:cell
of Land containing One hundred acres more or less scituated in ye Pish of
Christ Church in ye County of Lancastr: aforesd. being pte: of a dividend of
land formerly belonging to JOHN BRYAN of ye Pish: aforesd., bounded as followeth; Begin at ye REEDY BRANCH and running cross ye woods Northerly to
WM: CARTERs line and soe alonge ye sd. CARTERs line to EDWD. GIBSONs line,
soe alonge ye sd. GIBSONs line to ye GULFE where Mr. EDWD. GIBSONs corner
tree standeth, soe from thence as ye GULFE runns to ye head of NANTY POYSON
CREEK, soe downe ye sd. Creek to ye place where it first began; being parte of a
dividend of land formerly given to ye sd. BRYAN by JOHN MORRISS, deced., and
since sold & duly conveyed to JOHN CARROLL &c., and ye sd. MARK GENDRON &
MARY his Wife from them their heires doe fully make over unto the afsd. JOHN
GRASSON his heires & assignes for ever; To have and to hold to ye sd. JOHN
GRASSON his heires & assignes for ever (except nine choice white Oakes for
Plank) and ye sd. MARK GENDRON & MARY his Wife for themselves doe firmly
granted wth: sufficient warranty from all p:sons whatsoever claiming ye same
In Wittness whereof wee have hereunto sett our hands & fixed our seales the
day & year on ye other side above written
Signed sealed & delivered in presence of us
    GEO; FLOWER,   MARK GENDRON
    THO: MARTIN   MARY M GENDRON
    Recognitr in Cur Com Lancastr: 10 9br. 1703 et record
        p.   JOS: TAYLOE, Clk

p.   THIS INDENTURE made ye 7th day of Decembr: in ye 2d yeare of ye
71   reigne of or: Sovr: Lady Anne ye first &c., in ye yeare of or: Lord God
     1703, Betweene JNO: SHAW of ye Pish: of Xt. Church of ye County of Lan-
caster, Carpenter, & REBECCA his Wife of ye one part and SAMLL. BROMELEY of
ye Pish: of White Chapple in ye County afsd., Ship Carpenter, & MARGARET his
Wife of ye other pte., Wittnesseth yt. for consideracon of Nine thousand pds. of
good & merchantable tobbo conveniently paid in ye County of Lancaster unto
ye sd. JNO: SHAW his heires or assignes as followeth, that is to say, three thousand pounds of tobacco at or upon ye 25th day of this instant Decembr: and
three thousand pounds more of ye sd. tobbo at or upon ye 10th day of Octobr:
next ensueing and three thousand pounds ye residue thereof at or upon the
10th day of Octobr: wch: shall fall in ye yeare 1705; have sold unto ye sd.
SAMLL. BROMELEY & MARGARET his Wife & their heires or assignes, one dwelling house, one tobbo house with fifty acres of land now in ye possession of
WM: COTTERELL scituate & being in ye Pish of White Chappell & County aforesd.
bounded as followeth; Beginning at a marked corner white Oake standing by
an old corner red Oak stump on ye Northwest side of a Creek formerly called
POWELLS CREEK, from ye sd. white Oake North by West fifty poles crossing ye
head of a small Creek to a corner red Oake sapling standing by ye side of an Old
Field, thence East by North one hundred & sixty poles to a red Oake stump standing near a corner red Oake of JOHN FLOWERs, thence along FLOWERs line of
marked trees South by East fifty poles to a red Oake stump standing near by
DEEP BOTTOM BRIDGE, thence West by South by marked trees one hundred &
sixty poles to ye white Oake where it first began; To have & to hold with all ye
houseing fenceing orchards advantages thereunto belonging unto ye sd.

SAMLL. BROMELEY & MARGARET his Wife their heires for ever, and ye sd. JNO: SHAW & REBECCA his Wife their heires shall p:mitt ye sd. SAMLL. BROMELEY & MARGARET his Wife their heires at all times for ever quiet & peaceable possession wth:out any molestacon

p.   from any p:son wt:soever;   In Wittness whereof ye said JOHN SHAW &
72   REBECCA his Wife have hereunto sett their hands & seales ye day &
       month above written
Sealed and delivered in ye presence of
    ROBT. SCHOLFIELD,   JOHN S SHAW
    PETER P KILLGORE   REBECCA X SHAW
    Recognitr in Cur Com Lancastr: 8th die Decembris 1703 et record
              p.   JOS: TAYLOE, Clk.

    KNOW ALL MEN by these presents yt: I JOHN SHAW of ye Pish: of Xt. Church County of Lancster am firmly bound unto SAMLL. BROMELEY of ye Pish: of White Chappell in ye County of Lancaster in ye just quantity of eighteen thousand pounds of merchantable tobbo; as Wittness my hand & seale ye 7th day of Decembr: 1703
    THE CONDICON of this obligacon is such yt. if ye above bound JNO: SHAW keep all ye articles wch: on his parte ought to be kept and performed mentioned in a Deed of Sale bearing date even wth: these presents, Then this pr:sent obligacon to be oid or else to bee & remaine in full force
Sealed & delivered in ye presence of
    ROBT: SCHOLFIELD,   JOHN S SHAW
    PETER P KILLGORE
    Record 8th die Decembr: 1703 p. JOS: TAYLOE, Clk

    THIS INDENTURE made ye 3d day of Novembr: in ye 2d yeare of ye reigne of or: Sovr. Lady Anne ye first &c., and in ye yeare of or: Lord God 1703, Between SAMUELL BROMELEY of ye Pish: of White Chappell in ye County of Lancaster, Ship Carpenter, & MARGARET his Wife of ye one part and WM: ROBINSON of ye Pish: & County aforesd. of ye other part;   Wittnesseth that for ye just

p.   quantity of six thousand & five hundred pounds of good & merchant-
73   able tobacco conveniently paid in ye said County of Lancaster as fol-
       loweth, yt: is to say, three thousand pounds of ye same at or upon ye 25th day of Decembr: next ensueing ye date hereof and three thousand five hundred pounds ye residue hereof at or upon ye 10th day of Octobr: wch: shall follow being in ye yeare 1705, the sd. SAMLL. BROMELEY & MARGARET his Wife have sold to ye sd. WM. ROBINSON Seventy five acres of woodland ground now in ye possession of ye sd. BROMELEY & being in ye Pish: of White Chappell & County of Lancastr: afsd., between ye land of ye sd. BROMELEY, ye land of JOS: HAIL, ye land of GILES ROBINSON and ye land of STEPHEN TOMLIN, To have & to hold ye sd. pr:misses with all advantages belonging unto ye sd. WM: ROBINSON his heires & assignes without hinderance from any persons;   In Wittness whereof ye sd. SAMUELL BROMELEY & MARGT., his Wife, have hereunto sett their hands & seales the day month and yeare above written
Sealed & delivered in ye pr:sence of
    MIL: WALTERS,   SAMLL: BROMELEY
    ELIZA: BALL   MARY BROMELEY

Recognitr in Cur Com Lancastr: 8 die Xbr. 1793 et record
p.   JOS: TAYLOE, Clk

KNOW ALL MEN by these presents yt: I SAMLL. BROMELEY of ye Pish: of White Chappell in County of Lancastr: & MARGARET my Wife are firmly bound unto WM: ROBINSON in ye just quantity of Eleven thousand pounds of good tobacco to be convenient to Water in County of Lancastr: unto ye sd. WM: ROBINSON his certain Attorney or assignes whatsoever to wch: payment well & truely to be made we bind ourselves our heires firmly by these presents;   As Wittness our hands & seales ye 3d day of Novembr: 1703
THE CONDICON of this obligacon is such yt: if ye above bounden SAMLL. BROMELEY

p.   and MARGARET his Wife they or their heires shall in all things observe
74   all ye condicons which ought to be observed mentioned in a certain In-
denture made betweene ye sd. SAMLL. BROMELEY & MARGARET his Wife and ye above named WM: ROBINSON, Then this pr:sent obligacon to be of none effect or else to remaine in full force
Sealed & delivered in ye presence of
MIL: WALTERS,   SAMLL: BROMELEY
ELIZA: BALL   MARGT BROMELEY
Record 8th die xbr: 1703   p.   JOS: TAYLOE, Clk.

THIS INDENTURE made this 8th day of Decembr: 1703 betweene JNO: CHILTON, SENR. of Lancaster County, Planter, of ye one part and ROBT: CARTER of ye same County of Lancastr:, Esqr., of ye other part; Wittnesseth that ye sd. JNO: CHILTON, SENR. for ye sume of Forty pds. Sterling good & lawfull money of Engld. hath granted to him ye sd. ROBT. CARTER his heires and assignes for ever all yt: messuage & tract of land in County of Lancastr: in ye Pish: of Christ Church being ye Plantacon whereon ye sd. JOHN CHILTON now liveth and which he, ye said JNO: CHILTON, for a valuable consideracon bought of WM; CLAPHAM formerly of this said County, deced., as by Deed bearing date ye 11th day of Novr. 1672 and acknowledged in ye Court of ye sd. County ye 13th day of ye same month appeares, being part of a divident whereon ye sd. CLAPHAM lived & dyed, wch: sd. land in ye aforesd. Deed is mentioned to be bounded as followeth, (vizt), Lying on ye Westermost end of ye said CLAPHAMs Devidend

p.   comonly called MARGARIES, Begining at a marked Pine standing on ye
75   side of ye Eastermost Branch of COROTOMAN RIVER ye land formerly
HUGH KINLEY, deced., line belonging to EDWD. DALE and from thence to a marked white Oake standing on or neer ye side of ye Creek wch: divides ye land of said CLAPHAM from ye land of Lieut. Coll. JOHN CARTER, together wth: all houses fences & enclosures belonging;   To hae and to hold unto ye sd. ROBT. CARTER his heires & assignes for ever; And ye sd. JOHN CHILTON, SENR., for himselfe his heires ye said Land will warrant & defend by these presents from the claim of any p:sons wt:soever

p.   In Wittness whereof ye parties to these presents have interchangeably
76   sett their hands & seales
Signed sealed & delivered in presence of us
WM: LISTER,   JOHN CHILTON
HANCOCK LEE

12th of April 1704. JOAN CHILTON acknowledged her Dower
Test   JOS: TAYLOE, Clk
Recognitr in Cur Com Lancastr: 8th die Decembr: 1703 & record
p   JOS: TAYLOE, Clk

KNOW ALL MEN by these pr:sents yt: I JOHN VINCENT of POVE-
INGTON wth:in ye Pish: of Tinum in ye ISLE of PURBECK & County of DORSETT,
Gent., send Greeting. Whereas HENRY VINCENT, late of Copley Pish in ye County of WESTMORELAND & Collony of Virginia, Father of ye sd. JOHN VINCENT,
dyed possessed of a messuage of land in NOMINIE wth:in ye Pish of Copley in ye
County of WESTMORELAND. Now Know yee yt: I ye sd. JOHN VINCENT, Son &
heire of ye abovesd. HENRY VINCENT, Coxson, deced., doth by these pr:sents
appoint my trusty friend & Brother in Law, JAMES TAYLOR, of Washington
Pish: in ye sd. County of WESTMORELAND my true & lawfull Attorney in my
place & behalfe to have regard to all my lands plantacons & demands whatsoever yt: shall belong or be due to me as by Pattent may more at large appeare
from ye Sectys. Office of yt: Collony & allsoe impowering my sd. Attorny to
make survey of my abovesd. land & to wage Law wth: any yt: shall oppose ye
same & after quiet survey made by my sd. Attorny impowering him allseo to
lett ye sd. lands for one or two yeares not exceeding three & allsoe to receive ye
sd. rents & to sue for ye same and allsoe receive all such debts rents which are
due to me in Virginia afsd. and to sue for ye same

p.   confirming by these presents wt:soever my sd. Attorny doe to be good
77   in Law as if my selfe were personally pr:sent. In Wittness whereof I
          have sett my hand and seale ye 20th day of Septembr: 1703
Sealed & delivered in ye presence of
      THO: GRAVES,   JNO: VINCENT
      CHA: ANCKETILL, ROB: GROVE
      WM: LORD,   CHA: HAYWOOD
   Probatr Letr Attor. in Cur Com Lancastr: nono die Fbry. 1703/4 p sacramt.
THO: GRAVES, CHA: ANCKETILL, ROBT: GROVE et record
                  p.   JOS: TAYLOE, Clk

      MARGURITTE LADY CULPEPER, THOMAS LORD FAIRFAX and CATHA: his
Wife, Proprietors of ye Northern neck of Virginia to all to whom &c., this present writeing shall come send Greeting in our Lord God everlasting. Whereas
JOHN CURTIS of NORTHUMBERLAND County did on ye 8th day of July last sett
forth to our Office yt: ELIZABETH MOON afterwards HAZELLWOOD, ye Daughter
of ABRAHAM MOON, deced., formerly of MIDDLESEX County was seized in fee of
800 acres of land lying and being in ye County of Lancaster wch: land was first
granted unto ABRAHAM MOON, her Father, by Pattent bearing date ye 13 day of
February 1653, and from him descended upon her, ye sd. ELIZABETH, his only
Daughter and heire, who being so seized dyed leaveing no heires behind her
nor disposeing thereof by Will, by means whereof ye sd. Land escheate to ye
Proprietors; And yt: he ye sd. JOHN CURTIS was Brother by ye half blood and
next of kin to ye sd. ELIZABETH, and mooved to be prefered to a grant of ye
escheat; Whereupon a Certificate according to ye rules of ye Office issued to
make ye same publique at ye Court Door of ye County in wch: ye land lyes, wch:
being returned wth: attestacon under ye hand of Mr. JOSEPH TAYLOE, Clark of
ye Court of ye sd. County, certifying yt: ye same was made publick two Court
dayes successively; And ye six months being

p.   expired and no person appeareing to controvert ye title to ye sd. Escheat
78   Know yee therefore yt: we for ye composition to be paid and ye annuall
        rent herein refered have granted unto ye said JOHN CURTIS all ye right
and intrest of ye sd. eight hundred acres of land being in ye County of Lancaster as aforesd. upon ye head of MYRATTICO CREEK and upon ye North side of ye
Southeast Branch of ye sd. Creek, bounded as followeth;   Soueast upon a Branch
known by ye name of MACHMAPS BRANCH which divideth this Land and the
land formerly surveyed for JOHN SHARPE, Northeast unto ye woods, Northwest
upon METTOTOSSON SWAMP, Southwest upon NANSUNSIA BRANCH being ye
Southeast Branch first mentioned, Together with all rights belonging (Royal
Mines excepted);   To have & to hold ye sd. eight hundred acres of land with all
profitts belonging to him ye sd. JOHN CURTIS his heires for ever, paying to us
our heires and assignes, Proprietors of ye sd. Northern Neck yearely on ye
Feast of St. Michaell the Archangell, ye fee rent of one shilling Sterling
money for every fifty acres of land hereby granted; Provided yt: if ye sd. JOHN
CURTIS his heires shall not pay ye annual rent for ye space of two whole
yeares after ye same shall become due, then it may be lawfull for us or:
assignes to reenter and hold ye same as if this grant had never been passed.
Given at or: Office in Lancaster County wth:in or: said Proprietary under our
Seale.   Wittness our Agent and Attorny fully authorized thereto, dated ye 18th
day of December in ye second yeare of ye reign of or: Sovr. Lady Ann by ye
grace of God &c., 1703
JOHN CURTIS, his Escheat Deed for 800
        acres of land in Lancastr: County   ROBERT CARTER
                JAMES INNIS, Clk. of Proprietors Office
        On ye back side of ye Deed was this following -
        Whereas I ye wth:in named JOHN CURTIS, SENR., for a valuable consideracon
to me paid have sold unto ROBERT CARTER of Lancastr: County, Esqr., his heires
and assignes ye wth:in mentioned tract of land and appertanances thereto belonging by a pair of Indentures beareing date herewth: I have therefore
assigned and made over and do hereby assigne

p.   and make over unto ye said ROBERT CARTER his heires all my right and
79   interest to me belonging to ye wth:in mentioned eight hundred acres of
        land;   In Wittness wereof I have hereunto sett my hand and seale this
fourth day of February 1703
Signed sealed and delivered in presence of us
        JOHN LOMAX, JNO: BABE,   JOHN CURTIS
        JOHN STEWART, MARGARET UPTON
        Recognitr in Cur Com Lancastr: nono die Febry. 1703 et record
                p   JOS: TAYLOE, Clk.

        THIS INDENTURE made this 4th da of Febry. 1703 Betweene JOHN CURTIS,
SENR. of NORTHUMBERLAND County of one part and ROBERT CARTER of Parish
of Christ Church in Lancastr: County, Esqr., of other part;   Witnesseth that ye
sd. JOHN CURTIS, SENR. for two hundred pounds Sterling of lawfull money of
England hath sold unto ye sd. ROBERT CARTER his heires for ever eighty hundred acres of land bounded as followeth,   Southeast upon a Branch which hath
been known by ye name of MACHEMAPS BRANCH, Northeast unto ye woods,
Northwest upon METTOSSON SWAMP, Southwest upon NANSUNSIA BRANCH
being ye Southeast Branch first mentioned; which sd. land was first taken up
by ABRAHAM MOONE, deceased, formerly of MIDDLESEX County bearing date

ye 23d day of Febry. 1653, and from him descended upon ELIZABETH MOONE his only Daughter and heire and for want of heire of ye sd. ELIZABETH hath been lately escheated by JOHN CURTIS, her half Brother as appeares by Deed from ye Proprietors Office dated ye 18th day of Decemer last and hath been lately surveyed at ye request of ye said JOHN CURTIS by EDWIN CONWAY, Surveyor, who hath

p.   found therein eight hundred acres according to ye sd. Pattent as by his
80   Survey abearing date (blank) appeares; To have and to hold the sd. tract of land unto said ROBERT CARTER his heires and assignes for ever freely exonerated from all manner of gifts grants executions, to hold wth:out any lawfull incumbrance of him ye sd. JOHN CURTIS his heires

p.   In Wittness whereof ye parties have interchangeably sett their hands
81   and seales dated ye day and year first above written
Signed sealed & delivered in ye presence of us
JNO: LOMAX, JOHN BABE,   JNO: CURTIS
JOHN STEWART, MARGARETT UPTON
Recognitr in Cur Com Lancastr: nine die Febry. 1703 et recordr.
        p   JOS: TAYLOE, Clk
On ye back side of ye Deed were these following Indorsmts.
Memoand: That full and peaceable possession and seizin was given and delivered by ye wth:in named JOHN CURTIS of ye messuage tenements & tract of land wth:in mentioned wth: all appertenances thereto belonging and appertaining according to ye true intent and meaning of ye wth:in Deed unto ye wth:in named ROBERT CARTER, Esqr., by delivering of possession of ye Mantion House in ye name of ye whole this 7th day of Febry. 1703. In presence of us whose names are hereunto subscribed
    GEO: ✗ SMITHER
    JANE BUSH
WM: MANN, Tennant on ye abovesd. land delivered up possession of ye Tenement he lives upon unto ye sd. ROBERT CARTER by ye consent and in ye presence of ye sd. JOHN CURTIS and (?) tennat to ye sd. CARTER giveing him, ye sd. CARTER quiet possession of ye Mansion House he lives in, in ye name of ye whole tenement & appertenances in ye name of ye whole thereunto belonging in ye presence of us
    GEO: ✗ SMITHER
    JANE BUSH
    Recordr. p JOS: TAYLOE, Clk.

p.   Att a Grand Assembly holden at JAMES CITTY ye 24th day of Septr. 1692
82   An Act for ye Naturalizacon of JEREMY PACKQUETT,
Whereas at a Grand Assembly holden at JAMES CITTY 20 day of Septr. in ye 23 yeare of ye reigne of our Sovr. Lord ye King yt: now is and in ye yeare of our Lord God 1671, it was enacted & ordained yt: any Stranger desireing to make this Country the place of their constant residence might upon their pettition to ye Grand Assembly & upon takeing ye Oathes of Allegiance & Supremacy, be admitted to a Naturalizacon; Whereupon JEREMY PACKQUET an alien makeing humble suit as afsd. Act therefore enated by ye Governour, Councell & Burgesses of ye Grand Assembly, inter alia, be & is by vertue hereof & ye sd. aforecited Law wherein this is grounded capable of traffique & tradeing takeing up & purchaseing conveying deviseing & inheriting of lands

& tenements and from hence forth be & is declared deemed & holden in all
constructions of Law, stated vested & indulged wth: all previledges Libertyes
Immunitys wt:soever (relateing to ye Collony) yt: any naturall born English
man is capable of according to ye true intent & meaning of ye sd. Act.

   Cop Test JAMES MINGE, Clk, Ast. p temp
   Record May 8th 1704 p JOS: TAYLOE, Clk.
   26th Decembr: 1672. Reced. then of Mr. JEREMY PACKQUETT ye at: of
1200 lbs of tobbo being for his Naturalizacon

Testes FORTUNATUS SYDNER   I say reced. p me.
   THO: HAYNES   JNO: STRETCHLY
   Recordr. 8th May 1704 p. JOS: TAYLOE, Clk.

p. KNOW ALL MEN by these presents that wee WILLIAM SMITH of ye Citty
83 of WATERFORD, Alderman, Owner of ye one halfe of ye Adventure Ketch
   of WATERFORD burthen about fifty Tonns, now lying at ye Key of ye sd.
Citty, JAMES MACKRELL of ye sd. Citty, Mercht., Owner of ye one sixth of sd.
Vessell and GEORGE VILLIERS of said Citty, Merchant, Owner of one third of said
Ship, for & in consideracon of ye sume of two hundred & five pounds Sterling
to us in hand paid before ye perfecting hereof by HENRY STEVENS of ye Citty
of CORK, Marriner, ye receipt whereof wee hereby doe acknowledge & have
bargained & sold unto HENRY STEVENS ye sd. Ship, "ADVENTURE," wth: all her
furniture & apparell now to her belonging & appertaining; To have and to
hold ye sd. Ship to him his heires or assignes for ever, And wee ye sd. WM.
SMITH, JAMES MACKRELL & GEORGE VILLIERS their respective part of ye sd.
Ship to ye sd. HENRY STEVENS his heires & Exrs. warrant & defend from all
p:sons claiming from by or under them; In Wittness whereof they have here-
unto sett their hands & seales the 28th of Aprill Seventeen hundred & one 1701.
Sealed & delivered in presence of us
   PEIRE CONDON, ANTHONY PYLE, SENR.   WILL: SMITH
   JACOB MINNS, JUNR.   JA: MACKRELL
   SAMLL. TAYLOR, Notrus Publicus 1701 GEO: VILLIERS
 The above Ketch is sold p HENRY STEVENS as p his Bill of Sale in PHILADEL-
PHIA ye 27 Octobr: 1701 to Mr. JNO: CARY, Mercht.
Wittnesses present. WM: HALL, Publique House
   JNO: BUDD, a Brewer
   JNO: DAVIS, Mate of ye Ketch
 KNOW ALL MEN by these presents that I HENRY STEVENS of PHILADELPHIA,
Marriner, Owner of ye "FRIENDSHIP" Ketch of PHILADELPHIA burth of about
forty five Tonns now being at ye Wharf of PHILADELPHIA for & in considera-
con of ye sume of Five hundred & fifty pounds currant money of this place to
me in hand paid before ye pr:fecting hereof by JOHN CARY, Mercht., of PHILA-
DELPHIA, ye receipt whereof I doe hereby acknowledge, have sold and doe by
these presents fully and absolutely sell unto said JOHN CARY ye sd. Ketch ye
"FRIENDSHIP," wth: all her furniture & apparrells

p. now of her belonging & appertaining; To have and to hold ye Ketch to
84 him his heires or assignes to his or their propr use for ever, and I ye sd.
   HENRY STEVENS ye sd. Ketch to ye sd. JOHN CARY do for my selfe my
heires warrant & defend from all people claiming from by or under him. In
Wittness whereof I have hereunto sett my hand & seale in PHILADELPHIA this
twenty seventh of Octobr: seventeen hundred & one 1701.

Signed sealed & delivered in presence of us
     WM: HALL,   HENRY STEVENS
     JNO: BUDD, JNO: DAVIS
     Recordr. 20th June 1704   p.   JOS: TAYLOE, Clk.
     Reced. of Mr. JOHN CARY five hundred & fifty pounds currt. PHILADELPHIA
money being in full payment of ye within mentioned "FRIENDSHIP," Ketch;
Wittness my hand and seale this twenty seventh day of Octobr: seventeen hundred & one. 1701
Signed sealed & delivered in presence of us
     WM: HALL,   HENRY STEVENS
     JNO: BUDD, JNO: DAVIS
     Recordr. 20th June 1704   p. JOS: TAYLOE, Clk

     KNOW ALL MEN by these presents yt: I JNO: CARY of CECILE County in ye
Province of MARYLAND, Gent., Owner of ye "EXPECTACON Ketch of MARYLAND"
burthen about forty five tonns now being at ye RIVER of SASSAFRAS for & in
consideracon of ye sume of One hundred & thirty pounds Sterling money of
England to me in hand paid before ye p:fecting hereof by JOSHUA SWEATMAN,
Merhcant of MARYLAND, have sold unto ye sd. JOSHUA SWEATMAN ye sd. Ketch
ye "EXPECTACON" wth: all her furniture & appurtenances unto her belonging;
To have & to hold ye Ketch to him his heires or assignes for ever and I ye sd.
JNO: CARY ye said Ketch to ye sd. JOSHUA SWEATMAN doe forever warrant & de-
fend from all people claimeing under me either for Mortgage or Loanes of
Money yt: have or may be done before ye signing of these presents.   In Witt-
ness whereof I have hereunto sett my hand & seale in SASSAFRAS RIVER in
MARYLAND   this 20th day of June Seventeen hundred & three,   1703
Sealed & delivered in pr:sence of us
     JOHN (? STUKEY)   JNO: CARY
     PHILIP HOPKINS, JOHAH RICHARDSON
     Recordr. 20th July 1704   p JOS: TAYLOE, Clk

p.   Reced. of JOSHUA SWEATMAN one hundred and thirty pounds of cur-
85   rant money of MARYLAND being in full payment of ye above men-
     tioned "EXPECTACON" Ketch. as Wittness my hand & seale in SASSAFRAS
RIVER in MARYLAND 20th day of June Seventeen hundred & three   1703
Test JOHN (? STUKEY),   JNO: CARY
     PHILIP HOPKINS, JOHAH RICHARDSON
     Att ye Instance of Mr. NEHEMIAH JONES, it is ordered that these three Bills of
Sale should be recorded and is recorded
          p   JOS: TAYLOE, Clk

     JAMES CAMELL records his mark of Cattle & Hoggs according to ye
antient mark of Mr. THO: MARSHALL (deced), vizt./   a Crop & hole in the right
eare & an under keele in the left
     Recordr. 1th July 1704   p JOS: TAYLOE, Clk.

     WM: HOWARD records one Cow Calf called Sloe & all her increase for his
Daughter, MARTHA HOWARD & hir heires marked as follows (vizt), a cropp on
ye right eare & under keele on ye left

     KNOW ALL MEN by these presents that whereas I JOHN MOTT of ye Coun-
ty of Lancastr: haveing a sufficient warrant granted to me at ye Proprietors

OFFICE for ye Northern Neck for a certain p:cell of land scituate in Lancastr: County on a Branch of MORRATICO being in quantity two hundred & forty acres and haveing paid ye composition for so much bearing date ye 13th day of March 1684/5, wch: sd. land was formerly taken up by me JOHN MOTT & THO: CHATTWIN & JNO: CARPENTER, we being copartners together. Now Know yee that I JOHN MOTT haveing ye grand Warrts., for ye sd. 240 acres of land, doe give & grant a third part of ye same unto WM: WOOD of ye County of Lancastr: To have & to hold for him & his heires as is exprest in ye Warrant granted to me from ye sd. Office, he ye sd. WOOD paying ye annuall Quitt Rents for ye sd. third part which is in number eighty acres

p.   and allsoe his part of ye composition allready paid to me for ye whole
86   two hundred & forty acres which ye eighty acres being laid out & sur-
        veyed for Mr. THOMAS CHATWIN scituate in ye County aforesd. and is
bounded as followeth; scituate in Lancastr: County on a Branch of MORRATICO Begining at a Stake at ye end of CARPENTERs streight line & runneth E. 7 poles, thence N. W. 28 poles, thence N. 76 degs. E. 61 poles, thence N. 22 degs. E. 67 poles, thence N. W. 78 poles, thence S. W. 126 1/2 poles and finally S. E. along ye line of ye sd. CARPENTER 117 poles to ye place it began, wch: sd. land I do give 7 grant to WM: WOOD & his heires. In Wittness whereof I have putt my hand and seale the 16 day of Janry. 1695/6
Signed Sealed & delivered in presence of
        GEO: FINCH,   JNO: MOTT
        WM: GOODRIDGE
        Recognitr in Cur Com Lancastr: 7th die 7br: 1696 et record 14 die
                p.   JOHN STRETCHLEY, Clk Cur.
        Vera Copat Exact p.   JOS: TAYLOE, Cl, Cur.

        KNOW ALL MEN by these presents yt: I WM: WOOD of ye Pish: of St. Marys White Chappell in ye County of Lancastr:, Planter, for a valuable consideracon in hand secured to be paid, doe sell unto RICHD: ALLDERTON his heires or assignes yee wch. Deed of Sale wth: as full warranty & right to all intents & purposes as is & shall be made for ye same bearing date wth: these presents doe oblige my selfe & JANE my Wife to acknowledge ye same together wth: an In-deture of Sale for ye sd. Land att or: next Court; In Wittness whereof I have hereunto sett my hand & seale this 4th day of Septr. 1699
Signed sealed & delivered in presence of
        JOS: TAYLOE,   WM: WOOD, 1699
        JNO; MATHEW
        Recognitr. in Cur Com Lancastr: 4th die Septr. 1699 et recordr.
                p   JOS: TAYLOE, Clk.

        JOHN CONE, JUNR. doth discharge and acquitt my Father from all debts due to me upon ye Acct. of JNO: PILLs Estate or any other Debts due to me from ye date hereof; Wittness my hand the 23d of May 1687
        JNO: DICKSON   JNO: CONE, JUNR.
        Record. 25th July 1704

p.   KNOW ALL MEN by these presents that I THOMAS MACKEY, Mercht. doe
87   nominate & appoint WM: WOODBRIDGE of RICHMD. County to be my law-
        full Attorney for me & in my name and in ye names of Mr. GEO: MASON
and Mr. HUGH HAYWARD, my Employers, to receive every sum or sums of

tobaccoes wares goods merchandizes of wt: sort due to me or the abovesd. Mr.
GEO: MASON & Mr. HUGH HAYWARD of all & every persons resideing or being
in ye Collony of Virginia and to act and doe in the abovesd. pr:misses as amply
as I my selfe or my abovesd. Employers could doe if present and allsoe to make
any other Attorny as he shall see sitt in ye pr:misses. In Wittness whereof I
have hereunto putt my hand & seale this 29th day of May 1704
Signed sealed & delivered in presence of
     WM: WOODWARD   THO: MACKEY
     EDWD: TOMLIN
   Probat: Letr: de Attor: in Cur Com Lancastr: 14 June 1704 et recordr.
         p   JOS: TAYLOE, Clk.

     TO ALL TO WHOME these presents shall come. I HERBERT JEFFRYS, Esqr.,
Governr. & Capt. Genll. of Virginia send Greeting. Whereas his most sacred
Majtie was graciously pleased by his Royall Letters undr: ye Greate Seale of
England ye 10th day of Octobr: in ye 28th yeare of his reigne amongst other
things to continue & confirme ye antient powers & priviledges of granting
fivety acres of land for every p:son imported into tis his Majties. Collony of
Virga.,   Now Know yee that I ye sd. HERBERT JEFFRYS accordingly give & grant
unto WM: THERRIOT 3500 acres of land scituate in ye County of Lancastr: and
adjoying to ye head of CURROTOMAN RIVER, begining att ye point of ye mouth
of CLAPHAMS CREEK formerly called by that name att a marked corner red)
Oake, thence runing up the sd. Creek & Swamp as foll: (the next two lines marked
out)

p   N. W. 214 po. then N. by W. 24 po:, No. 20 degs. E. 20 po., N. E. by N. 108 po:
88   by E. 26 po. the severall courses of ye sd. Creek and Main Branch there-\
     of to a corner marked white Oake standing by ye side of the Main
Branch, thence N. E. by a line of marked trees 372 po: to another marked cor-
ner white Oake standing in a plain, thence S. E. 660 po. to a line of marked trees
to a marked corner Ash by a Run in a Branch which Branch issueth out of ye
Maine Swamp att ye head of COROTOMAN RIVER, thence downe ye Maine Swamp
& River ye severall courses wch: follow, which parts this land from ye land of
EDWIN CONWAY, W. S. W. 158 po:, then S. W. 218 po., to ye first stand, the said
Land is due as followeth; 1600 acres formerly granted to DOM: THERRIOTT by
Pattent dated ye 18th day of April 1662 and ye residue being 1900 acres surveyed in ye name of ye sd. DOM: THERRIOTT (deced), but by reason of ye Pattent
granted to ye sd. WM: THERRIOTT as being Sone & Heire to ye sd. DOMINICK, he
haveing found rights for ye 1900 acres whose names are in ye Records menconed underneath this Pattent; To have and to hold the sd. land with his due
share of all Mines wth: all woods all profitts whatsoever to ye sd. land to him ye
sd. WM: THERRIOTT his heires & assignes for ever in as ample manner as hath
been used since ye first Plantacon; To be held of or: Sovereigne Lord ye King
&c., provided yt: ye sd. WM: THERRIATT his heires doe not plant upon ye sd.
Land wth:in three yeares next ensueing, then it shall be lawfull for any Adventurer or Planter to make choice & seate thereon; Given undr. my hand &
Seale of the Collony ye 18th day of May 1678
WM: THERRITT his Pattent p 3500   HERBERT JEFFRYS
acres of Land in Lancastr: County
   Recordr: Test HENRY HARTWELL, Cl
   Recordatr: dicemo die 8br. 1704   p.   JOS: TAYLOE, Clk.

p.   TO ALL TO WHOME these presents shall come, I WM. BERKLEY, Knt.,
89   Governr: & Capt. Genll. of Virga., send Greeting in or: Lord God ever-
        lasting;   Whereas by informacon from ye Kings most Excellent Majties
directed to me, his Majties was graciously pleased to authorize sd. Governr: &
Councill to grant such portions of land to all Adventurers & Planters for mony
or transportacon of people into this Collony.   Now Know yee tht I ye sd. Sr. WM:
BERKLEY, Knt. Governr., &c., doe with ye consent of ye Councill of State give
unto DOMINICK THERRIATT of COROTOMAN in ye County of Lancastr: sixteen
hundred acres of land adjoying to ye head of ye sd. COROTOMAN RIVER bounding Easterly upon ye Main Branch of ye head of ye River which devides this
land from ye Land of Mr. EDWIN CONWAY, So: West upon an other Branch formerly called CLAPHAMS CREEKE;   No: West & No: East into ye Main Woods running No: Westerly, Northerly & North Easterly ye severall courses of ye sd.
Creeke to ye Main River or Swamp, No: Easterly 300 poles to another corner
white Oake, thence So: Easterly by marked trees 540 poles to a corner marked
Ash by a Main Run in a Swamp & downe ye River So. Westerly to ye place
where it began 630 pole, includeing the sd. quantity, the sd. Land being formerly granted to ye sd. THERRIATT by Pattent dated ye 2d day of June 1657 and
renewed in his Majties name by ordr. of ye Quartr: Court;   To have and to hold
ye sd. Land wth: all rights to ye sd. THERRIATT his heires & assignes for ever
&c

p.   Provided that if ye sd. DOMINICK THERRIATT doe not seate ye sd. land
90   within three yeares next ensueing, then it shall be lawfull for any
        Adventurer or Planter to make choyce & seate the same.   Given att
JAMES CITTY undr: my hand & the Seale of the Collony this 18th day of March
1662, and in the 15th yeare of or: Sovereigne Lord King Charles ye 2d. &c.
DOMINICK THERRIATT his Patt: for
1600 acres of land   WILLIAM BERKLEY
        Test PHIL: LUDWELL, Cl. Office   THO: LUDWELL, Secty.
        Recordr. 10th die 8br: 1704 p. JOS: TAYLOE, Clk

        THIS INDENTURE made ye 4th day of September in ye 11th yeare of ye
reigne of or: Sovereigne Lord Wm., by the grace of God King of England &c.,
and in ye yeare of or: Lord 1699;   Between WM: WOOD of the Pish: of St. Marys
White Chapple in County of Lancaster, Planter, of ye one part and RICHARD
ALDERSON of sd. County & Pish: of the other part;   Witnesseth yt. ye sd. WM:
WOOD for seven thousand one hundred pounds of good legall tobbo. & casque &
one bull Staff of neer foure yeares old to him in hand allready secured to be
paid, hath sold unto ye sd. RICHARD ALDERSON in his actuall possession by virtue of this Indenture by transferring uses into possession all that p:cell of land
late in the possession of ye sd. WM: WOOD, being in ye Pish: of St. Marys White
Chapple in County of Lancastr: and bounded (vizt),   Beginning att a Stake on a
Branch of MARRATICO att ye end of CARPENTERs streight line wch: runs N. E.
seven pole, thene North West 28 pole, thence North 76 degrees E. sixty one pole,
thence North 22 degrees

p.   East 67 pole, thence Northwest 78 pole, thence Southwest 126 pole & a
91   halfe and finally South East allong ye sd. CARPENTER 117 pole to ye place
        where it first began; containing Eighty acres of Land together with all
houses gardens stables and orchards & all appurtenances whatsoever to ye sd.
land belonging, together with such writeings which can come by wth:out sute

in Law;   To have and to hold unto ye sd. RICHD: ALDERSON his heires & assignes
for ever and ye sd. WM: WOOD doth hereby promise & oblidge himselfe that he
& JANE his Wife shall in p:son acknowledge the sd. Land at ye next Court to be
held for ye sd. County of Lancastr: In Wittness whereof to this present Deed I
have sett my hand & seale this day & yeare first above written
Signed Sealed & delivered in presence of us
    JOSEPH TAYLOE,   WM: WOOD
    JNO: MATHEW
    Recognitr in Cur Com Lancastr: decimo tertio die 7bris: 1699 p WM: WOOD et
JANE his Uxor et record   p.   JOS: TAYLOE, Clk

    THIS INDENTURE made ye 2d day of 8br: 1704 and in ye 3d yeare of ye
reigne of or: Sovereigne Lady Anne by the grace of God of England &c., Betweene SAMLL. BROOMLY of ye Pish: of St. Marys White Chapple in ye County
of Lancastr:, Ship Carpenter, and MARGARET his Wife of ye one part and
WILLIAM ROBINSON of the Pish: & County aforesd., Plantr., of the other part;
Wittnesseth that ye sd. SAMLL. BROMLEY and MARGT. his Wife for consideracon of Foure thousand pounds of good & merchantable tobbo. & one Bullock,
three thousand pounds of ye sd. tobo: and the sd. Bullock to be paid unto ye sd.
BROMLEY att or before ye last day of December now ensueing and one thousand pounds, ye residue thereof, to be paid by the sd. WM: ROBINSON att or before ye last day of December which shall be in ye yeare of or: Lord 1705, by
these presents hath sold unto ye sd. WM: ROBINSON his heires & assignes
Seventy five acres of Land in ye Pish: & County aforesd. and bounded as hereafter mentioned.   The land being the one moiety of one hundred & fivety acres
seventy five thereof formerly sold by the sd. BROMLEY & MARGT. his Wife unto
ye sd. WM: ROBINSON, the bounds and courses of the sd. one hundred & fivety
acres of land are as followeth;

p.   vizt., Begining att a corner Pignut Pochiccory standing by the side of
92   MOUNT NODDY SWAMP neer unto an old corner Pockhiccory of JOHN
      BAILYs, thence running by a new line of marked trees West by North
203 poles to a corner white Oake standing on a Plaine neer the head of a
Branch, thence running South by West by marked trees 100 poles to a corner
red Oake standing in MRS. PRITCHARDs line of marked trees, thence East one
quarter North by marked trees 42 poles to an old corner red Oake of MRS.
PRITCHARDs standing by the Path leading from FRANCIS FRIZELLs to GILES
ROBINSONs on ye West side thereof, thence running South South East one quarter Easterly neer unto an old line of marked trees of the sd. MRS. PRITCHARDs
thirty seven poles to a corner red Oake, thence East one halfe South by marked
trees 198 poles to a corner red Oake standing by ye Maine Swamp side, thence
up the sd. Maine Swamp the severall courses thereof to ye first mentioned Pignut Pochiccory where it first began, the sd. one hundred & fivety acres of land
the sd. SAMLL. BROMLY & MARGT. his Wife by these presents doe give unto ye
sd. WM: ROBINSON his heires and assignes and alsoe all profits and appertenances belonging;   To have and to hold for ever subject nevertheless unto ye
Quitt Rents unto her Majestie, her heires & successors and SAMLL. BROMLEY &
MARGT. his Wife for ye consideracon aforesaid will for ever warrt: & defend by
these presents;   In Wittness whereof the sd. SAMLL. BROMLEY & MARGT. his
Wife have hereunto sett their hands & seales the day month & yeare above
written

Signed sealed & delivered in ye presence of
    MIL: WALTERS,   SAMLL. BROMELEY
    TOBIAS PHILLIPS   MARGT. BROMELEY
    Recognitr in Cur Com Lancastr 11th die 8bris 1704 et recordr
            p.   JOS: TAYLOE, Clk

p.
93
    THIS INDENTURE made this 10th day of (blank) 1703 Betweene EDWD. GIBSON of the Pish: of Xt. Church Lancastr. County, Gent., of ye one part and ROBERT CARTER of ye sd. Pish: & County of ye other part; Wittnesseth that ye sd. EDWARD GIBSON for seventeene thousand pounds of sound merchantable sweet sented stem'd tobbo. paid by the said CARTER hath granted unto ye sd. ROBERT CARTER his heires & assignes for ever all that tract of land scituate in the aforesd. Pish of Christ Church in ye County of Lancastr: containing at least 375 acres being the Plantacon whereon the sd. EDWD. GIBSON now liveth being bounded as followeth (vizt), Begining att a corner Gum tree of JOHN KELLEYs standing att ye mouth of a small Cove which issueth out of TABBS CREEK on ye South West side & thence downe the Maine Creeke att severall courses to ye mouth of a Creeke which issueth out of ye Maine Creeke which sd. Creeke parts this land from BRYAN GROVEs Land, thence up the said Creeke att sevll: courses to a corner pochiccory standing in ye sd. GROVEs line att ye head of the sd. Creeke just by NANTEPOYSON PATH, thence allong ye sd. line to a corner white Oake standing just by JOHN MERRIS corner tree, thence allong a line of marked trees South West by West to a corner white Oake standing on ye East most side of JOHN MERRIS ROADE just by the Roade side, thence allong the sd. Roade att severall courses to a corner white Oak standing by the Roade side att a place called ye GULPH, thence by a line of new marked trees North by East to a corner Ash standing in ye GUM SWAMP, thence by a line of new marked trees North East to a corner Gum tree standing by the edge of a Swamp in JOHN KELLEYs line, thence allong the sd. KELLEYs line of marked trees at severall courses to ye Gum gree where it first began, which sd. land is part of a devidend of Twelve hundred acres belonging to TOBIAS HORTON and by him sold unto TEAGUE CORRELL and descended from ye sd. TEAGE unto ABRAHAM CORRELL, his Son & heire, by Deed of Indenture lawfully executed p ye sd. ABRAHAM bearing date ye seventeenth day of 8br: in ye yeare of or: Lord 1686, with all its rights houses gardens commodities & appurtenances whatsoever; To have and to hold

p.
94
    unto ye sd. ROBERT CARTER his heires & assignes from any manner of p:sons whatsoever att all times for ever he may lawfully ocupye ye said tract of land; In Wittness whereof the parties have interchangeably sett their hands & seales to two Indentures of ye same tenor & date
Signed Sealed & delivered in presence of us
    JOHN BABE,   EDWARD ⊕ GIBSON
    MARY SWAN, ELIZABETH LOMAX
    Recognitr in Cur Com Lancastr: 13th day 8bris: 1703 et record
            p. JOS: TAYLOE, Clk.

p.
95
    Virga. May ye 16th 1705. Exchange for 7 lb.=10 sh=00 pence
    Att twenty dayes sight of this my first Bill of Exchange, my second or third not paid, pray cause to be paid to Mr. JNO: SHAW or ordr: the summe of seven pounds ten shillings Sterling mony it being for value reced., here att time make good paymt. and place it to ye acct. of yor: humble Servt.

To Mr. JONATH: MATHEW & JNO:
   GOODWIN, Merchts. in London   JOHN LOMAX
Second & Third of ye same tenor
   Recordr 26th die May 1705   p. JOS: TAYLOE, Clk

    Mr. CORBIN. Virga: 7br: ye 18th 1704. Exchange L. 5=00=00.
    Att thirty dayes after sight of this my third p exchange, my first & second
not paid, pray pay or cause to be paid unto JNO: SHAW (or ordr.) ye sume of five
pounds Sterling money, it being for foure barrells of Pitch reced. here at time
make good paymt. and place it to ye acct. of Sr. yr: humble Servt.
To Mr. THO: CORBIN, Mercht. in
   PHILLPOT LANE LONDON   ROBT: TAYLOE
   Recordr. 26th die May 1705   Test   JOS: TAYLOE, Clk.

    Virginia. KNOW ALL MEN by these presents that I RICHD. CUDLIP
Comandr. of ye good Ship, "CORBIN" doe acknowledge & confesse my selfe indebted unto JNO: SHAW, Chyr., on board the sd. Ship the full & just sume of five
pounds lawfull mony of England, whih sd. sume I promise to pay att or before
ye 21st of Augt. next ensueing the date hereof; as Wittness my hand this 25th
day of Febry. in ye yeare of or: Lord one thousand seven hundred four & five
1704/5.
Test   BENJ: SUTTON   RICHD: CUDLIP
   Recordr 26th die May 1705   Test   JOS: TAYLOE, Clk.

p.   KNOW ALL MEN by these presents that I THO: BANKS, Cooper & Steward
96   on board the Ship, "CORBIN" Mr. RICHD. CUDLIP Comandr., doe acknow-
    ledge & confesse my selfe indebted unto JNO: SHAW, Chyr., on board ye
sd. Ship the full & just sume of two pounds, five shills: lawfull money of England which sd. sume I promise to pay att or before ye 21th day of August next
ensueing ye date hereof, dated the first day of March in ye yeare one thousand
seven hundred fower & five 1704/5; as Wittness my hnd
Test   RICHD: CUDLIP   THO: BANCKS
   RICHD: BEVIS, JOSEPH HILL
   Recordr. 26th die May 1705   Test   JOS: TAYLOE, Clk

    THIS INDENTURE Wittnesseth tht HENRY ANDERSON, Son of WM. ANDER-
SON, Carpenter, and wth: ye consent of my Mother, ANN ANDERSON, doth putt
himselfe Apprentice to Mr. DAVENPORT of ye County of Lancastr: in ye Collony
of Virga:, Ship Wright, his heires & assignes to learne ye Trade & Calling of a
Ship Wright or Carpenter which ye sd. DAVENPORT useth to be taught and wth:
his heires & assignes, and after ye manner of an Apprentice to dwell & serve
the sd. DAVENPORT according to ye Law of Orphans untill he is ye age of 21
yeares, he being eleven yeares of age ye first day of Febry. next ensueing ye
date hereof, all wch: time the sd. Apprentice agrees wth: ye sd. DAVENPORT his
heires & assignes well & truely to   serve, his secrets shall keep, observe his
commandmts. lawfull & honest shall gladly doe, he shall not be absent or pro-
long himselfe but in all things as a good and faithfull Apprentice shall behave
towards his sd. Mastr., dureing ye time aforesd., ye sd. Trade which he now
useth shall teach or cause to be taught the best way he can to learne him to
reade & write and dureing the aforesaid terme of yeares to provide him with
apparell meat drink and all other necessaries and att ye expiracon of sd. terme
to give unto ye sd. HENERY ANDERSON all his then working tooles and one suit

of good apparell.   In Wittness whereof the parties named hath interchange-
ably sett their hands & seales this 28th day of Apr: 1704
Signed sealed & delivered in presence of us
      JNO: LAWRIE,   HENRY ANDERSON
      JAMES WETHERSPOON   WM: DAVENPORT
   This done p my consent, as wittness my hand.
                                     ANN ANDERSON
    Recordr June 14th 1704 p. J. T., Clk.

p.   KNOW ALL MEN by these presents that I JOHN HALL of ye County of
97   Lancastr:, Planter, for a valuable consideracon in hand paid me by
       JAMES LAWRIE of ye abovesd. County, Marrinr:, have granted unto ye
sd. JAMES LAWRIE a certaine p:cell of land containing fivety acres being in ye
Pish: of White Chapple in ye County of Lancastr: lying upon ye Creeke called
PARTING CREEKE and runing up allong the sd. Creeke from a Cove called
SPRING COVE parting the sd. Land from CORDEROY DAVIS his Land & runing
from the head of ye sd. Cove up into ye woods to a marked red Hiccory, N. E. by
E. 47 poles and from ye sd. Hiccory allong by the line of NOAH ROGERS untill it
comes into ye sd. PARTING CREEKE as by survey & Pattent thereof more fully
doth appeare, wch: sd. p:cell of land is a Plantacon that formerly belonged unto
WM: WEST it being part of a devident of land containing 300 acres formerly
Pattented and taken up by THO: HARWOOD bearing date ye 14th day of 9br: 1649,
wth: all houses fences enclosures belonging to ye aforesd. land;   To have and to
hold unto JAMES LAWRIE his heires or assignes for ever in as large manner as
are exprest in ye original Pattent of the sd. land and by the Rents & provisoes
mentioned wth: warranty against all persons whatsoever, and the sd. JNO:
HALL wth: JANE his Wife doth covenant wth: ye sd. LAWRIE his heires to acknowledge these presents at ye next Court held for ye County of Lancastr:; In
Wittness whereof the sd. JNO: HALL doth hereunto putt his

p.   hand and seale this 12th day of May 1700
98   Signed sealed & delivered in presence of us
    JOHN MALLIS   JOHN HALL
    JOHN RANKIN   JANE HALL
   Recognitr in Cur Com Lancastr: decimo quarto die 9bris: 1704 et recordr
         p   JOS: TAYLOE, Clk

   Dr. Sister.   Virga: July ye 10th 1705
   Since my last to you by way of BRISTOLL wch: gave you an acct. of my
Brothers death, I have had noe opertunity to write to you untill this time,
dureing wch: space I have made it my businesse to veiw ye state of yor:
affaires in Virginia and haveing made what progress I possibly could doe in ye
time, I send you this to acquaint you this with first.   Then it may suffice to lett
you know that my Brother, haveing contracted some debts in or: parts on his
own & the Ships acct. wee durst not intermedle with any of his Estate but what
could be done by the bye for fear of being made Extors. in or: owne wrong; and
soe be made lyable for his debts here, soe that my Brother, WM., advised ye
Mate, (vizt., Mr. RICHD. CUDLIP) to sell his Estate att ye most wch: he did to
great advantage as you will find by ye enclosed accts. his wearing clothes were
sold for Thirty pounds one shill: & two pence, and wee find by Mr. CUDLIP his
accots. that he has sold other goods of his amounting to nine pounds five shills:
wch: he is actually yor: debtor for.   I urged him all that I could wth: ,modesty

to draw Bills in yor: name for ye mony or to give me an obligacon to pay you ye mony in England when he arrived there but could bring him to neither of those proposalls soe I gott him to signe ye accts. all which I have gott recorded in or: Office and the originalls I have herewith sent you as allsoe a memord: of what goods were left unsold, part of ye abovesd. goods were sold (as you will find by ye Accts. signed by CUDLIP) to one THOMAS CLARKSON who was a Seaman hired by the month in or: Country and his wages were due here soe Mr. CUDLIP gave me a Note on Mr. GAWIN CORBIN for his debt being Nine pounds, five shill., I cant yet advise you wither it will be paid or noe, Mr. CORBIN being down at JAMES RIVER, the Ships will be come away before I can demand it, But if I gett it paid, it shall be sent by the next occasion. I have sent you a Bill of MADAM GRIFFINs for two pounds ten shill: drawn on Mr. CORBIN being for goods sold by my Brother in his life time. I find an Acct. of Capt. JNO: TARPLEYs in my Brothers books, the balla. being eleven pounds, one shill: & one penny. I demanded in yor: name and he owned but foure pounds to my Brother, WM:, to be weavered wch: you will heare on by the next occasion allsoe. Mr. JNO: SHAW, Chyr., of ye Cabin

p.
99
to whome you are obliged for this care in yor: affaires has sent me a memorand: to send you of Sugr: & mony lent you from JAMAICA wch: you will find inclosed comes to L. 10=12s. My Brother left some goods wth: me to sell for him wch: was a p:cell of old Shop Keepers (vizt) boots shoos & slipers &c., amounting to L. 7=10, which I sold to a Shoomaker att a lump but am forced to sue for ye moneys & allsoe commence suit in my owne name to blind ye world yett you may be sure of an honest Acct. when recovered. You may informe yr:selfe of Mr. SHAW, ye Chyr., who is the most intiligable Gent. on board ye Ship and knows ye most of yor: concerns and of the truth of all yor: affaires and will assist you in what lyes in his power. It is convenient to be private in where you receive cense, it being known may oblidge you to pay more away then you would be willing. I sent last weeke to know my Brothers pleasure wth: Cozn. CHARLES, who resolves to keep him here and if you dont send for him to bind him Apprentice to ye sea. I know not more I have to enlarge upon but recomending you to ye p:tection of Allmighty God who best knows how to provide for ye Widdow & Fatherless, I conclude in all sincerity dr. Sister your affectiont: & luving Brother
To MRS. RUTH TAYLOE
BASINGHALL STREET, LONDON   JOS: TAYLOE
Under Cover to Mr. BEN: TAYLOE, Bedford
Street, Covent Garden, London
Recorded July ye 10th 1705   p   JOS: TAYLOE, Clk

Janry. ye 18th 1704/5. An Acct. of ye sale of Capt. ROBT. TAYLOEs	Clothes		
Imprs. To a flock bed, 1 rugg, 1 blankett, 2 pillos	1	4:	6
To a black Coat, 1 wast coat, 1 pr. breetches	5	15:	0
To Pillow beer	0	2:	6
To 2 pr. linnin Britches	0	11:	6
To 1 pr. slippers	0	1:	9
To 1 Quilt	1	5:	0
To 1 Wt. shirt	0	10:	6
To 1 pr. shoos	0:	5:	0
All these severall things sold to THO: CLARKSON	L. 9:	15:	9

Mr. RICHD: CUDLIP on ye Acct. of THOMAS BROUGHTON
Dr. to WIDDOW TAYLOE

To a light collerd. wastcoat	1:	5:	6
To a wide coat	2:	0:	0
To 1 pr. silk brittches & 1 dimetty waistcoat	1:	14:	6
To 2 pr. linnin brittches	0:	11:	6
To 1 pr. of shoos	0:	7:	0
To 1 pr. of Leather Stockings	0:	12:	6
L.	6:	11:	0

RICHARD COOKE, Carpenters Mate, Dr.

p. To a light cloath coat	2:	2:	0
100 To blew waistcoat	1	10:	0
To 1 Shirt, 1 pr. dimetty breetches	1	1:	0
To 1 hankercheiffe & 2 old night capps	0	7:	6
To 2 pr. of linnin breetches	0	12:	0
To 1 pr. old shoos	0	4:	0
	5	16:	6

JOHN MACKENNY. Dr.

1 pr. of striped drawers & a wast coat	0	7:	6
To 1 hatt	0	10:	0
To 2 pr. of linnin breetches	0	11:	6
	1	9:	0

THO: MONK, Carpenter, Dr.

To 1 flannell waist coat	0	6:	0
To 1 pr. of leather stockins	0	11:	0
	0	17:	0

Capt. RICHD. CUDLIP, Dr.

To a rumall hanckerceife & 1 pr. of gloves	0	5:	6
To 1 Cane	0	10:	0
To 1 Capp	0	3:	0
To 1 pr. of breetches	0	12:	6
To 1 pr. of stockins	0	2:	0
To 1 hatt & pr. of slippers	0	5:	9
To 1 knife & fork & 1 pr. of slippers	0	4:	0
	2	2:	9

WM. BARE, Dr.

To 1 furr capp	0	12:	6
To pr. of linnin Breetches	0	11:	6
To 1 old perriwigg	0	8:	6
	1	12:	6

THOS: DUNBABIN, Dr.

To 1 pr. of linnin breetches	0	5:	9
To 1 Chest	0	7:	0
	0	12:	9

FORTUNATUS DAVENPORT, Dr.

To 1 Bible & psalme booke	0	5:	0

ABRAH: MASTERS Dr.

To sold wastcoat	1	3:	6
Sum of Sale	30	1:	2

RICHD: CUDLIP,
Mr. RICHARD BEVIS, Dr. to WIDDOW TAYLOE

To a black capp	0	4:	6
To 1 shirt	0	12:	0
	0	16:	6

p.   Sum totale is   L.   30: 17: 8
101   Recordr: July 10th 1705 p JOS: TAYLOE, Clk.

Memorand: of goods left belonging to Capt. ROBERT TAYLOE, not disposed
of -- To 1 case of bottles; To 2 Quadrants & Veines, To 1 Nocturnell, To 1 Cloak,
To 3 table Clothes & Napkins, 1 dozn., To 1 case of Drawers, To 1 close stoole pan;
To Mantesse; To 1 great punch bole; To lesser ditto, To 6 books of Navigacon, To
2 Devidrs; To 2 Compasses, To 2 Attlasses; To 1 Crown & 1 Ryall

Goods sold p Mr. RICHARD CUDLIP at ye Mast by ay of Auction

	L	30:	10:	2
To 370 1/2 lbs. of white Sugr.		9:	5:	0
To 310 lbs. of ditto course		5:	3:	4
To 17 1/2 galls. Rum		3:	10:	0
To 8 1/2 galls. Lyme Juce		1:	5:	6
Sum totall is		49:	5:	0

p RICHD: CUDLIP

Mr. BEVIS Acct.	0:	16:	6
	50:	1:	6

RICHD: CUDLIPs Receipts for wages signed p his own hand

May ye 25th 1704 of ROBERT TAYLOE, for	L. 4:	1:	0
JNO: SHAW ditto	0:	12:	7
RICHD: BEVIS ditto	5:	0:	0
THO: BANKS ditto	4:	10:	6
THO: MONK ditto	4:	9:	0
THO: MONK more ditto Augt. 1704	0:	15:	0
JNO: MACKENNY ditto	1:	19:	8
WM: BARE ditto	5:	10:	6
JOHN GLASSCOCKs ditto, Cooke	1:	6:	0
BENJ: SUTTON ditto	1:	5:	0
RICHD: COOKE, ditto	5:	15:	0
THO: DAVIS, ditto	1:	15:	6
ABRAH: MASTERS ditto	1:	2:	2

p. BENJ: PEIRCE ditto	1:	2:	2
102 THO: BROUGHTON, ditto	6:	19:	0

All ye above named have signed to ye Booke
JNO: MALSCET, JOHN ANGOON, PETER CORRONETT, PETERS de PERRUE,
Frenchmen shipt on Board ye Cabin disburst for Clotheing   10: 12: 3
Recordr 10th July 1705   p JOS: TAYLOE, Clk.

July ye 9th 1704. Sent my Wife a Bill of six pounds upon Mr. JNO: COMBEs next ye Admiralty Office Gate, London from JOHN ELDRIDGE, Leiut. & JNO: SHALES, Capt. of hir Majties Fire Ship, "YE EARL GALLY" att JAMAICA by Mr. BLACKMAN, Leiut. on board ye "NORWICH" Man of Warr by ditto/ 1 casque of fine wt. sugr: qt. 135 lbs.

Do sent by Mr. COLLINS, Cheife Mate of Capt. LOVE from GUINNY in Sterl: English mony five pound twelve shills: & in Spanish Dollars four pound, ten shill: Sum   totall   10: 12: 0

A Copy taken from Capt. ROBERT TAYLOEs Booke for Memrd.

JOS: TAYLOE, Clk

Ye 10th July 1705 p idem   JOS: TAYLOE, Clk.

THIS INDENTURE made this 12th day of Apr: in ye yeare of or: Lord 1705; Betweene JOHN WADE, Eldest Son of JOHN WADE, late of ye County of Lancastr: (deced),, RICHD: FRISTER & LETTICE his Wife, one of ye Daughters of ye sd. JNO: WADE (deced), and ABIGALL WADE of ye one pte, and Capt. WM: FOX of ye Pish: of St. Marys White Chapple in ye County of Lancastr:, Gent., of ye other parte; Wittnesseth that ye sd. JOHN WADE, RICHARD FRISTER & LETTICE his Wife and ABIGALL WADE for ye sume of five shills. of lawfull money of England hath sold lunto ye sd. Capt. WM: FOX all that tract of land being in ye Pish: of St. Marys White Chapple in ye County of Lancastr: upon ye North East side of a Southeast Branch of MORRATICOE CREEKE lyeing Northwest upon ye Land of ABRAHAM MOONE, North East into ye Woods upon a Swamp up on ye head of ye sd. Branch, South West upon ye sd. Branch, the Plantacon being now in ye tenure of ye sd. JNO: WADE and the reversion and profitts of ye premisses

p.   To have and to hold unto ye sd. Capt. WM: FOX his heires or assignes
103   dureing the terme of one whole yeare paying yearly att ye Feast of St.
        Michall ye Arch Angell yearly rent of one Pepper Corn to him and his
heires;   In Wittness whereof the p:ties first above written have sett their hands and affixed their seales the day & year first above written
Signed sealed & delivered in ye presence of

JOHN DARE,   JOHN WADE
JAMES ATTCHISSON,   RICHD: FRISTER
WM: KELLY   LETTICE FRISTER
                                  ABIGALL WADE

Recognitr: in Cur Com Lancastr: dicimo tertio Janry: 1705 et recordr

p JOS: TAYLOE, Clk.

Note upon this Deed was this endorsmt:

Memorand. That this day ye 12th day of Apr: in ye yeare 1705, JNO: WADE, RICHD. FRISTER and LETTICE his Wife and ABIGALL WADE partys to these presents delivered actuall possession of ye Manner House and other houses upon the within mentioned tract of land wch: Livery and Seizin by twigg & turff in ye name of seizin of ye whole to ye sd. Capt. WM: FOX his heires & assignes.
In presence of us   WM: DARE,

SAMLL: FOX,   MIL: WALTERS,
BRYON STOTT

THIS INDENTURE made this 13th of April 1705; Betweene JOHN WADE of ye Pish: of NORTH FARNHAM in ye County of RICHMOND in ye Dominion of Virginia, Planer, Eldest Son

p.   of JOHN WADE, late of the Pish: of St. Marys White Chapple in County of
104   Lancastr: in ye Dominion aforesd., Cordwainder, (deced), RICHD: FRIS-
        TER and LETTICE his Wife, one of the Daughters of ye aforesaid JOHN
WADE, (deced) of the one part and Capt. WM: FOX of the Parish of White Chapple in ye County of Lancastr:, Gent., of ye other part;   Wittnesseth that the said
JOHN WADE, RICHD: FRISTER & LETTICE his Wife & ABIGALL WADE, in consideracon of One hundred pounds have granted unto Capt. WM: FOX in his actuall
possession now being by virtue of a bargaine & sale for one whole yeare and
by force of ye Statute for transferring of uses into possession, all that Planta-
con & tract of land consisting of five hundred acres in ye Pish. of St. Marys
White Chapple in ye County of Lancastr:, the sd. Land being granted to one
SHARP, late of ye sd. County of Lancastr:, (deced), by Pattent bearing date ye
fourth day of Septembr: 1655, relacon being had may att large appeare, and to
JNO: SHARP, Son & heire of ye sd. SHARP (deced), now allsoe (deced) by his
Deed bearing date ye seaventh day of December 1680 sold said to one THOMAS
THOMSON, late of ye aforesd. County of Lancastr: now allsoe (deced), as in ye
said Deed of Bargain & Sale remaineing upon Record in ye Court of Lancastr:
Conty and by him, ye sd. THOMAS THOMPSON, by his Deed of bargaine & sale
remaineing upon Record of ye Court of Lancastr: County Court aforesd. sold
unto JOHN WADE, Father of aforesd. JOHN WADE, party to these presents and by
ye sd. JOHN WADE (deced), by his Last Will in writeing bearing date ye 2d day of
March 1687/8 and remaineing upon Record upon ye Records of Lancastr:
County devised ye sd. Land to him, JOHN WADE, party to these presents and
other his Children, the said tract of land being now or late in ye occupacon of
ye sd. Capt. WM: FOX or his assignes and all other land and hereditaments in ye
County of Lancastr: whrein the said JOHN WADE, RICHD: FRISTER and LETTICE
his Wife and ABIGALL WADE or any of them have any Estate

p.   of free hold and inheritance in;   To have and to hold the sd. tract of land
105   unto ye sd. Capt. WM: FOX his heires & assignes for ever, quietly to hold
        and enjoy the sd. Plantacon wth:out trouble of them ye sd. JOHN WADE,
RICHD: FRISTER and LETTICE his Wife and ABIGALL WADE their heires and
assignes

p.   In Wittness whereof ye parties first above named have putt to this
106   Indenture of Release their hands and affixed their seales the day and
        year first above written/1705.
Signed Sealed and delivered in presence of
        WM: DARE,   JOHN WADE
        JAMES ATTCHISON,   RICHD: FRISTER
        WM: KELLY   LETTICE FRISTER
                                            ABIGALL WADE
        Recognitr in Cur Com Lancastr: dicimo tertio die Juny 1705 et recordr
                    p   JOS: TAYLOE, Clk.

p.   RICHMOND ss. TO ALL CHRISTIAN PEOPLE to whome this pr:sent
108   writeing shall come, JOHN WADE of ye County of RICHMOND, Planter,
        and JANE his Wife, RICHARD FRISTER & LETTICE his Wife, and ABIGALL
WADE send Greeting. Know yee yt: whereas certaine Indentures betweene
JOHN WADE, RICHD. FRISTER & LETTICE his Wife and ABIGALL WADE of one part
& Capt. WM: FOX of ye other part purporting a bargaine saile and release of a
certaine plantacon in ye County of Lancastr. Now the said JOHN WADE and

JANE his Wife, RICHD. FRISTER & LETTICE his Wife and ABIGALL WADE have appointed Mr. WM: DARE their true & lawfull Attorney to acknowledge the before mentioned Indentures & to acknowledge ye rights of Dower hereby ratifying whatsoever or: sd. Attor: shall doe in ye pr:misses;   In Wittness whereof the p:ties hereby menconed to these presents have sett their hands and seales this 13th day of Aprill 1705

Signed Sealed & delivered in ye presence of
      WM: KELLY,   JOHN WADE
                                         JANE WADE
                                         RICHD: FRISTER
                                         LETTICE FRISTER
                                         ABIGALL WADE

    Probatr: Lettr. de Attor: in Cur Com Lancastr: 13th die Junii 1705 p WM: KELLY et recordr   p   JOS: TAYLOE, Clk

p.   THIS INDENTURE made the 28th day of October in the tenth yeare of ye
108   reigne of or: King Lord William &c., 1698 Betweene ROGER WILLIAMS of
         the Pish: of Christ Church in the County of Lancaster of the one part
and ROBERT DENHAM of the aforesd. Pish: and County of the other part;   Wittnesseth that ROGER WILLIAMS for the sum of Six thousand pounds of good legall tobacco hath sold unto the sd. ROBERT DENHAM his heires or assignes all that parcell of land containing One hundred acres as by the Survey and Platt thereof will appeare and bounded as followeth (vizt.) the sd. land lying and being upon the Eastermost Branch of COROTOMAN in the County aforesd. commonly called MILLSTONE POINT and formerly in the occupacon of the sd. ROGER WILLIAMS, runing into ye woods about halfe a mile to a head line of marked trees and bounded on either side with natural bounds, vizt., two Swamps, one dividing the sd. land from the land of JOHN GIBSON; and the other from ye Land of THOMAS BLANCH, and was taken up by the sd. ROGER WILLIAMS in copartnership with WILLIAM LAWRENCE (deced), and by them, ye sd. WILLIAMS and LAWRENCE, divided betweene themselves in the said LAWRENCEs life time, the moiety whereof hereby granted together with all houses fences woods and apertainances apertaining and all the right of ROGER WILLIAMS to the same; To have and to hold to the sd. ROBERT DENHAM his heires or assignes ever more

p.   In Wittness whereof the parties have hereunto sett their hands and
109   seales the day and yeare above written
     Signed sealed & delivered in the presence of
     JOS: TAYLOE   ROGER WILLIAMS
     RICH: HAYNIE
    Recognitr in Cur Com Lancastr: 10th die Novembris 1698 et recordr 16th die
             p   JOS: TAYLOE, Clk
    Recognitr in Cur Com Lancastr: 12th July 1704 p WM: BALL, Attor: de ROBERT DENHAM et recordr.   p   JOS: TAYLOE, Clk

KNOW ALL MEN by these presents that I ROBERT DENHAM of the County of Lancastr: doe owe unto MARTHA HAYNES of the abovesd. County the full sum of Eight thousand pounds of every way good sound merchantable tobacco and caske to be truely paid I bind my selfe my Exectrs. or Administratrs: for the whole and in the whole as Wittness my hand and seale this 31st day of October 1702
    THE CONDICION of the above obligacon is such that if the above bound

ROBERT DENHAM shall truely pay unto MARTHA HAYNES the full sume by the
five and twentieth day of December come twelve months which will be in the
yeare 1703, according to the provisoe mentioned in a Deed of Indenture
bearing date the Eight & twentieth day of October 1698, Then if the abovesd.
ROBERT DENHAM and ELENOR his Wife doe att ye next Court holden for the
County of Lancastr: after the 25th day of Decembr: and in the yeare 1703

p.   lawfully surrender in Court the above mentioned Deed to MARTHA
110   HAYNES her heires for ever according to ye tenour of the abovesd.
        Lease of Indenture as above the sd. p:cel of land wth: every of their
appurtenances in ye sd. Indenture mentioned and allsoe if ye said MARTHA
HAYNES her heires may peaceably and quietly hold and enjoy the abovesd.
p:cell of land acquitted from all maner of former grants and incumbrances,
That then the abovesd. obligacon to be of none effect otherwise to stand in full
force
Signed sealed and delivered in pr:sence of us
        WILLIAM BALL,   ROBERT DENHAM
        HANNAH BALL
        Recognitr in Cur Com Lancastr: 12th die Julii 1704   et recordr
                        p   JOS: TAYLOE, Clk.

        KNOW ALL MEN by these presents that I ROBERT DENHAM of the County
of Lancastr:, Planter, hath appointed WM: BALL, Gent., of the aforesd. County
my true and lawfull Attorney for me to acknowledge unto Mr. RICHD: FLINT
and MARTHA his Wife a certaine Deed of Indenture bearing date the 28th day
of October 1698 according to a Bond made bearing date the 31st day of October
1702 made to her, the above named MARTHA, then Widow and Relict of EDWARD
HAYNES of the abovesd. County; which sd. land is now in the occupacon of the
sd. MARTHA now Wife to ye above named RICHD: FLINT, then and therefor me
and in my name to delivr: as my act and deed unto the above named RICHD:
FLINT or MARTHA his now Wife, their heires or assignes, one Deed of Indenture of land whereunto I have allready sealed bearing date 28th day of October
1698 made betweene me, ye sd. ROBERT DENHAM and MARTHA now Wife to ye
abovesd. RICHD: FLINT, according to ye tenor of the sd. Indenture unto ye sd.
MARTHA her Executrs. or assignes for ever from me my heires or assignes or
any other p:sons whatsoever that may have any claime and what my above
named Attorney doth in this case, I doe acknowledge to be as authentick as if I
my selfe were p:sonally pr:sent.   In Wittness whereof I have hereunto sett my
hand and seale this 4th day of July 1704
Signed sealed and delivd: in presence of us
        HANNAH BALL,   ROBERT DENHAM
        SUSANNA PAYNE
        Recognitr: in Cur Com Lancastr: 12th die Julii 1701 et recordr
                        p   JOS: TAYLOE, Clk.

p.   KNOW ALL MEN by these presents that I ROBERT DENHAM of the County
111   of Lancaster make over unto MARTHA FLINT, now Wife of RICHD: FLINT,
        all my title and interest of the within Indenture of Lease wth: warranty
from me my heires unto MARTHA FLINT her heires;   As Wittness my hand this
4th day of July 1704
Signed sealed and delivered in pr:sence of us
        HANNAH BALL,   SUSANNAH PAYANE   ROBERT DENHAM

Recognitr in Cur Com Lancastr: 2 July 1704 et p WM; BALL, Attor: of ROBT:
DENHAM et recordr: p   JOS: TAYLOE, Clk

    TO ALL TO WHOME this present writeing shall come, THOMAS LOE of
Couny of Lancastr: in RAPPAHANOCK RIVER in Virginia sendth Greeting.
Know ye that ye sd. THOMAS LOE for Fifteen pounds of good and lawfull mony
of England paid by JOHN HARRIS, Plantr., of County aforesd. hath sold unto the
sd. JOHN HARRIS, Fifty acres of land in the County aforesd. in as full manner as
the same was sold to ye sd. LOE,   Begining at a markd. red Oake standing neer a
Creeke commonly called ABBYES CREEKE and runing up ye sd. Creeke to a
marked Hickory being the corner tree of JOHN HARRIS his land and so runing
along the sd. HARRIS his line to the line that divides the land of JOHN BERRY
(deced), and the land of the sd. LOE, and from thence a streight course to ye
place first specified;   To have and to hold the sd. land unto ye sd. JOHN HARRIS
his heires and assignes for ever, and that ye sd. LOE and MARTHA his Wife
shall att ye next Court held for ye County aforesd. acknowledge ye pr:misses to
be ye right of the sd. JOHN HARRIS;   In Wittness whereof the said THOMAS LOE
hereunto sett his hand and seale the 10th day of May 1704
Signed sealed & delivered in the presence of us
    JOHN BROWN   THOMAS LOE
    JOHN ✝ FAIREMAN
    Recognitr in Cur Com Lancastr: 14th Junii 1704 et recordr
        p   JOS: TAYLOE, Clk

p.   RECEIVED of THOMAS LOE the just sume of Nine pounds Sterling (or one
112   Mare and fifteen pounds or to ye value thereof in land) concluded be-
      tweene them which ye said WALTER ANISS sold to Mr. JOHN HARRIS, I
say reced. by me, WALTER ANNISS, likewise reced. to ye value of three pounds,
ten shillings in Cattle, I say reced. by me, WALTER ANNIS, likewise reced. one
KEEL BOAT valued to three pounds, ten shillings, I say reced. by me WALTER
ANNIS.   The total sume in all one and thirty pounds
Test   MATHEW MYARS   WALTER ✘ ANIS
    JOHN ✝ FAIREMAN

    TO ALL CHRISTIAN PEOPLE to whome this present writeing Indented
shall come in the year of our Lord God everlasting 1703,   Whereas HENRY
CARTYS of the Pish: of St. Marys White Chappell in ye County of Lancastr:,
Planter, did by his Deed dated the thirtieth of Aprill 1693 did give unto JOSEPH
BALL of the sd. Pish:, Gent., three hundred acres of land being in ye sd. Pish: of
White Chapell and County of Lancastr:, being pte. of a Pattent for Nine hundred and sixty acres formerly granted unto Mr. CHARLES GRYMES and dated
twenty sixth of December Anno Domini 1653, and renewed by Pattent dated the
Eighth day of Octobr: Anno Domini 1657; and upon a survey was found within
the bounds of the sd. Pattent one thousand acres; the three hundred acres of
land beginning at a   red Oake on West side of a Swamp which partes the same
from the land of the sd. JOSEPH BALL, and runing thence West and by North
one hundred and thirty eight poles to a small white Oake saplin, thence North
and by East one hundred and ninety poles to a Stake in CARPENTERs Field,
thence East and by South one hundred and ninety and eight poles to a red Oake
in MOTTs line, thence along sd. MOTTs line South West sixty six poles, and South
East one hundred and twelve poles to land of the sd. BALLs, thence along the
line of the said BALL South West and by West one hundred thirty four poles to a

red Oake on East side of the head of the sd. Swamp and then down the Swamp South twenty two degrees West seventy eight poles to ye first mentioned red Oake, the place where it first began as in and by the sd. Deed relacon being thereunto had more at large may appeare,   NOW THIS INDENTURE WITTNESSETH that JOSEPH BALL of the Pish; of White Chappell in the County of Lancastr:, Gent., for the love and affection which I have and doe bear unto my Son in Law, RAWLEIGH CHINN, of ye sd. Pish: and County, Gent., doe give and by these presents have granted unto ye sd. RAWLEIGH CHINN and his heires for ever one hundred and ninety acres of land being a parte of the sd. three hundred acres of land in Lancastr: County bounded as followeth, vizt., Beginning at the formr: marked red Oake standing on the Westward side of a Branch of Capt. SAMUELL FOX's his MILL which sd. Branch divides this from the lands formerly granted to THEOPHILUS HONE, from the sd. red Oake

p   runing West and by North one hundred and thirty eight poles, thence
113   North and by East two hundred ninety poles to ye East and South line of
        the aforesd. Pattent, thence along the sd. line East and by South to a Branch of MOUNT TIERALL, thence along the said Branch its severall courses to a marked Gum standing in the sd. Branch at ye head thereof; thence South twenty eight degrees West twenty six poles to a white Oake, thence South twenty four degrees East one hundred and nine poles to another white Oake standing nigh the head of the first mentioned Branch, thence down the sd. Branch South three degrees West eighty six poles to ye place where it first began with all the timber woods swamps &c. within the bounds aforesd. To have and to hold unto the sd. RAWLEIGH CHINN his heires for ever; Provided he shall pay the Quitt Rents for ever hereafterwards due for the said ninety acres unto the right Honourable the Lord Proprietors and their Agent if the same be lawfully demanded;   And the sd. JOSEPH BALL doth covenant for himselfe and heires with the sd. RAWLEIGH CHINN and his heires that the sd. JOSEPH BALL will warrt. the sd. land so given from him and his heires and doth covenant that he will when requested acknowledge these pr:sents in the open Court of the County of Lancastr: before her Majties: Justices of the Peace for better confirming of these presents;   In Wittness whereof, I have hereunto sett my hand and seale this Twelfth day of February in the year above menconed
Signed sealed & delivd. in the pr:sence of us
    GEORGE FINCH,   JOSEPH BALL
    MARY ⨂ JOHNSON, EDWARD JEFFERYS
    Recognitr in Cur Com Lancastr: 12th die Aprilis 1704 et recordr
            p.   JOS: TAYLOE, Clk.

    These are to impower you, WILLIAM DARE, to appeare for me in all actions wherein I am concerned in Lancastr: County Court and to prosecute or defend the same in effect and for your soe doing this shall bee your warrant
                                                    CHALOTE BERTRAND

    KNOW ALL MEN by these presents yt: I WILLIAM SIMONS of the County of Lancastr:, Joyner, doe appoint my loveing Wife, SARAH SIMMONS to be my Attorney to appeare for me and in my stead to all such matters as I have depending in the Lancastr: County Court, as Wittness my hand the 11th day of September Anno 1704

Signed and delivered in the presence of
GEORGE TURBERVILE   WILL: SIMON

p.   THIS INDENTURE made the tenth day of February one thousand seven hun-
114   dred and one & two and in the thirteenth yeare of the reigne of or: Sovereigne
        Lord King William by and betweene JOHN RHOODES of ye Couny of Lancaster
and Pish: of Christ Church of the one pt: and JOSEPH TAYLOE of the sd. County and
Pish: of the other part;   Wittnesseth that ye sd. JOHN RHOODES for the severall clauses
hereaafter exprest doth covenant and agree with the said JOSEPH TAYLOE to serve
him the full terme of five whole yeares commencing from the fourth day of this instant February in any such service or employmt. as he the said JOSEPH shall employ
him according to ye custome of the Country and in like kind in consideracon whereof the sd. JOSEPH doth promise with sd. JOHN RHOODES to allowe him good and sufficient cloathing washing lodging and dyet dureing the sd. terme of five yeares, and
for the two first yeares, viz., 1702 and 1703, to keep him wholely to Schoole, excepting
in time of planting and tending of Corne and at the expiracon of the whole five
yeares to give him, the sd. JOHN, one good sute of wearing apparell and three barrells
of Indian Corne, to ye true p:formance of which Indenture and every article thereof
wee have hereunto sett our hands and seales allowing that the same shall be within
three months inroll'd in Court and there transmitted to Record
Signed sealed and delivered in presence of us
        DANLL: McCARTY   JOHN RHOODES
        THO: WALTER   JOS: TAYLOE

        Virginia, RAPPAHANCK: RIVER   May the 15th 1704
        KNOW ALL MEN by these pr:sents that I THOMAS PETER, Mercht. in Glasgow in
the Kingdom of Scotland doe herey ordain and constitute my well beloved Friend,
DAVID CROSSE, Mercht., in the City aforesd., to be my lawfull Attorney here in Virginia for me to demand and sue for recover and receive all such debts of money or
tobacco that is due to me upon Bond, Bill of Exchange or any other accompt, and for
default of paymt. use all lawfull meanes for recovery thereof, and before any Judges
or Justices in all business concerning me as my Agent or Factor granting by these
presents unto

p.   my sd. Attorney lawfull authority to give acquittances upon the receipt of any
115   sumes of mony or tobacco or any other things whatsoever as the cause shall
        require, ratifying and confirming effecuall and irrevocable all and whatso-
ever my sd. Attorney ·doe or cause to be done about the pr:misses;   In Wittness whereof I have sett my hand and seale the day and yeare above written
Signed sealed and delivd. in the presence of us
Test RICHD: FLINT,   THOMAS PETER
      MARTHA FLINT

        Lancaster County ss. THIS INDENTURE made the sixteenth day of October 1704
Betweene JOHN SHARP of the Pish: of St. Marys White Chappell, Planter, of one part
and ROBERT HOPKINS of the Pish: of Christ Church and County aforesd. of other part;
Wittnesseth that the sd. JOHN SHARP for the consideracons hereafter exprest hath
granted to farm letten unto the sd. ROBERT HOPKINS all that my Plantacon Lands
lying and being in the County aforesd. and Pish: of St. Mary White Chapell, whereon
ELINOR PRICE, Widow, late lived, with all houses barns orchards gardens and profitts
whatsoever apertaining with liberty of ingress and egress dwelling into the sd. Plantacon or Lands for the full space of twelve yeares commencing from the Nativity of

our blessed Lord and Saviour Jesus Christ now next comeing and from thence to be compleated and ended with liberty of Timber to build fences, make tobacco hogsheads as may for him the sd. ROBERT be necessary dureing the sd. terme with liberty of fishing fowling hunting and hawking so far as I the sd. JOHN by the first grant now have dureing the sd. terme of twelve yeares, paying yearely upon the Nativity of our Lord and Saviour Jesus Christ the fee Rent of five hundred pounds of good tobacco in one hogshead to conaine the same, allwayes provided that if the Rent aforesd. shall be unpaid by the space of one month after the same shall become due then it shall be lawfull for him ye sd. JOHN his Executrs: or Administraters into the sd. Lands and re-enter and abide as tho this Lease had never been made and the sd. ROBERT HOPKINS doth further agree that at the expiracon of the full terme he shall deliver the sd. Plantacon to ye sd. JOHN his heires or lawfull assignes in tenantable repaire. In Witt-ness whereof the p:tys to this Indenture have sett their hands and seales the day and yeaare above written, and it is further agreed that ye sd. ROBERT shall build one twenty foot dwelling house and one thirty foot tobacco house within the terme afore-sd and plant an Orchard, the said SHARP his heires or assignes finding the trees

p.   Signed sealed and delivd: in the presence of
116   JOS: TAYLOE,   JOHN SHARP
      ANN TAYLOE   ROBERT HOPKINS

     Mr. TOM: CHILTON Dr. July 12th 1703.

To 4 Cowes and Calves at L. 2: 10s.	10.....00.....00
To 4 Sheep at 10s p.	02.....00.....00
To 1 Mulata Girle named KATHARINA COLLINGS	10.....00.....00
To 1 Iron Pott and pott hooks	00.....08.....09
To 1 Frying Pan	00.....02.....06
To 23 Gees at 2s p	01.....06.....00
To 10 Ganders at 1s. 6d.	00.....15.....00
To a Feather Bed and Bolstr:	04.....03.....00
To 12 Henns and 1 Cock at 6d p	00.....06.....06
To 8 1/4 Pewter at 10d p	00.....06.....10 1/2
To 1 Blankett	00.....07.....00
To 1 p Pott Racks	00.....01.....00
To 1 Chest	00.....05.....00
	30.....01.....07 1/2

    July 12th: 1703. Then reced. of Mr. THO: LOE the full contents of the within Accot. upon the Account of my Wife's portion, reced. p me.
                                 TOM: CHILTON his ⋔ marke

    KNOW ALL MEN by these presents that I JANE KELLEY doe by these pr:sents appoint Captn. HENRY FLEET to be my true and lawfull Attorney in my name to ack-nowlidge my thirds of Sixty two acres of land sold by my Husband, CHARLES KELLEY to WM: SIMONS and his heires, as Wittness my hand this 8th day of Xber: 1704
Test   HEN: FLEET, JUNR.   JANE ✠ KELLEY her marke

p.   KNOW ALL MEN by these presents that I ANN ANDERSON, Wife of WILLIAM
117   ANDERSON have assigned and in my stead and place by these presents doe
      authorize and make JOHN LAWRIE of Lancaster County, Carpentr:, my true and lawfull Attorney for my use to acknowledge these Indentures of my Son, HENRY ANDERSON and WILLIAM DAVENPORT to be done by my order and knowledge and con-sent of these same and doe impower JOHN LAWRIE to acknowledge the same as if I

were present my selfe;   In Wittness whereof I the sd. ANN ANDERSON have sett my
hand and seale this 28th day of Aprill 1704
Wittness   ANN CHOUNING,   ANN ANDERSON
         JAMES WALTERS

     March 8th: 1703/4
     These are to impower WILLIAM DARE to appeare for me in all actions de-
pending in Lancastr: County Court wherein I am concerned and to prosecute the
same to effect
Teste RICHD: FLINT   HUGH LADNOR

     THIS INDENTURE made this 30 day of March in the yeare one thousand seven
hundred and five Betweene JOHN BUSH of the Pish: of St. Marys White Chappell in the
County of Lancaster, Planter, and MARGARET his Wife, of the one part and WILLIAM
HOWARD of the Pish; and County aforesd., Inn holdr: of the other part;   Wittnesseth
that the sd. JOHN BUSH and MARGARET his Wife for the sume of thirty pounds of good
and lawfull mony of England pd. by the said WILLIAM HOWARD, doth by these presents hath granted unto the said WILLIAM HOWARD his heires and assignes for ever
all that tract of land being in the aforesd. Pish: of St. Marys White Chapell in ye
County of Lancastr: being Two hundred acres or thereabouts being the Plantacon
whereon the sd. JOHN BUSH now liveth, bounded as followeth, vizt., Beginning at a
white Oake standing in the MINE BRANCH betweene PEAVINE CREEKE and GRIMES his
Old Field, thence runing South along a line of

p.   marked trees to a Branch of HOGGS HED NECK, from thence North West downe
118   the new PLANTATION NECK SWAMP mouth; thence East up the NEW PLANTA-
       TION NECK SWAMP to a line of marked trees, thence South across NEW PLANTA-
TION NECK to a Branch that runneth betweene the sd. LUCKHAMs and JOHN BUCK-
STONs, thence downe the sd. Branch to a line that parts this land from the land of
JOHN BUXTON, thence cross the sd. Branch to a corner Pear tree standing in JOHN
BUXTONs Cornefield, from thence runing Westerly to a Branch which divides this
from the land of SAMLL: STEELE,   from thence downe that Branch to the mouth of it,
from thence up the Maine Swamp to the white Oake where it first began, with all and
singular its rights houses gardens and ppertainances whatsoever appertaining,   To
have and to hold unto the sd. WILLIAM HOWARD his heires and assignes for ever; And
the said JOHN BUSH and MARGARET his Wife will warrant these pr:sents from the
claimes of any p:son whatsoever

p   In Wittness whereof the parties first above mentioned have hereunto sett
119   their hands and seales the day and yare above written
       Signed sealed and delivered in the presence of us
       JOS: TAYLOE   JOHN BUSH
       ANN TAYLOE, DICK SANDERS   MARGT. CO BUSH, her marke
       Recognitr in Cur Com Lancastr: 13th die Junii 1705 et recordr
                 p.   JOS: TAYLOE, Clk

     KNOW ALL MEN by these presents that I JOHN BUSH and MARGT. my Wife are
bound unto WILLIAM HOWARD his heires or assignes in the full amount of One hundred pounds of good & lawfull money of England.   Sealed wth: our seales and dated this
30th day of March 1705
     THE CONDICION of this obligacon is such that whereas the above JOHN BUSH hath
conveyed unto WM: HOWARD two hundred acres by Deed bearing equall date with

these pr:sents; Now if the sd. JOHN BUSH and MARGT. his Wife fullfill all covenants in the sd. Deed and at all times hereafter defend him, ye sd. WILLIAM, from any disturbance that may arise by dispute of the title to the sd. Deed and secure to him ye sd. WILLIAM, his heires and assignes a sure possession of the sd. Land, That then this obligacon to be void and of non effect or else to remaine in full force

Signed sealed and delivd: in the presence of us

    JOS: TAYLOE, ANNE TAYLOE,   JNO: BUSH
    DICK: SANDERS   MARGT: ∞ BUSH

     June 13th 1705. Recorded.   p. JOS: TAYLOE, Clk.

p.   THIS INDENTURE made this eighth day of August 1705 and in the fourth yeare
120   of the reigne of or: Sovereigne Lady Ann, Queen of England &c., betweene
        JOHN LUCKHAM of the County of Lancastr: Pish: of St. Marys White Chapell, Planter, of one part and WILLIAM HOWARD of the same County and Pish:, Inn holdr: of the other part; Wittnesseth that the said JOHN LUCKHAM in consideracon of the sume of Two thousand foure hundred pounds of tobacco and caske to him paid, by these presents hath sold unto the said WILLIAM HOWARD his heires or assignes one certaine tract of land lying in the County of Lancastr: and Pish: aforesd. formerly belonging to JOHN BUSH and by him sold to the aforesd. JOHN LUCKHAM by Deed dated May the 25th 1698 and recorded in the said County the August following; the said Land being bounded; Beginning at a line runing South to a Branch of BARTHOLOMEW WOODs and soe runns thence West North West another Branch and along the sd. Branch to the lower end of the Neck and across the Neck East to another Branch of MARATICOE, runing thence downe the sd. Branch into the Maine Branch which parts JOHN BUXTONs land from the land of JOHN BUSH, soe runing up the sd. Maine Branch into the sd. line of BARTHOLOMEW WOODs; To have and to hold the sd. Plantacon wth: all houses timber woods moors unto ye sd. WILLIAM HOWARD his heires or assignes for ever; paying to ye Cheif Lord of the Fee the usuall Rents reserved to him and I the sd. JOHN LUCKHAM doe further promise that I have a good warrantable right in the sd. p:cell of land and doe warrt. and will for ever defend quiet possession of every p:cell of ye sd. land to be enjoyed by him ye sd. WILLIAM, his heires and assignes; In Wittness whereof I have sett my hand and affixed my seale the day and yeare first above   written

Sealed and delivered

    JOS: TAYLOE,
    JOHN BRADLEY   JOHN ✝ LUCKHAM

     Recognitr in Cur Com Lancastr: 12th die 7bris: 1705 et recordr.
                p   JOS: TAYLOE, Clk

p.   TO ALL CHRISTIAN PEOPLE to whome these presents shall come, Know yee
121   that I JOHN BUSH of the County of Lancastr:, Plantr., for a valuable sume of
        tobacco in hand allready reced., have sold unto JOHN LUCKHAM of the aforesd. County, Plantr., a p:cell of land; To have and to hold for ever with profitts in as large manner whatsoever as may have been expressed and the sd. JOHN BUSH doth bind him selfe to maintaine and warrt. the sale of the p:cell of land peaceably and further I oblige my selfe to give the sd, LUCKHAM possession and for the true p:formance of every article herein expressed, I the aforesd. JOHN BUSH have hereunto sett my hand and seale this 25th day of May 1698

Signed sealed and delivered in the presence of

    JOHN MILLER,   JOHN BUSH
    WILLIAM MILLER

KNOW ALL MEN by these pr:sents that I JOHN LUCKHAM doe assigne unto WM: HOWARD all my right to ye within mentioned Land as I my selfe had to ye same and will for ever defend to him, the sd. WM., his heires and assignes for ever;   As Wittness my hand and seale this 8th day of August 1705
Sealed & delivered in presence of
    JOSEPH TAYLOE   JOHN LUCKHAM
    JNO: BRADLEY
     Recognitr in Cur Com Lancastr: 12th die 7bris: 1705
          p   JOS: TAYLOE, Clk

p.   THIS INDENTURE made the twelve day of July in the yeare of or: Lord one
122   thousand six hundred ninety nine Betweene JOHN HUTCHINGS of the Pish: of
      Christ Church in the County of Lancastr: in the Collony of Virginia of the one part and WILLIAM LISTER of the said Pish: and County of the other part;   Wittnesseth that the sd. JOHN HUTCHINGS for a valuable consideracon hath grante unto WILLIAM LISTER his heires or assignes, a certaine tract of land being in the Pish: and County aforesd. and bounded Beginning at the head of a small Branch that runneth of CARO-TOMAN nigh unto the House of JOHN FLOYD, deced., at a white Oake in a valley near to Mr. FLOYD and runing from thence South unto a marked Gum and from the sd. Gum South and by West by a line of marked trees near the path that goes out of FLEETS BAY to the said HUTCHINGS House unto a corner red oake, and runing thence North & by West by a line of marked trees unto a corner red Oake standing in GABRIEL THAT-CHERs line and runing due East to a corner red Oake sapling and runing from thence by a line of marked trees South and by West over the Branch it first began, and soe up the South side of the sd. Branch unto the white Oake where it first began;   To have and to hold the sd. land unto the sd. WM: LISTER his heires and assignes for ever, and I JOHN HUTCHINGS doe hereby promise to warrant for ever and to defend ye sd. WIL-LIAM LISTER against all manner of persons, and I doe hereby further promise to acknowledge this conveyance in Court and that ELENOR my Wife shall likewise acknowledge and relinquish her right of Dower that shee now hath unto the sd. tract of land;   In Wittness whereof I have hereunto sett my hand and seale the day and yeare first above written
Signed sealed and delivered in the presence of
    RICHARD BALL,   JOHN HUTCHINGS
    GEORGE CHILTON,   JOHN MOTT
     Recognitr in Cur Com Lancastr: 13th die Septr 1699 et record 15th die p   JNO:
HUTCHINGS

p.   KNOW ALL MEN by these presents that I WILLIAM LISTER of the County of
123   Lancastr: doe hereby assigne over all my right of the within parcell of land
      with all appertainances thereunto belonging unto JAMES KIRK him his heires and assignes and I doe hereby bind my selfe to acknowledge this unto ye sd. KIRK at the next Court to be held for this County. Wittness my hand and seale this 23d day of June 1702
Signed sealed and delivered in presence of us
    JOHN TURBERVILE,   WM: LISTER
    JEREMY INNYS,   CHRIST: KIRK
     Recognitr in Cur Com Lancastr: 5th die July 1702 et recordr
          p   JOS: TAYLOE, Clk

     KNOW ALL MEN by these presents that I JAMES KIRK of the County of Lancastr: doe assigne over all my right of the within mentioned p:cell of land wth: all the appurtenances belonging unto CHRISTOPHER KIRK, JUNR., his heires and assignes and I doe hereby bind my selfe to acknowledge this within Deed unto ye sd. CHRISTOPER KIRK, JUNR., aforesd. at the Court held for this County of Lancastr: and that my Wife, ELIZABETH, shall acknowledge her right of Dower also;   As Wittness my hand and seale this eighth day of May 1705

Signed sealed and delivered in the presence of us

GABRIELL X THATCHER,   JAMES KIRK
GEO: WALE

Recognitr in Cur Com Lancastr: 13 June 1705 et recordr
              p   JOS: TAYLOE, Clk

KNOW ALL MEN by these presents that I JAMES TISDLEY of LEVERPOOLE in the Kingdome of England, Mercht., doe nominate and appoint my true and trusty Friend, THOMAS CARTER of the County of Lancastr: in Virginia my lawfully Attorney to demand all debts that shall be due to me by Bill or Account and upon none paymt. thereof to arrest and imprison any persons that shall be defective in the pr:misses aforesd. & I doe further ratiefie and allowe all my said Attorney shall lawfully doe in ye pr:misses as if I my selfe were present.   In Wittness whereof I have hereunto sett my hand & seale this 18th day of May 1704

Signed sealed in presence of

HEN: CARTER,   JA: TYSDLEY
PETER CARTER

p.   KNOW ALL MEN by these presents that I WILLIAM LAWSON of the City of
124   BRISTOLL, Merchant, have appointed THOMAS WHITE of the County of Lancastr:
        and Pish: of White Chapell in Virginia my true and lawfull Attorney for me to demand and receive of all and every persons resideing within the Collony of Virginia all such debts and sumes of mony as is oweing or belonging to me by the sd. p:sons and upon none paymt. thereof to sue imprison and prosecute for ye same and upon such sute proceed to Judgment and execution and to execute all other reasonable thing whatsoever for discharging the same as needful to be done, giveing my sd. Attorney my full and absolute power in the pr:misses holding firme all and whatsover my sd. Attorney shall lawfully doe whereunto I have here sett my hand and my seale this 13th day of October 1703

Signed sealed and deliv'd in the presence of us

JOHN STOTT   WILLIAM LAWSON
RICHARD WELLCH

WHEREAS ROBERT YOUNG and THOMAS CARPENTER of Lancastr: County did joyntly purchase a certaine tract of land scituate betweene the Branches of MARI-TICOE CREEKE in ye County of Lancastr: aforesd: NOW KNOW YE that I the sd. THOMAS CARPENTER, Survivor of the sd. purchase for severall good and valuable conderacons have released and by these presents doe for ever quitt claime unto the one moiety and halfe the sd. tract of land with all the houses thereupon standing;   To have and to hold the one moiety of the sd. tract of land unto THOMAS YOUNG, Executor of ye aforesd. ROBERT YOUNG, and his heires for ever according to the true meaning of the sd. ROBERT YOUNG's Last Will and Testamt.   In Wittness whereof I the sd. THOMAS CARPENTER have sett my hand and seale the fifth dy of May in the fourth yeare of the reigne of or: Sovereigne Lady Ann, Queen of England &c., and in the year of or: Lord 1705

Signed sealed and deliv'd. in the pr:sence of

MILES WALTERS,   THO: ∫ CARPENTER

JON: *J* SIMMONS, BRYAN YOUNG

p.   THIS INDENTURE made the fourth day of May one thousand seven hundred
125   and five Betweene THOMAS CARPENTER of the County of Lancastr: Planter, of
         one part and THOMAS YOUNG of the County aforesd. of the other part; Wittnes-
seth that THOMAS CARPENTER for the just sume of Five thousand poudns of good and
merchantable tobacco, part thereof being paid, and the residue to be paid by the said
THOMAS YOUNG his heires before the tenth day of December next ensueing the date
herein have granted unto the sd. THOMAS YOUNG his heires and assignes the one
moiety and halfe of MILL called by the name of MARATICOE MILL and Fifty acres of
land adjoyning being in the County of Lancastr: at the head of MORATICOE CREEKE; To
have and to hold with all and singular the pr:misses unto the sd. THOMAS YOUNG his
heires and assignes for ever; subject unto the Quitt Rents which grow due for the sd.
land unto her Majesty her heires and successors; And THOMAS CARPENTER for the
consideracon aforesd. the sd. hereby granted Mill and Land will for ever warrant and
defend unto the sd. THOMAS YOUNG his heires for ever wth:out trouble of him ye sd.
THOMAS CARPENTER his heires and assignes or any other persons whatsoever; In
Wittness whereof the sd. THOMAS CARPENTER hath hereunto sett his hand and seale
ye day month and yeare above written
Sealed and deliv'd in the presence of
        MILES WALTERS,   THO: *C* CARPENTER
        JON: *J* SIMMONS, BRYAN YOUNG

p.   KNOW ALL MEN by these presents that I THOMAS CARPENTER for a valuable
126   consideracon paid by THOMAS YOUNG have released for ever quitt claimed unto
         a certaine MILL called MORATTICOE MILL and Fifty acres of land adjoyning
being at the head of MORATTICOE CREEKE in County of Lancastr: unto aforesd. THOMAS
YOUNG his heires and assignes for ever; In Wittness whereof I THOMAS CARPENTER
have hereunto sett my hand and seale the fifth day of May in ye yeare of or: Lord
1705
Signed sealed and deliv'd in ye presence of
        MILES WALTERS,   THO: *T* CARPENTER
        BRYAN YOUNG, JON: *J* SIMMONS

        THIS INDENTURE made the fourth day of August in the fourth yeare of the
reigne of or: Sovereigne Lady Anne &c., and in the yeare of or: Lord seven hundred
and five; Betweene WILLIAM SHORT of the Pish: of Christ Church and County of Lancastr: and ELISABETH his Wife of the one party and LEONARD KNIGHT of the Pish: of
WICKCOMOCO in County of NORTHUMBERLD. and his Wife of the other party; Wittnesseth that ye sd. WILLIAM SHORT and ELISABETH his Wife in consideracon of other
lands by the sd. LEONARD KNIGHT and ANN his Wife conveyed to ye sd. WILLIAM
SHORT and ELISABETH his Wife and the heires of the said WILLIAM SHORT in exchange whereof and the sd. WILLIAM SHORT and ELISABETH his Wife acknowledge
themselves fully satisfied and clearly acquitted & dischargeth the sd. LEONARD
KNIGHT and ANN his Wife a certaine tract of land containing Two hundred and fif-
teene acres being in FLEETS BAY in the Pish: of Christ Church in the County of Lancastr: bounded as followeth, vizt., Beginning at a marked Pine tree standing a little
below the mouth of a Creeke which issueth out of TABBS CREEEKE by ye side of the
Maine Creeke near unto ROBERT HUFFs House, thence down ye Maine Creeke by
severall courses thereof to a corner marked red Oake or marked line of ABRAHAM
CORRELLs standing by the sd. Maine Creeke, thence South 26 degrees West 32 poles to
a corner

p.   Cedar post of the sd. ABRAHAM CORRELLs, thence along the sd. CORRELLs line
127   W. N. W. 30 poles to a corner Chesnutt tree or white Oake standing near ROBERT
       HUFFs Plantation; thence along ye sd. CORRELLs line South 26 degrees W. 238
poles to a marked corner Pine in MORRIS his line, thence W. by N. by a line of
marked trees 118 pole to a corner Pohickorey, thence N. W. by N. by a line of marked
trees 60 pole to a corner white Oake standing in Low Pine Ground, thence by a line of
more marked trees N. E. to oye head of the first mentioned small Creeke and down the
sd. small Creeke by severall courses thereof which brought upon a streight line is
248 pole to ye corner Pine at the mouth of ye sd. small Creeke where it first began,
the sd. land being part of a tract of 1280 acres of land formerly belonging to TOBIAS
HORTON as may appear by Pattent bearing date the 16 day of June 1662, and after in
the possession of ABRAHAM CORRELL and by him made over by Deed of Sale unto
BRYAN GROVE as by the same Deed bearing date ye 7th of May 1691 it may and doth
appeare, and by the sd. BRYAN GROVE made over unto ye sd. WILLIAM SHORT by his
Deed of Sale bearing date the 7th day of My 1691, and now by the sd. WILLIAM SHORT
and ELISABETH his Wife made over unto ye sd. LEONARD KNIGHT and ANN his Wife; To
have and to hold the sd. tract of lnd and all buildings fences and every part thereof
unto the sd. LEONARD KNIGHT and ANN his Wife and ye heires and assignes for ever
against him ye sd. WILLIAM SHORT his heires and all other persons whatsoever
claiming under him and will warrt. and for ever defend by these presents;   In Wittness whereof the said WILLIAM SHORT and ELISABETH his Wife have interchangeably sett their hands and seales the day and year above written
Signed sealed and delivered in the presence of
        EDWARD ⊕ GIBSON,   WILLIAM SHORT
        WALTER ⋈ JAMES   ELIZABETH SHORT
        JOHN ROBERTSON
     Recognitr in Cur Com Lancastr: 12th die 7bris: 1705 p WM: SHORT et ELIZTH:, Uxor, et
recordr   p   JOS: TAYLOE, Clk

p.   THIS INDENTURE made the fouteenth day of February in the yeare of our Lord
128   one thousand seven hundred and foure Between GABRIELL THATCHER of Xt.
        Church Pish: in ye County of Lancastr: of the one part and JAMES KIRK of the
aforesd. Pish: and County of the other part;   Wittnesseth that whereas the abovesd.
GABRIELL THATCHER for divers consideracons and a valuable consideracon hath sold
unto ye aforesd. JAMES KIRK his heires a Neck of Land lying near COROTOMAN RIVER,
Beginning at a Chesnutt standing at the mouth of a small Branch runing out of a
Creeke called HUTCHING his CREEKE, runing up the head of a valey to a marked red
oake from thence across the Neck to a small red Oake standing at ye head of a Branch
runing out of THATCHERS MILL DAMM, down that Branch to a marked white Oake
standing at ye Branch, from thence runing to ye sd. HUTCHING his CREEKE and soe
downe the sd. Creeke to ye place where it first began;   which sd. land not being at this
time surveyed or estimated how many acres but according to the bounds before mentioned hath confirmed unto the sd. JAMES KIRK all those messuages woods waters
rents and profitts of all the pr:misses and benefitt whatsoever of me the sd. GABRIELL
THATCHER;   To have and to hold the sd. messuages unto the sd. JAMES KIRK and his
heires and assignes for ever; And I the sd. GABRIELL THATCHER have granted for me
and my heires that we will grant unto the sd. JAMES KIRK and his heires the land
aforesd. wth: ye appurtenances belonging against all people for ever;   As Wittness
my hand and seale the day and yeare first above written
Signed sealed and deliv'd in presence of
        CHRIST: KIRK,   GABRIELL THATCHER
        THO: KIRK,   WILL: LAWRANCE

Recognitr in Cur Com Lancastr: 14th die March 1704/5 et recordr
        p   JOS: TAYLOE, Clk

     THESE ARE TO IMPOWER you to appeare for me in all actions that I am con-
cerned in in Lancaster County Court and the same to prosecute and defend and for soe
doing this shall be your sufficient warrant; Wittness my hand this Tenth day of
March 1704/5
To Mr. WM: DARE,   WM: MANN
     Attorney at Law these

p.   I doe hereby appoint you to be my Attorney in any cause I have or may have
129   in Lancastr: County Court and in the same to act and doe as I my selfe might if
     pr:sent for which this shall be yor: warrant; Wittness my hand this 8th day of
November 1703
To Mr. DANIELL McCARTY   JAMES ROGERS
     Attorney at Law these

     THIS INDENTURE made this Twenty sixth day of February in the third yeare of
the Reigne of or: Sovereigne Lady Anne &c., And in the year of or: Lord God one
thousand seven hundred and four; Betweene JOHN SHARPE, Son and heire of JOHN
SHARPE, late of the County of Lancastr: in the Dominion of Virginia, deceased, which
was the Son & heire of JOHN SHARPE formerly of the County and Dominion aforesd.,
Planter, deced., of the one part and Capt. WILLIAM FOX of the Pish: of St. Marys White
Chappell in the aforesd. County & Dominion, Gentleman, of the other part; Witnesseth that the said JOHN SHARPE for the sume of one hundred pounds of Sterling mony
of England hath granted unto Captain WILLIAM FOX his heires and assignes for ever
all that p:cell of land being in ye Pish: of St. Marys White Chappell in the County of
Lancastr: and in the Dominion of Virginia which was granted unto JOHN SHARPE,
Grandfather to the sd. JOHN SHARPE, party to these presents by one Pattent bearing
date the fourth day of September 1655, and remaining upon Record in her Majties:
Court of Record in Lancastr: County; Beginning upon the North East side of a South
East Branch of MORATICOE CREEKE lying Northwest upon the land of ABRAHAM MOON,
North East into the woods upon a Swamp upon the head of the sd. Branch, South West
upon ye sd. Branch containing five hundred acres of land wth: all appurtenances
together wth: all houses barns orchards pastures woods profitts whatsoever to the sd.
tract of land or to any part of them belonging

p.   now late in the occupacon of the said JOHN SHARPE or his assignes and alsoe all
130   estate right of him the sd. JOHN SHARPE to the same; To have and to hold unto
     the sd. Captain WILLIAM FOX his heires and assignes for ever o ye only proper
use and behoofe of the sd. Captain WILLIAM FOX his heires and assignes against him
the sd. JOHN SHARPE his heirs and every other p:son whatsoever claiming undr: him

p.   kept harmless by the said JOHN SHARPE from all anner of grants or sales; In
131   Wittness whereof the sd. JOHN SHARPE to this present Indenture hath sett his
     hand and affixed his seale the day and yeare first above written
Signed sealed and delivered in the presence of
     RICHD: FLINT   JOHN SHARPE
     WM: DARE
     Recognitr in Cur Com Lancastr: 14th die March 1704/5 et recordr
           p   JOS: TAYLOE, Clk.

p.   KNOW ALL MEN by these presents that I WILLIAM FOX of the County of Lan-
132   castr:, Gentleman, am firmly bound unto MARGARET SHARP, Widdow, and JOHN
        SHARP, Planter, of the County aforesd. in the sume of Five hundred pounds of
Sterling money of England to be paid to the sd. MARGARET and JOHN SHARP their or
either of their heires &c. to the which payment to be made I bind my selfe my heires
firmly by these presents;   Sealed with my seale dated this Twenty sixth day of February in the third yeare of the reigne of or: Sovereigne Lady Anne by the grace of God
of England &c., Queen, Defendr: of the faith &c., 1704
        THE CONDICON of this obligacon is such that whereas JOHN SHARP hath by one In-
denture of bargaine and sale conveyed to ye above bounden WILLIAM FOX a certaine
tract of land in the County aforesd. upon a Creeke called MORATICOE CREEKE which
was granted to JOHN SHARP, Grandfather of the sd. JOHN SHARP party to these presents by Deed of Grant bearing date the 4th of September 1655 and remaining upon
Record in her Majties. Court of Record of Lancastr: County Court. Now Know ye that if
the above bounden WILLIAM FOX his heires shall well and truely save harmless &
keep indemnified the above named MARGARET SHARP and JOHN SHARP their & either
of their heires and either of their goods and chattles from all maner of causes of
action concerning the sd. land and pr:misses in the before menconed bargaine and
sale specified wth:out any manner of fraud or collusion; Then this obligacon to be
void and of none effect or else to stand in full force
        RICHD: FLINT,   WILLIAM FOX
        WM: DARE

        July the 5th day 1705
        I THOMAS WOOSLEY doth hereby this Letter of Attorney impower GEORGE CHIL-
TON, JUNR. to act in my stead, to pay and receive this impower by me
Wittness   THOMAS CLACKSON   THOMAS WOOSLEY
        THOMAS LO

p.   JAMES HILL records for his three Children, vizt., SARAH CULLIN, ELIZTH:
133   CULLIN & KATHERINE CULLIN one black Mare wth: a blaze on her face,
        branded on ye buttock wth: I   C.,   wth: all her future encrease equally to be
devided betweene them
        Recorded ye 20th 8br: 1705   p.   JOS: TAYLOE, Clk.

        THIS INDENTURE made this 22d day of November 1705. Betweene JOSEPH TAY-
LOE of Lancastr: County of the one part and ROBERT HUGHES of the County of RICHMD:
of the other part;   Wittnesseth that ye sd. JOSEPH TAYLOE doth grant to farm lett unto
the sd. ROBERT HUGHES all that my Plantacon houses pastures lands & appurtenances
being in the Pish: of NORTH FARNHAM together with One hundred acres of land lying
next to ye sd. Plantacon aforesd., Together wth: ye Stock thereon of Cattle & Hoggs
being in quantity as follows, vizt., four Cows, two Heifers & one Steere of two yeares
old as alsoe three breeding Sows & one barrow hogg & four shoats of a yeare old for
the full terme of foure whole yeares commencing from ye 25th of Xbr. next ensueing
this p:sent date to ye full end & terme aforesd., fully to be complated. In consideracon
whereof the sd. ROBERT HUGHS doth agree wth: ye sd. JOSEPH TAYLOE att ye full end &
terme aforesd. to rendr: unto ye sd. JOSEPH TAYLOE his heires or assignes the prin-
ciple Stock of Cattle & Hoggs and halfe their encrease conditioned that if any dye p
casualty or sickness, the sd. JOSEPH is to p:take of the loss thereof and it is further
agreed that he the said ROBERT shall annually pay the sume of Five hundred pounds
of good legall tobbo: & casque of the growth of the Plantacon or otherwise provided it
be lawfully demanded and att ye end of ye sd. terme shall returne possession of the

lands & pr:misses aforesd. to ye sd. JOSEPH TAYLOE his heires or assignes in good tenantable repaire;   In Wittness whereof wee have hereunto sett our hands & seales the day and year abovesd.

Sealed and delivered in presence of us

    JNO: NEWMAN,   JOS: TAYLOE

    ROGR: WILLCOX   ROBERT HUGHS

    Lancastr: Recorded the 22d day of 9br: 1705 per agreemt. of both partys

           p   JOS: TAYLOE, Clk

p.   KNOW ALL MEN by these presents that I JOHN BENDALL of ye County of ESSEX
134   in the Collony of Virginia, Planter, doe appoint my Freind, JOSEPH TAYLOE,
Clerk of the County of Lancastr., to be my lawfull Attor: for me and in my name to acknowledge unto ROBERT POLLARD his heires and assignes fivety acres of land being part of seventy acres of land left me by my Father, WM: BENDALL, (deced), lying in the Pish of White Chapple in Lancastr: County joyning to ye lands whereon ye sd. ROBERT POLLARD now liveth, ratifying what my sd. Attor: shall act or doe in ye pr:misses as if I were personally present.   In Wittness whereof I have hereunto sett my hand and seale this Sixth day of Xbr. 1705

Test   THO: (? BRASTER)   JOHN BENDALL

       JUDITH FARR

    Recognitr in Cur Com Lancastr: 12th Xbris: 1705 et recordr

           p   JOS: TAYLOE, Clk

THIS INDENTURE made this 19th day of August 1699 and in the 11th yeare of ye reigne of or: Sovereigne Lord King William &c.   Betweene FRANCISCOE FRIZELL and MARY his Wife of the one part of the County of Lancastr: and WILLIAM MOORE of ye sd. County of ye other part;   Wittnesseth that ye sd. FRANCISCOE FRIZELL and MARY his Wife in consideracon of Foure thousand pounds of tobacco to be paid att three intire payments by WM: MORE his heires &c., to the sd. FRANCISCOE FRIZELL as appeares by Bill given from undr: the hand of WILLIAM MOORE unto ye said FRANCISCOE FRIZELL his heires & bearing equall with the tener of this date, Therefore I FRANCISCOE FRIZELL by these presents have sold unto ye sd. WM: MOORE all that our parts tract or p:cell of land which is already devided betweene me, FRANCISCOE FRIZELL and NOAH ROGERS scituate near the mouth of COROTOMAN upon the head of a small Creek and adjoyning to ye plantacon of Mr. WM: BALL and the Plantation of JOHN HALL, the moeity whereof being Fourty seaven acres and a halfe more or less togeather with all houses apple trees which is my own proper part of the Orchard upon the land in ye possession of NOAH ROGERS togeather with all trees woods & underwoods belonging to ye sd. WILLIA MORE his heires &c.   To have and to hold in as ample manner as is exprest in the originall Pattent and will for ever warrant & defend against any

p.   persons whatsoever.   In Wittness whereof wee have sett or: hands and seales
135   the day & year first above written

    Signed sealed & delivered in presence of us

    WM: BAYLIE,   FRANCIS FRIZELL

    JOSEPH DUKESHALE   MARY FRIZELL

    Recognitr in Cur Com Lancastr: 13th die Xbris 1699 et recordr sixto dicimo die

           p   JOS: TAYLOE, Clk.

KNOW ALL MEN by these presents that I WM: MOORE of the County of Lancastr: in Virginia and HANAH my now Wife doe for divers good causes bequeath and assigne all or: right of the within specified Deed of Sale bearing date ye 19th day of August 1699 unto JAMES GAYNER of the County of NORTHUMBERLAND his heires & assignes for ever in as large manner as it to us granted and Deed of Sale doth express, togeather wth: all appurtenances and priviledges belonging, I ye sd. WM: MOORE and HANAH my Wife doe by these presents oblidge us or: heires to acknowledge the sd. Deed in the County Court of Lancastr: next Octobr: insueing the date hereof; In Testimony thereof wee have hereunto sett or: hands & seales this 11th day of September 1705

Test   BENJ: BROWNE   WM: MOORE
       FRANCISCOE FRIZELL   HANAH MOORE
       Recognitr in Cur Com Lancastr: 12th die Xbris 1705 et recordr
                    p   JOS: TAYLOE, Clk

       KNOW ALL MEN by these presents that I WM: HUNTER of PRINCES ANNE County doe impower JAMES WETHERSPOONE of Lancastr: County to be my true and lawfull Attor: to aske demand sue for and arrest all p:sons that are indebted to me. I doe further impower my sd. Attor: to impower one or more Attornys undr: him and to revoake them att his pleasure and I doe further impowr my sd. Attor: to imprison & take out of prison att his pleasure and I doe firme & good all as my sd. Attor: shall doe lawfully in my business as if I my selfe were p:sonally pr:sent; As Wittness my hand this 13th day of Xbr: 1705

Signed sealed in presence of
       JOHN MULLIS,
       ANTHONY HICKSON   WM: HUNTER
       Recognitr in Cur Com Lancastr: 13th die Xbris 1705 et recordr.
                    p   JOS: TAYLOE, Clk

p.   TO ALL CHRISTIAN PEOPLE to whome these presents shall come, I RANDOLPH
136   MILLER send Greeting for and in consideracon of the love good will & affection wch: I have unto JNO: MILLER of Lancastr; County, hath given and confirmed unto ye sd. JOHN MILLER his heires & assignes Ninety foure acres of land being in the County aforesd. now in ye holding & occupacon of the sd. RANDOLPH MILLER, being part of Two hundred & fivety acres of land bought by Mr. EDWARD SAUNDERS in NORTHUMBERLD. County and bounded as herein exprest, Begining att a white oake standing in a line belonging to Mr. SAUNDERS, runing along an old line to a Chesnutt Stake standing in Mr. CONWAYs line, devideing from this land & twenty one links from a marked Hickory & about three foot from a small red Oake saplin & ten foot from a marked Hiccory to ye Northward of the sd. Stake, from thence along Mr. CONWAYs line tohis sd. line Stone by the Road leading from ye MILL comonly called FOX MILL and stretching thence downe ye sd. Road to ye sd. RANDOLPH MILLERs line and soe long that line to ye first mentioned Oake, and all & singular the rights profitts wth: all other advantages to ye sd. land; To have and to hold unto ye sd. JOHN MILLER his heires and assignes for ever in as large & ample manner as are exprest in ye sd. originall Sale made to ye sd. RANDOLPH MILER; In Wittness whereof I have hereunto sett my hand and seale ye 13th day of March 1705/6

Signed sealed & dd. in ye presence of us
       THO: WHITE   RANDOLPH MILLER
       Recognitr in Cur Com Lancastr: ye 13th March 1705/6 et recordr
                    p   JOS: TAYLOE, Clk.

p.   Stampt. Paper. (Seal) KNOW ALL MEN by these presents that I THOMAS EDGAR
137   of LEVERPOOLE in ye County of Lancastr:, Mercht., have appointed my loveing

Freinds, JOHN McMILLAN of LIVERPOOLE, Mercht., & JAMES KENNAN of DRUMFRIES in the Kingdome of Scottland, Mercht., my true & lawfull Attorneys to demand and receive of all such portions of the goods chattles estate of JOHN EDGAR of ASETAGE in County of SOMERSETT in MARYLAND (deced), late Brother of me the sd. THOMAS EDGAR & on non paymt. of such part of the sd. goods or estate for me and in my name to sue for arrest imprison & secure for the same and upon such to proceed to execution upon such sd. p:sons in prison to hold untill payment be made wth: all costs & damages sustained to doe all things whatsoever as the same shall be needfull to be done, giveing my sd. Attorneys absolute power in the pr:misses ratifying all & whatsoever my sd. Attorneys shall lawfully doe about ye pr:misses by these p:sents.   In Wittness whereof I have hereunto sett my hand and seale the 21th day of Febry: 1705 Sealed and delivered in p:sence of us

     DANLL. COLLETT,   THO: EDGAR
     THOMS: BOND

Att a Court held for Lancastr: the 12th day of June 1706, ye sd. DANLL. COLLETT & THOMAS BOND made Oath in open Court that they see ye wth:in Lettr. of Attorney sealed & delivered to ye uses therein exprest.
Test   JOS: TAYLOE, Clk. & is recorded in ye sd. County of Lancastr: p the same.
            JOS: TAYLOE

    ABIGALL JENKINS records for her Son, HENERY JENKINS, a young Mare named Flower & a young Heifer of two yeares old named Nancy
        Test   JOS: TAYLOE, Clk

p.   (Seale). MARGTT. LADY CULPEPER, THOMAS LORD FAIRFAX and CATHERINE
138   his Wife, Proprietors of the Northern Neck to all to whome these presents come
      send Greeting. Whereas GEORGE BUSH, JOHN BUSH and ABRAHAM BUSH of the County of Lancastr: hath repaired to ye Office kept by our Agents for us in the Northern Neck and hath upon suggested that there is a certaine p:cell or devidend of land in White Chapple Pish: in County of Lancastr: belonging to us not yet granted to any p:sons and thereupon paid ye composition for two hundred forety three acres whereof he obtained a warrt. ye first day of August 1695, directed to one of our Surveyors to survey, & give Bond in ordr: to obtaine the grant wth: warrant being duely returned together wth: ye Plott & bounds thereof to or: sd. Office.   Know Yee that wee for the composition pd. by them ye sd. GEORGE BUSH, JOHN BUSH and ABRAHAM BUSH doe hereby grant to them all that p:cell of land being in White Chapple Pish: in ye County of Lancastr: bounded as followeth: Beginning att an old marked Poplar of ABRAHAM BUSHes standing on ye South side of MORRATICOE MILL SWAMP by a Path that leads from ye sd, BUSHes to RICHARD WELCHes, from the Poplar up the Maine Swamp South East eighty poles to a Branch, thence South crossing the sd. Branch eighty two po. to a corner white Oake standing on the South side thereof, from the white Oake up the said Branch South thirty degrees Easterly forty po: thence South thirty two po: to an old corner Spanish Oake Stake standing on Mr. THOMAS CHATTINs line, South West 55 po: to an old corner Spanish Oake standing by the sdie of the sd. Branch, thence Southwest by West 117 po: to a corner Gum standing on ye side of a Branch in the sd. CHATTINs line, thence Northwest by marked trees bounding upon HENERY STONAM 84 po: to a corner red Oake standing on a small Hill, thence by marked trees W. 62 degrees Westerly 38 po: to a corner Oake of the sd. STONAMs standing just by a Path that leads from STONAMs to ROWLEYs, thence alogne STONAMs line W. S. W. 55 po: to a Stake drove down in JOB HILLs Corne Feild neer a corner red Oake of the sd. STONAMs, from thence West by North through JOB's Corne Feild 44 po: to a corner Dogg wood standing neer JOBEs Corne Feild Fence, from ye Doggwood Westerly

8 po: to a corner red Oake wch: goes by the name of ROBERT YOUNGs, thence North upon the sd. YOUNGs 84 po: to a Stone Hill by an Oake Stump in the sd. YOUNGs Old Feild neer his dwelling House, from the Stone East by marked trees bounding upon the land formerly granted to ABRAHAM BUSH & PETER ELMORE 254 po: to a Stake standing in ABRAHAM BUSHes Old Feild neer the sd. BUSHes Old Dwelling House, from the Stake North by a line of Stakes & marked trees 150 po: bounding upon the sd. BUSH to the corner Poplar where it first began; containing and being now laid out for a hundred fivety three acres of land together wth: all profitts;   To have and to hold together wth: all rights in anywaise appertaining to ye sd. GEORGE BUSH, JOHN BUSH & ABRAHAM BUSH their heires or assignes for ever

p.   they paying to us Proprietors of ye sd. Northern Neck yearely ye fee rent of
139   six shillings provided that if they shall not pay the annual rent soe then ye
        same be unpaid ye space of two whole yeares, then it shall be lawfull for us or our heires or Agents into ye above granted pr:misses to reenter as if this grant had never passed;   Given att or: Office in STAFFORD County wth:in or: Proprietary undr. or: Seale. Wittness our Agents WM: FITZHUGH & GEORGE BRENT fully impowered thereto or either of them dated the 13th day of Janry: 1695/6
Registred p WM: FITZHUGH, JUNR.   WILLM: FITZHUGH
Recorded p   WM: HOWARD
                p. JOS: TAYLOE, Clk

        TO ALL TO WHOME these may concerne, Know yee that I JUSTIN STEELE of the Citty of BRISTOLL, Mercht., doe appoint Mr. NICHOLAS SMITH of RICHMOND County in Virginia my lawfull Attorny to demand all such debts belonging to ye above STEELE, to sue attach prosecute ye sd. p:sons, to compound and acquittances and other sufficient discharges to make for me and to doe all things whatsoever concerning the pr:misses as fully as if I my selfe could doe if I were p:sonally pr:sent.   In Wittness whereof I have hereunto sett my hand & seale this 10th day of July 1705
Signed sealed & delivered in presence of
        HUGH LADNER,   JUSTIN STEELE
        MARTHA RINE
     Probatr Lettr. Attor in Cur Com Lancastr: 12th Julii 1705 p sacramt. HUGH LADNER et
recordr   p   JOS: TAYLOE, Clk.

p.   KNOW ALL MEN by these pr:sents that I HUGH BRENT of the County of Lancas-
140   tr: doe owe & stand justly bound unto HUGH BRENT, JUNR., of the said County
        his heires or assignes in the just sume of Two hundred pounds Sterling money of England as Wittness my hand and seale dated the 12th day of Febry: 1704
        THE CONDICON of the above obligacon is such that if the above bounden HUGH BRENT, JUNR. will injoy a certaine tract of land given unto him by the above bounden BRENT & bounded as followeth, (vizt), Begining on ye INDIAN CREEKE on TOBIAS HORTONs line & running from ye sd. Creeke up along the sd. HORTONs line to a marked Pine and running Easterly from thence along a line of marked trees to a marked corner Pine standing neer ye yead of POCKENCES COVE and running from ye sd. Pine down ye Cove to ye sd. INDIAN CREEKE and so running up the severall courses of ye Maine Creeke to ye place where it began; wch: sd. tract of land with all houses profitts belonging excepting ye Orchard & Ground it stands on and Cartway from ye sd. Orchard to be fourty yards below or above ye Cartway that now is which sd. Orchard & Cartway ye above bounden BRENT doth reserve to himselfe out of this tract of land and the sd. BRENT, JUNR. shall fully and quietly injoy ye sd. tract of land excepting

before excepted dureing his life and in case ye sd. BRENT, JUNR. shall marry and he
should happen to dye before his said Wife that then his Wife after his death dureing
her widowhood shll accordingly injoy the sd. land & noe longer then she remaines a
widow and not to make any manner of waste of any timber but for ye use of the Plantacon and further ye above bounden BRENT doth oblidge himselfe not to disturbe
him, ye sd. BRENT, JUNR. dureing his life nor his Wife in case of his death dureing
her widowhood. Now if ye sd. BRENT, JUNR. and his Wife in case of Marriage will
according to this condicon peaceably hold ye sd. land wth:out ye Leave or trouble of
him ye sd. BRENT or through any means, then this obligacon to be void or else to
stand in free power and this Bond never to be out of date notwithstanding any Law or
usage to ye contrary. As Wittness my hand & seale the day & date abovesd.
Signed sealed & delivered in presence of
    WM: LISTER,   HUGH BRENT
    JOHN STOWER
    Recorded the 9th day of July 1706 att ye instance & request of JAMES HAINES
                p. JOS: TAYLOE, Clk

p.   Virginia. ye 5th of August 1706. Excha: for L. 39:11:0 Coll. CARTERs. Att
141   thirty dayes sight pay this my third of Exchange, my first nor second being
       paid unto Mr. ROBERT HALL or ordr: thirty nine pounds, eleven shillings for
value of him here reced and place to Acct. as p advice from
To ARTHUR BALYE, Esqr. in London   ROBERT CARTER

    Virginia August ye 21st 1706. Excha: for L. 02:00;00 Mr. DAREs.
    Att twenty dayes sight of this my third Exchange my first and second not paid, pay
or cause to be paid unto Mr. ROBERT HALL, Mercht., or ordr: ye sume of two pounds
Sterling for value here reced. att time make good paymt & place it to Acct. of Sr. yr.
humble Servt.
To Mr. JNO: GOODWIN, Mercht. in London   WM: DARE

    Virginia. June ye 19th 1706. Exchange for L. 50:00:00
    Gentlemen: Att twenty dayes sight of this my third bill of Exchange, my first or
second not paid, pay or cause to be paid unto Mr. ROBERT HALL or ordr: ye sume of
fivety pounds Sterl., mony, it being for value reced. here att time make good payment
and place the same to Acct., as p advice from Gentlemen yor: humble Servt.
To Mr. MICAJAH PERRY & COMPA. Merchts.   A. SWAN
      in London   5=3=4

    Virgnia June ye 10th 1706. Excha. for L. 5: 18: 8
    Att twenty dayes sight of this my third of Excange, my first and second not paid,
pay or cause to be paid to Mr. ROBERT HALL, Mercht., the sume of five pounds eighteen shillings & eight pence Sterl. mony, it being for value reced. here att time make
good payment & place it to ye Acct. of Sr. yor: humble Servt.
To Mr. PATRICK MacADAMS, Mercht.   ANDR: JACKSON
      in London

    Virginia. June ye 20th 1706. Exchange for L. 6: 10: 00
    Sr. Att thirty dayes sight of this my third of Exchange my first & second not paid,
pay or cause to be paid to Mr. ROBERT HALL or ordr: ye sume of six pounds, ten shillings Sterl. mony, it being for value received here att time make good payment and
place the same to Acct. of Sr. yor: humble Servt.
To Mr. JNO; GOODWIN, Mercht. in London   ROWLAND LAWSON

p.   Virginia June ye 20th 1706. L. 5 =9 =0
142   Att twenty dayes sight of this my third of Exchange my first and second not
          paid, pay or cause to be paid to Mr. ROBERT HALL or ordr: ye sume of Five
pounds, nine shillings Sterl. mony it being for value received here att time make
good paymt. and place it to ye Acct. of yor: humble Servt., as p advice
To Mr. THO: COATES, Mercht. in
          White Haven   WILLIAM SMITH

          Virginia June ye 20th 1706. Excange for L. 4 =15 =0
          Sr. Att thirty dayes sight of this my third of exchange my first and second not paid,
pay or cause to be paid unto Mr. ROBERT HALL or ordr. the sume of Four pounds, five-
teen shillings Sterl. mony, it being for value received here att time make good payment and place to Acct. of yor: Servt., to comd.
To Mr. DAVID ARBUTHNOTT, Mercht.   ISAAC HARVEY
          in Waymouth

          Virginia May 23d 1706.   Exchange for L. 5 =18 =4
          Sr. Att thirty dayes sight of this my third of Exchange my first and second not paid,
pay or cause to be paid unto ROBERT HALL, Mercht., or ordr., five pounds, eighteen
shillings & four pence Sterl. mony, it being for value received att time make good
payment and palce it to ye Acct. of
To Mr. DAVID ARBUTHNOTT, Mercht.   Sr. yor: humble Servant
          in Waymouth   JOSEPH BALL, SENR.

          Virginia. June ye 20th 1706.   Exchange for   L. 9 =7 =3.
          Sr. Att twenty dayes sight of this my third of Exchange my first and second not
paid, pay or cause to be paid to Mr. ROBERT HALL or ordr. the sume of Nine pounds,
seaven shillings & three pence Sterl. mony, it being for value received att time make
good payment and place it to the Acct. of Sir, yor: humble Servt.
To Mr. JNO: PEMBERTON, Mercht.   WM: WHITESIDE
          in Leverpoole

          Virginia Apr: ye 23d. 1706.   Exchange for L. 22 =18 =2.
          Att thirty dayes sight of this my third of Exchange my first and second not paid,
pay or cause to be paid to Mr. ROBERT HALL or ordr: the sum of Twenty two pounds,
eighteen shills: & two pence Sterl. mony, it being for value received here att time
make good payment and place it to the Acct. of Sr. yor: humble Servt.
To MR. MacADAMS in London   WM: LISTER

p.   Virginia June ye 10th 1706   Exchange for L. 40 =00 =00
143   Sr. Att twenty dayes sight of this my third of Exchange, my first and second
          not paid, pay or cause to be paid to Mr. ROBERT HALL, Mercht., the sume of
Forty pounds Sterl. money, it being for value reced. here att time make good payment
and place it to ye Acct. of yor: humble Servt.
To PATRICK MacADAMS in London   ANDRW: JACKSON

          Virginia May ye 28th 1706.   Exchange for L 1 =8 =0.
          Sr. Att twenty dayes sight of this my third of Exchange my first and second not
paid, pay or cause to be paid unto Mr. ROBERT HALL, Mercht., the sume of One pound,
eight shills: Sterl. mony, it being for value received here att time make good payment and place it to ye Acct. of yor: humble Servt.

To ARTHUR BALIE, Esqr., Mercht. in London   WM: ARMISTEAD
          This Bill is endorsed p THO: GRAVES
                              JNO: ROBINSON & THOM: HARDING

     Virginia. May ye 11th 1706.   Cr. L. 4 =19 =4
     Sr.   Att thirty dayes sight of this my third of Exchange my first and second not paid,
pay unto JNO: ROBINSON or ordr. ye sume of four pounds, nineteen shlls. and four
pence Sterl. and place it to Acct. of Sr.
To Mr. FRANCIS CATHMEAD,   RICHD: PASSATT
     Mercht. in Lond.   This Bill is endorsed p JNO: ROBINSON & THOM: HARDING

     Virginia August ye 12th 1706. Exchange for L. 7 =13 =4
     Sr.   Att thirty dayes sight of this my third of Exchange, my first and second not
paid, pay or cause to be paid to Mr. ROBERT HALL or ordr. the sume of seaven pounds,
thirteene shills. & four pence Sterl., it being for value reced. here att time make payment and place it to ye Acct. of Sr. yor: humble Servt.
To Mr. THOMAS ROBINSON, Mercht. in London   RAWLEIGH DOWNEMAN

     Virginia August ye 20th 1706.   Excha. for L. 3 =7 =7.
     Att thirty dayes sight of this my third of Exchange, my first and second not paid,
pay or cause to be paid to Mr. ROBERT HALL or ordr: the sume of Three pounds, seaven
shills. & seaven pence Sterl. mony, it being for value received here, att time make
payment and place the same to Acct. of yor: humble Servt.
To ARTHUR BAYLIE, Esqr., Mercht. in London   JNO: STEPTO

p.   Virginia July ye 12th 1706. Exchange for L. 11 =3 =6
144   Sr.   Att thirty days sight of this my third of Exchange, my first or second not
         paid, pay or cause to be paid to Mr. ROBERT HALL or ordr: the sume of eleven
pounds, three shills: & six pence Sterl. mony, it being for value reced., here att time
make payment and place the same to Acct. of yor: humble Servt.
To Mr. WM: DAWKINS, Mercht., in London   DAVID   DICKIE marke of

     Virginia Novembr: ye 16th 1705. Exchange for L. 25 =00 =00
     Sr.   Att twenty dayes sight of this my third Bill of Exchange, my first or second not
paid, pay or cause to be paid to Mr. ROBERT HALL or ordr: the sume of Twenty five
pounds Sterl. mony, it being for value reced. here, att time make good paymt. and
place ye same to ye Acct. of Sr. yor: humble Servt.
To ARTHUR BAYLIE Esqr. in London   THO: PINKARD

     Virginia. Novembr: ye 15th 1705. Exchange for L. 24 =00 =00
     Att twenty dayes sight of this my third Bill of Exchange, my first or second not
paid, pay or cause to be paid to Mr. ROBERT HALL or ordr: the sume of Twenty five
pounds Sterl. mony, it being for value reced. here, att time make good paymt. and
place ye same to ye Acct. of Sr. yor: humble Servt.
To ROBERT SENR., Esqr. in Londaon   URIAH ANGELL

     Virginia. Novembr: 15th 1705. Exchange for L. 26 =5 =00
     Sr.   Att twenty dayes sight of this my third Bill of Exchange, my first or second not
paid, pay to Mr. ROBERT HALL or ordr: the sume of Twenty six pounds, five shills.
Sterl. mony, it being for value reced. here,   att time make paymt. and place ye same to
ye Acct of yor: humble Servt.
To Mr. ROBERT BRISTOW, Esqr., Mercht. in London   JNO: BRASON

Virginia. April ye 23d. 1706. Exchange for L. 40 =00 =00
     Sr. Att forty dayes sight of this my third of Exchange my first and second not paid,
pay or cause to be paid to Mr. ROBERT HALL or ordr: the sume of forty pounds Sterl.
mony, it being for value reced. here, att time make good paymt. and place it to ye
Acct. of Sr. yor: humble Servt.
To Mr. JNO: GOODWIN, Mercht. in London   W: LISTER

     Virginia April ye 22d. 1706.   Exchange for L. 7 =17 =9
     Sr. Att twenty dayes sight of this my third of Exchange, my first or second not paid,
paye or cause to be paid to Mr. ROBERT HALL or ordr: the sume of seaven pounds,
seaventeene shills: & nine pence Sterl. mony, it being for value reced. here, att time
make good paymt. and place it to ye Acct of ye SHIP MAN of "FEILD FRIGITT"
To Mr. JNO: GOODWIN, Mercht. in London   JNO: BURFORD

p.   Virginia. Janry. ye 26th 1705. Exchange for L. 10 =0 =0
145   Sr. Att twenty dayes sight of this my third of Exchange, my first or second not
         paid, pay or cause to be paid to Mr. ROBERT HALL or ordr: Ten pounds Sterl.
money it being for value received here, att time make good paymt. and place it to ye
Acct. of yor: humble Servt.
To Capt. ANTHONY (? GESTER) Mercht.   ROWD. LAWSON
in London, liveing in Rattcliffe Highway

     Virginia. Apr. ye 22th 1706. Exchange for L. 11 =3 =00
     Sir. Att thirty dayes after sight of this my third p Exchange, my first or second not
paid, pay unto Mr. JAMES HAINES, Smith, or to his ordr., ye just sume of Eleven
pounds three shills., it being for value reced. at ye time make good paymt. and place it
to ye Acct. of Sr. yor: humble Servt.
To Mr. JNO: GOODWIN, Mercht., in London   W: LISTER
     On the back of this Bill is the following assignemt.
     I doe hereby assigne ye wth:in Bill of Exchange to Mr. ROBERT HALL or his ordr:
May the first 1706   JAMES HAYNES, Smith

     Virginia June ye 8th 1706.   Exchange for L. 14 =00 =00
     Sr. Att twenty dayes sight of this my third Bill of Exchange my first or second not
paid, pay or cause to be paid to Mr. HENRY LAWSON or ordr: the sume of fourteene
pounds Sterl. mony. for value reced., here, att time make good paymt. & place it to ye
Acct. of Sr. yor: humble Servt.
To ARTHUR BAYLIE, Esqr., Mercht. in London   JOHN C\ BROWN marke of
     On ye back of ye wth:in mentioned Bill to Mr. ROBT. HALL or ordr. this being my
ordr: and you will oblidge Sr. yor: humble Servt.   HENERY LAWSON

     Virginia May ye first 1706.   Exchange for L. 14 =00 =00
     Att thirty dayes sight of this my third Bill of Exchange, my first or second not paid,
pay or cause to be paid to Mr. ROBERT HALL or ordr: ye just sume of Fourteene pounds
Sterl. mony, it being for value reced. here, att time make good paymt. and place the
same to Acct. of Sr. yor: humble Servt.
To ARTHUR BAYLIE, Esqr., Mercht. in London   JAMES HAINES, Smith

     Virginia Apr. ye 23d 1706.   Exchange for L. 30 =00 =00
     Sr. Att twenty dayes sight of this my third of Exchange, my first or second not paid,
pay or cause to be paid to Mr. ROBERT HALL or ordr: the sume of Thirty pounds Sterl.

Sterl. mony, it being for value reced. here, att time make good paymt. and place it to
ye Acct. of Sr. yor: humble Servt.
To ARTHUR BAYLIE, Esqr., Mercht. in London   WM: LISTER

p.   Virginia. May ye 2d. 1706.   Exchange for L. 36 =00 =00.
146   Sr.   Att sixty dayes sight of this my third Bill of Exchange my first nor second
           not paid, pay unto Mr. ROBERT HALL or ordr., the sume of Thirty six pounds
Sterl. for value received here and place to Acct. as p advice from yor: humble Servt.
To ARTHUR BAYLIE, Esqr., Mercht. in London   HANCOCK LEE

        Exchange p L. 21 =10 =0.   Virginia Febry ye 18th 1705/6
     Sr.   Att sixty dayes sight of this my third of Exchange, my first or second not paid,
pay or cause to be paid to Mr. ROBERT HALL or ordr: the sume of Twenty one pounds,
ten shills, Sterl. mony, it being for value reced., here, att time make good paymt. and
place it to ye Acct. of Sr. yor: humble Servt.
To Mr. NICHO: GOODWIN, Mercht. in London   ANTHO: HAYNIE
        Sr.   Pay wth:out further advice

        Virginia. Apr. ye 20th 1706.   Excha: for L. 28 =00 =00
     Sr.   Att thirty dayes sight of this my third of Exchange, my first or second not paid,
pay or cause to be paid to Mr. ROBERT HALL or ordr., the sume of Twenty eight pounds
Sterl. mony, it being for value reced. here, att time make good paymt. and place it to
ye Accot. of Sr. yor: humble Servt.
To Mr. JNO; GOODWIN, of London, Mercht.   ROBERT LAWSON, JUNR.

        Virginia Apr: ye 24th 1706.   Excha. for L. 4 =14 =00
     Sr.   Att twenty dayes sight of this my third Bill of Exchange, my first or second not
paid, pay or cause to be paid to Mr. ROBERT HALL or ordr: the sume of Four pounds,
fourteene shills. Sterl. it being for value reced. here, att time make good paymt. and
place it to ye Acct. of Sr. yor: humble Servt.
To Capt. ANTHONY GESTER Mercht. in London   MARK ATTKINS, Chyr.

        Virginia. March ye 18th 1705/6.   Excha. for L. 3 =00 =00
     Sr.   Att twenty dayes sight of this my third of Exchange my first or second not paid,
pay or cause to be paid to RICHARD CHICHESTER or ordr. the sume of Three pounds
Sterl. mony, it being for value reced. here, att time make good paymt. and place it to
ye Acct. of ye Ship, "AFRICA" from Sr. yor: humble Servt.
To Mr. JNO: BURRIDGE, Mercht. in Lyme   WM: READ
     Endorsed RICHARD CHICHESTER

        Virginia. Sept. ye 12th 1705.   Excha. for L. 10 =10 =00
     Sr.   Att twenty dayes sight of this my third of Exchange, my first or second not paid,
pay or cause to be paid to RICHD: CHICHESTER, Esqr., or ordr: ye sume of Ten pounds,
ten shills, Sterl., it being for value reced. here, att time make good paymt. and place
it to Acct. of Sr. yor: humble Servt.
To Mr. JNO: BURRIDGE, Esqr., Mercht. in Lyme   W. ALLERTON
     Endorsed RICHARD CHICHESTERl GEO: ESKRIDGE

        Virginia. May 28th 1706. Excha. for L. 3 =00 =00
     Sr.   Att twenty dayes sight of this my third of Exchange my first or second not paid,
paid or cause to be paid to RICHD: CHICHESTER or ordr: ye sume of three pounds Sterl.
mony being for value reced. here, att time make good paymt. and place it to ye Acct.

of the Ship, "GLOCESTER" I am Sr. yor: humble Servt. to comand
Mr. MICAJAH PERRY & COMPA. Merchts.   EDW: ELLIS
    in London

    These Third Bills were recorded ye 24th of August att ye request of Mr. ROBERT
HALL   p. JOS: TAYLOE, Clk.

p.   Virginia March 11th 1705.   Excha. L. 11 =00 =00
147   Sr. Att thirty dayes sight of this my third Bill of Exchange, my first nor
    second not being paid, pay unto GEORGE LOYD or ordr: the sume of Eleven
pounds Sterling mony of England, it being for value here reced., att time make good
paymt. & place it to ye Acct. of vor: Servt.
To Mr. MICAJAH PERRES, Mercht. in London   TIMOTHY T HAY
    Endorsed by GEORGE LOYDE, MICH: BROMLEY & RICHD: CHICHESTER

    Virginia August 27th 1706   Exchange for L. 10 =05 =00
    Sr. Att twenty dayes sight of this my third of Exchange my first or second not paid,
pay or cause to be paid to RICHARD CHICHESTER, Esqr., or ordr: the sume of Ten
pounds, five shills., Sterl. mony, it being for value here reced., att time make good
payment & place it to ye Acct. of 'SEAFLOWER CARGOE," from Sr. yor: humble Servt.
To Mr. PETER SEMHOUSE,   LEWIS POWE
    Mercht. in White Haven   Endorsed p RICHD: CHICHESTER
    Recorded ye 2d day of Septr. att ye instance of Mr. ROBERT HALL
        p   JOS: TAYLOE, Clk.

    Febry. ye 18th 1703/4.   Exchange L. 10 =00 =00
    Sr. Att thirty dayes sight of this my third Bill of Exchane my first or second not
paid, pay or cause to be paid unto JNO: HALL or ordr. the full sume of Ten pounds
Sterl. mony; att time make good paymt. & place to Acct. of Sr. yor: humble Servt.
To Capt. JNO: HIDE, Merchant in Fanchurch Street   WM: ANDERSON
    On this Bill was this London endorsment.
    I assigne all my right & title of this Bill unto EDWD. ATTWOOD as Wittness my hand
            JNO: HALL
    I assigne this Bill back to JNO: HALL, Wittness my hand
            EDWD. ATTWOOD

p.   Virginia PRINCES ANNE County. Mr. EDWARD ATTWOOD produceing to me a
148   Bill of Exchange bearing date ye 18th of February 1703/4 drawn on Capt. JNO:
    HIDE, Mercht. in London, by one WM: ANDERSON & passed to ye aforesd. ATT-
WOOD by JOHN HALL of Lancastr: County and the sd. ATTWOOD hath this day declared
before me on his corporall Oath that he hath never received any part or whole of the
aforesd. Bills. Given undr: my hand this 20th of Janry: 1705/6
            JOHN RICHISON
    The aforesd. Bill & this Affidavit is recorded att ye instance of Mr. JNO: HALL
        p   JOS: TAYLOE, Clk

    ARTICLES of AGREEMT. had made indented & agreed upon the 10th day of Apr:
in ye 5th yeare of the reigne of or: Sovereigne Lady Anne &c., and in ye yeare of or:
Lord God 1706; Between ROBERT GIBSON of the Pish: of Christ Church in ye County of
Lancastr:, one of the Admrs. of the Estate of MOTTR: WRIGHT (deced) of the one part
and JOSEPH BELFEILD of the Pish: of Sittenbourn in County of RICHMD, Chyr., one
other of the Admrs. of ye Estate aforesd. of ye other part; Wittnesseth that whereas

for the avoiding of all doubts varriances & strifes that might grow betweene ye aforesd. parties touching their administratorship of the sd. Estate, and the true execution of the same and concerning the residue or plussage of the goods chattles & other things belonging to ye sd. Estate after ye debts & Legacies discharged, each of the sd. parties have faithfully promised and doe severally covenant & grant to & with each other and with the heires administrators of each other by these presents in manner and forme following (that is to say), That each of the sd. parties covenanteth & granteth severally for himselfe his heires with ye other of them or either of them shall not att any time willingly or wittingly conceale withdraw or keep close from ye heires or Admrs. of them or either of them any such goods chattles debts credits or other things as hath come or shall happen to come to him or their or any other hands or knowledge that were or did or ought to belong to ye sd. Estate of the sd. MOTTR: WRIGHT (deced), to ye intent the same or any part thereof should not be recovered used or ordered by the same Admr. to their & either of their propr: benifitt & advance and that each of the sd. p:ties shall possess the goods chattles Negroes or other things they now have in possession in peace wth:out disturbance of the other his heires or any of them or any other p:sons from or undr: him them or either of them and it is further greed betweene the sd. parties that whereas there is money due to ye sd. Estate from Coll. JOSEPH BALL, it is therefore agreed and concluded that ye sd. ROBERT GIBSON shall have & receive the sd. money lett it be more or less provided that ye sd. ROBERT GIBSON pay unto the sd. Coll. JOSEPH BALL

p.   the sume of twelve pounds Sterl. for the Board of the sd. JOSEPH BELFEILD his
149   Wife and it is allsoe agreed upon betweene the sd. parties that ye sd. JOSEPH
       BELFEILD shall receive & have the sume of Twenty five pounds Sterl. due at
Lady Day last past from Mr. JOHN LOYD for Rent and that ever hereafter the sd. JOSEPH BELFEILD doe receive but ye one third part and the sd. GIBSON to receive two thirds ye other moyetie yearly as the same shall become due from ye sd. LOYD, And it is covenanted & fully agreed by & betweene ye sd. parties and the sd. parties doe severally covenant and grant to & with either of them by these presents that if att any time or times hereafter it should be found & approved that ye sd. Estate ought to be charged either by Law or Conscience wth: any other debts or sums of mony or other duties or other things whatsoever, then att this present is well known & doth appeare to ye sd. Admrs. or either of them or their heires, Admrs. or survivors of them shall att any time hereafter happen to be charged wth: any manner of other charges whatsoever by reason of the sd. Estate or by reason of the due execution of the Administratorship either in Law or otherwise that then each & either of the sd. Admrs. or survivors of them or either of them and Admrs. of such of them as then shall be dead and that their equall & indifferent costs according to oye part of the Estate they severally have in possession bear support pay & allow the same charges of them, any thing herein contained to ye contrary in any wise notwithstanding;   In Wittness whereof wee the parties above exprest have interchangeably sett or: hands & fixt or: seales the day & yeare above written
Signed seled & delivered in presence of
     JOHN TURBERVILLE,   ROBERT GIBSON
     JOHN ROBERTSON   JOSEPH BELFEILD
     Recorded 2d 8br: 1706   p   JOS: TAYLOE, Clk.

     KNOW ALL MEN by these p:sents that I ROBERT GIBSON of ye Pish: of Xt. Church in ye County of Lancastr: am firmly bound unto JOSEPH BELFEILD of ye Pish: of Sittenburn in ye County of RICHMOND, Chyr., the sume of one thousand pounds good & lawfull money of England, dated this tenth day of Apr: 1706.

THE CONDICON of this obligacon is such that if the above bounden ROBERT GIBSON doe at all times hereafter truely observe the covenants & payments wch: on his or their behalfe ought to be observed in certaine articles of agreement bearing even date wth: these pr:sents between the above bounden ROBERT GIBSON

p.   one of the Admrs. of the Estate of MOTTR: WRIGHT (deced), of the one part and
150   the above named JOSEPH BELFEILD one other of the Admrs. of the sd. Estate of
       the other part and wth:out fraud or coven according to ye intent of the sd.
agreemt., That then this obligacon to be void or else to remaine in full force
Signed sealed & delivered in presence of
       JOHN TURBERVILE   ROBERT GIBSON
       JOHN ROBERTSON
       Recorded ye 2d 8br: 1706   p   JOS: TAYLOE, Clk

       KNOW ALL MEN by these pr:sents that I JOSEPH BELFEILD of County of RICH-
MOND, Chry., am firmly bound unto ROBERT GIBSON of County of Lancastr: in ye sume
of One thousand pounds of lawfull money of England.   Sealed wth: my seale dated this
tenth day of Aprill 1706
       THE CONDICION of this obligacon is such that if ye sd. JOSEPH BELFEILD at all times
hereafter keeps all covenants which on his part out to be kept in a certaine agreement made betweene JOSEPH BELFEILD one of the Admrs. of ye Estate of MOTTROM
WRIGHT (deced), of ye one part and the above named ROBERT GIBSON one other of the
Admrs. of ye sd. Estate of the other part in all things according to ye true meaning of
the sd. agreemt., That then this obligacon to be void or else to remaine in full force
Signed seled & delivered in presence of
       JOHN TURBERVILE,   JOSEPH BELFEILD
       JOHN ROBERTSON
       Recorded ye 2d. 8br: 1706   p   JOS: TAYLOE, Clk.

       THIS INDENTURE made the thirteenth day of Febry. Ano. Dom: 1705/6, Be-
tweene ABRAHAM BUSH of the Pish of White Chapple in ye County of Lancastr:, Planter, of the one part and WILLIAM HOWARD of ye Pish; & County aforesd., Inn Holder
of ye other part;   Wittnesseth that ye sd. ABRAHAM BUSH for seaven thousand pounds
of good legall tobbo. paid or secured to be paid by the sd. WM: HOWARD doth acquit the
sd. WM: HOWARD his heires for ever and for divers other good causes

p.   hath granted unto the sd. WM: HOWAD his heires & assignes all that p:cell of
151   land containing Eighty four acres & one third of an acre late in ye tenure of
       him the sd. ABRAHAM BUSH, being part of Two hundred and fivety three acres
taken up by conveyance from ye Proprietors Office between GEORGE BUSH, JOHN
BUSH and ye said ABRAHAM BUSH bearing date ye 13th day of Janry: 1695/6, and
signed by Colo. WM: FITZHUGH, the Agent for the Proprietors aforesd., and by them,
ye sd. GEORGE BUSH, JOHN BUSH and ABRAHAM BUSH devided into three equall parts,
the moyety whereof hereby sold together wth: all houses orchards gardens stocks of
cattle & hoggs being the proper marke of him ye sd. ABRAHAM BUSH or otherwise
runing thereon by his assignmt. to ye sd. Eighty three acres and one third part of an
acre belonging, with all pastures timber & priviledges belonging and the profitts
title whatsoever of the sd. ABRAHAM BUSH together wth: all such escripts which he
hath in custody;   To have and to hold unto the sd. WM: HOWARD his heires & assignes
to be holden of the Cheife Lord of the fees freely & clearly acquitted

p.   from all claimes whatsoever;   In Wittness whereof the p:tis first above men-

tioned have hereunto sett their hands & affixed their seales the day & year first
above written
Signed sealed & delivered in the pr:sence of
    JOS: TAYLOE,   ABRAHAM BUSH
    JNO: SHARP   JANE BUSH
    Recognitr in Cur Com Lancastr: dicimo tertia die March 1705/6 et recordr
        p   JOS: TAYLOE, Clk.

      TO ALL TO WHOME these pr:sents shall come, I HERBERT JEFFRYS, Esqr.,
Governr: and Capt. Genll. of Virginis send Greeting;   Whereas his most sacred Majesty
hath been pleased undr: the Great Seale of England bearing date the 10th day of
Octobr: in ye eight & twentieth yeare of his Reigne among other things contained ye
antient priviledge of granting fivety acres of land for every person imported into
his Majties Collony of Virga.,   Now Know yee that I ye sd. HERBERT JEFFRYS, Esqr.,
Governr: &c., doe grant unto ABRAHAM BUSH Thirty five acres of land in Lancastr:
County, Begining att a marked Beach standing in a Banch of MARRATICOE CREEKE and
runing up the sd. Swamp S. S. Wt. 44 poles to a corner white Oake standing in ye sd.
Swamp, thence E: So: E: up another Branch 90 pole to a marked Ash, thence N: N: E: 74
pole to a marked white Oake standing in a Swap, thence West North West down ye
Swamp to the place where it first began, the sd. land bounding upon ABRAHAM BUSH
and PATRICK GRIMES, which sd. land being due for the transportacon of One

p.   person into this Collony, whose name is in the Records mentioned;   To have
153   and to hold the sd. land wth: all rights to him the sd. ABRAHAM BUSH is heires
       & assignes for ever;   paying for every fivety acres of land yearly the fee rent
of one shilling provided that if ye sd. ABRAHAM BUSH his heires or assignes doe not
seate upon the said land wth:in three yeares, that then it shall be lawfull for any
Adventurer or Planter to make choice & seate thereupon;   Given undr: my hand this
fifth day of Janry: 1677 and in ye 29th yeare of the reigne of or: Sovr: Lord King
Charles ye 2d. over England &c.
ABRAHAM BUSH Patent for 35 acres of land
      sold to WM: HOWARD   HERBERT JEFFRYS
    Recorded in ye Secretaries Office Janry. 5th 1677 p me EDW: HARRISON, Cl Cur
    Recorded at ye instance of WM: HOWARD
        p   JOS: TAYLOE, Clk

      MARGARITT LADY CULPEPER, THOMAS LORD FAIRFAX and CATHERINE his Wife,
Proprietors of ye Northern Neck of Virga: to all to whome these presents shall come;
Whereas JNO: BUSH of ye County of Lanastr. hath repaired to or: Office kept by or:
Agents in ye sd. Northern Neck and hath there suggested that a devidend of Land
scituate upon the Branches of MORRATICOE in ye County of Lancastr: belonging to us
not yett granted to any p:son and thereupon paid the composition for ßeventy   three
acres of land by means whereof he obtained a warrant directed to one of or: Sur-
veyors to survey & give bounds to ye same in ordr: to obtain this Grant, wch: warrant
being duely returned together wth: ye Plot & Bounds thereof to or: sd. Office,   KNOW
YEE therefore that in consideracon of the composition paid doe hereby grant to him
ye sd. JOHN BUSH all that p:cell of land lying upon the Branches of MARRATICOE in
the County of Lancastr: bounded as followeth; (vizt);   Begining att a marked white
Oake

p.   standing in ye sd. BUSH his line on a Point betweene ye sd. BUSHes & JNO: BUX-
154   TONs and on ye South East side of a Maine Branch from the white Oake up the

sd. Branch South eighty one degrees East thirty seaven pole, then North sixty nine degrees East twenty pole to a corner Gum standing a little wth:in ye sd. Swamp near BUXTONs Corne Feild, thence up the sd. Swamp South fourty foure degrees East fourty two pole to a corner white Oake standing in BARTH: WOODs line just by the side of the Branch, thence along WOODs line & STEPHEN WELLS line South fourty degrees W: one hundred and eight perches to a corner Spanish Oake standing neer the head of a little Branch in a line belonging to JNO: BUSH and his two Brothers, GEORGE & ABRA-HAM, from the Spanish Oake N. E. by E. 81 po. to a corner Spanish Oake standing on the side of a Branch, thence down the Branch N. 32 po., thence No. 30 degs. Wt. 40 po: to a corner wt: Oake standing in ye side of the line and thence W. crossing the sd. Branch 46 po: to ye wt. Oake where it first began; containing Seventy three acres of land together with all rights & benefitts belonging; To have and to hold the said Seventy three acres of land with all rights to him the sd. JOHN BUSH for ever; Provided that if the said JOHN BUSH shall not pay the annuall rent for the space of two whole yeares that then it shall be lawfull for us or: assignes to reenter and to hold in or: first right soe as if this grant had never passed; Given att or: Office in STAFFORD County wth:in or: sd. Proprietary undr: or: seale. Wittness or: Agents WM: FITZHUGH or GEORGE BRENT or either of them the 13th day of Janry. 1695/6
Registred p WM: FITZHUGH, JUNR.   WM: FITZHUGH
        Recorded att ye instance of WM: HOWARD
                    p   JOS: TAYLOE, Clk

        KNOW ALL MEN by these presents that I EDWARD ATTWOOD of Linhaven in PRINCES ANNE County have nominated & appointed my trusty & well beloved Kinsman, Mr. WM: HOWARD of Lancastr: County ORDINARY KEEPER my true & lawfull Attorney to recover & receive for me of JNO: HALL of Lancastr: County, ORDINARY KEEPER, all such debts undr: the sd. JOHN HALLs hand & seale dated ye 24th day of May 1704, and a Bill dated ye 9th day of June 1704, due to me, EDWARD ATTWOOD, from ye sd. JNO: HALL, giving and granting

p.   to my sd. Attorney full power to sue imprison and condemn the sd. JNO: HALL
155   his heires for me in any Court & in my name all & singular things wch: shall
        be necessary concerning the pr:misses as fully as I the sd. EDWD. ATTWOOD might or could doe about the same. In Wittness whereof I the sd. EDWD. ATTWOOD have hereunto sett my hand & seale this 7th day of Febry: 1705/6
Signed sealed & delivered in presence of us
        JNO; HAYES,   EDWARD ATTWOOD
        EDWD. HAYES
    Lettr. Attry. recordr 13th March 1705/6
                    p   JOS: TAYLOE, Clk.

        THIS INDENTURE made ye eighth day of March in ye yeare of or: Lord 1705 Betweene JOHN ALLDERSON of the Pish: of St. Marys White Chappell of the County of Lancastr:, Planter, of the one party and WILLIAM GOODRIDGE of the sd. County & Pish: Planter, of the other party; Wittnesseth that ye sd. JNO: ALLDERSON for the sume of seaven thousand pounds of good legall tobbo: & casque hath granted unto sd. WILIAM GOODRIDGE in his actuall possession and to his heires and assignes for ever, that messuage of land being in ye sd. Pish: of St. Marys White Chappell in County of Lancastr: and bounded as followeth, (vizt); Begining at a corner Chesnutt thence North North East sixty eight pole to a corner wt: Oake bounding upon the land of Mr. THOMAS CHATTWIN & JOHN MOTT, thence North West twenty eight pole to a corner pockhiccory saplin, thence East a quarter of a point North by marked trees two hundred twenty two pole to a corner red Oake of the said ALLDERSONs, thence West by South bounding upon the sd. ALLDERSONs line two hundred eighteene pole to ye place where it first began; includeing Eighty three acres of land wthall houses orchards fences & appurtenances whatsoever to the sd. tenemt.

p.   appertaining and ye sd. JOHN ALLDERSON and LYDIA his Wife shall in p:son
156   acknowledge ye sd. land att ye next Court to be held for the County of Lancas-
       tr: In Wittness hereof to this pr:sent Deed indented, I have hereunto sett my
hand and seale this eighth day of March as is above exprest
Signed sealed & delivered in presence of us
       GEORGE FINCH, SENR.   JOHN ALLDERSON
       ELIZABETH FINCH
       Recognitr in Cur Com Lancastr: 13th die March 1705/6 et recordr
              p   JOS: TAYLOE, Clk

       KNOW ALL MEN by these presents that whereas I JOHN MOTT of the County of
Lancastr: haveing a sufficient warrant granted unto mee att ye Proprietors Office for
the Northern Neck, for a certaine parcell of land scituate in Lancastr; County on a
Branch of MARRATICOE being in quantity Two hundred & fourty acres and haveing
paid the composition for soe much beareing date ye 13th day of March Ano: 1684/5,
which said land was formerly taken up by me, JOHN MOTT, & THO; CHATTIN & JNO:
CARPENTER, wee being copartners together. Now Know yee that I JOHN MOTT
haveing the grand warrant for the said Two hundred & fourty acres of land doe give
a third prt unto WM: WOOD of the County of Lancastr: To have and to hold for him &
his heires as is exprest in ye grant to me from the said Office, he ye sd. WOOD paying
the Rents for the sd. third part which is in number Eighty three acres, allso his part
of the composition all redy paid by me for the whole two hundred & fourty acres wch:
being laid out & surveyed for Mr. THO: CHATTIN scituate in Lancastr:County on a
Branch of MARRATICOE, Begining att a Stake ye end of CARPENTERs streight line &
runns N. E. seaven poles, thence N. W. 28 poles, thence 76 degrees E. 60 poles, thence
N. 22 degrees E. 67 poles, thence N. W. 78 poles, thence S. W. 126 1/2 poles & finally S.
E. along the line of the sd. CARPENTER 117 poles to ye place where it began, which sd.
land I doe grant to WM: WOOD & his heires; In Wittness whereof I have putt my hand
and seale ye 16th day of Janry. 1695/6
Signed sealed & delivered in p:sence of
       GEORGE FINCH,   JOHN MOTT
       WM: GOODRIDGE
       Recognitr in Cur Com Lancastr: 3 die 7bris: 1696 recordr 14th die
              p   JOS: TAYLOE, Clk
       On which is ye following endorsmt.

p.   KNOW ALL MEN by these presents that I WM: WOOD of ye Pish: of St. Marys
157   White Chappell in ye County of Lancastr:, Planter, for a valuable consideracon
       in hand secured to be paid, doe sell uno RICHD: ALDERSON his heires & assignes
ye wth:in Deed of Sale wth: as full warranty & right to all intents and purposes as
shalbe made for the same bearing date wth: these pr:sents and oblidge my selfe and
JANE my Wife, to acknowledge the same together wth: an Indenture of Sale for ye sd.
Land att or: next Court; In Wittness hereunto sett my hand & seale this fourth of
Septr: 1699
Signed sealed & delivered in p:sence of
       JOSEPH TAYLOE   WILLM: WOOD
       JOHN MATHEW

KNOW ALL MEN by these presents that I RICHD: ALDERSON of St. Marys White Chapple Lancastr: County, Planter, for a valuable consideracon in hand secured to be paid doe sell & sett over unto WM: GOODRIDGE his heires or assignes this wth:in Deed of Sale wth: as full warranty & right to all intents as it shall be made for the same bearing date wth: these presents and doe oblidge my selfe & ANNE my Wife to acknowledge the same together wth: an Indenture of Sale for ye sd. Land att or: next Court;   In Wittness I have sett my hand & seale this 19th day of Febry. 1705/6

GEORGE FINCH, SENR.   RICHD. ALDERSON
MARY MEEKES

Recognitr in Cur Com Lancastr: 13th die May 1705/6 et recordr
                    p   JOS: TAYLOE, Clk

THIS INDENTURE made ye 4th day of Septembr: 1699 Betweene WILLIAM WOOD of the Pish of St. Marys White Chapple in the County of Lancastr:, Planter, of the one part and RICHARD ALDERSON of the same Pish: & County of ye other part;   Wittnesseth that ye said WILLIAM WOOD in consideracon of the sume of Seaven thousand one hundred pounds of good legall tobbo: & casque & one Bull Staff of neer foure yeares old to him in hand already secured to be paid, have sold

p.   the sd. RICHD: ALDERSON in his actuall possession by the transferring of uses
158   into possession all that land late in the possession of him ye sd. WM: WOOD
being in ye Pish: of St. Marys White Chapple in County of Lancastr: and bounded as followeth; vizt., Begining att a Stake on a Branch of MARRATICOE att ye end of CARPENTERs streight line & runs N. E. 7 poles, thence N. W. 28 po:, thence N. 76 degrees E: 61 po:, thence N. 22 degrees E. 61 po:, thence N. W. 78 po; thence S. W. 126 1/2 po: and finally S. E. along the line of the sd. CARPENTERs 187 po: to the place where it first began; includeing Eight acres of land, together with all houses buildings barns and all Orchards timber water priviledges & appertenances whatsoever to oye sd. land belonging;   To have and to hold to ye sd. RICHD: ALDERSON his heires & assignes for ever and the sd. WM: WOOD doth hereby promise that he ye sd. WM: WOOD and JANE his Wife shall in p:son acknowledge ye sd. land att ye next Court held for the County of Lancastr: In Wittness whereof to this pr:sent Deed Indented I have hereunto sett my hand & seale this day & yeare first above written
Signed sealed and delivered in p:sence of
        JOS: TAYLOE,   WM: WOOD
        JNO: MATHEW

Recognitr in Cur Com Lancastr: 13th die 7bris: 1699 et recordr
                    p   JOS: TAYLOE, Clk

KNOW ALL MEN by these presents that I RICHD: ALDERSON for a valuable consideracon in hand received to be paid do sell unto WM: GOODRIDG his heires or assignes the wth:in Deed of Sale wth: full warranty & right as it shall be made for the same bearing date wth: these pr:sents and doe oblidge my selfe and ANN my Wife to acknowledge the same att or: next Court.   In Wittness whereof, I have sett my hand and seale this 19th day of Febry: 1705/6
Signed sealed & delivered in p:sence of
        GEO: FINCH, SENR.   RICHD: ALDERSON
        MARY MEEKES

Recognitr in Cur Com Lancastr: 13th die March 1705/6 et recordr
                    p   JOS: TAYLOE, Clk.

p.
159

    THIS INDENTURE made this twelfth day of June in the fifth yeare of or: Soveraigne Lady Anne &c., and in the yeare of or: Lord 1706, Betweene JOHN STOTT of ye Pish: of St. Marys White Chappell in County of Lancastr: in ye Dominion of Virginia, Planter, of the one part and FORTUNATUS DAVENPORT of the Pish: of NORTH FARNHAM in the County of RICHMOND, Shipwright, of ye second part; Wittnesseth that ye sd. JNO: STOTT for the sume of Thirty pounds Sterl., money & two thousand five hundred pounds of tobbo: to him paid. JOHN STOTT doth for himselfe his heires hath granted unto ye sd. FORTUNATUS DAVENPORT his heires & assignes for ever all that Devidend of Land in ye Pish: of St. Marys White Chappell in County of Lancastr: containing fivety acres of land and bounded as followeth, vizt., Begining att a marked tree of JOHN SIMPSONs and runing North North West to MARRATICOE CREEKE twenty five pole soe into ye woods South South West which sd.tract of land was granted to BRYAN STOTT, late of the County of Lancastr: aforesd. (deced), by Pattent bearing date ye 24th daye of August in ye 16th yeare of ye reigne of or: Soveraigne Lord King Charles ye 2d. &c., and in the yeare of or: Lord God 1664, as by the aforesd. Pattent in the Records of the Honorable Genll. Court for the Dominion of Virginia relacon being thereunto had and alsoe all that tract of land being in the Pish: County & Dominion aforesd. containing Fivety five acres of land and bounded as followeth, vizt., Begining att a marked red Oake the begining of a tract of eight hundred acres of land granted to Mr. BRYAN STOTT, from the sd. red Oake runing North eighty eight degrees West thirty poles to another red Oake a corner tree of a tract of land granted to Mr. BRYAN STOTT & THOMAS STOTT, thence North & by West two hundred & eighty poles, thence North North East fivety two poles to a marked red Oake which devides this from JOHN CALLIHANs Land, thence South & by East three hundred & thirty perches to ye first mentioned station, which tract of land bounded as aforesd. was first granted to ye sd. JOHN STOTT by Pattent beareing date ye 16th day of Xbr: in ye third yeare of ye reigne of or: Soveraigne Lady Anne &c., 1704, as by the sd. Pattent remaining in ye Proprietors Office for the Northern Neck relacon being had may more at large appeare and allsoe one certaine point or

p.
160

    parcell of land containing five acres of high land being in ye County & Dominion aforesd., betweene the Plantacon whereon one JOHN POTT now liveth & the Plantacon of the sd. JOHN STOTT, together with all rights & every part & p:cell thereof and all houses stables water courses & comodityes unto ye sd. FORTUNATUS DAVENPORT his heires & assignes for ever; To have and to hold at all times freely discharged from all former grants

p.
161

    and that he ye sd. FORTUNATUS DAVENPORT shall att all times for ever hold all the sd. pr:misses wth:out disturbance of ye sd. JNO: STOTT his heires or any person whatsoever wth: warranty agt: all men bee it by fines Deeds or any other lawfull meanes

p.
162

    In Wittness whereof the sd. JOHN STOTT to this pr:sent Indenture hath sett his hand and seale the day & yeare first above written/1706

Signed sealed & delivered
FORTUNATUS SYDNER   JOHN STOTT
ANTHONY SYDNER

Recognitr in Cur Com Lancastr: 12th die June 1706 by JOHN STOTT & MILES WALTERS Attor: of JANE STOTT, et recorded

       p   JOS: TAYLOE, Clk.

KNOW ALL MEN by these presents that I JANE STOTT, Wife of JOHN STOTT, have sett in my stead & place MILES WALTERS of the Pish: & County aforesd. to be my true & lawfull Attor: for me to acknowledge one Deed of Land granted to FORTUNATUS DAVENPORT of the County of RICHMD. in ye Pish. of NORTH FARNHAM, Shipwright, by the said JOHN STOTT of one hundred & ten acres of land as ye Deed doth express and in consideracon ye abovesd. DAVENPORT is to give the sd. JANE STOTT tenn shillings or the worth of it to her likeing, as Wittness my hand & seale this 12th day of June 1706 Signed sealed & delivered in p:sence of

EDWD: TOMLIN,   JANE STOTT
DUKE SAUNDERS

Lancastr: KNOW ALL MEN by these presents that wee JOHN STOTT & DUKE SAUNDERS both of the Pish: of St. Marys White Chapple in ye County aforesd. are firmly bound unto FORTUNATUS DAVENPORT of the County of RICHMOND, Shipwright, in the full sume of One hundred pounds Sterl., money of England dated this twelfth day of June 1706

THE CONDICION of this obligacon is such that if the above JOHN STOTT his heires & every of them shall truely keep all articles on the behalfe of the sd. JNO: STOTT in one certaine Indenture made by the sd. JOHN STOTT to ye abovesd. FORTUNATUS DAVEN-PORT; That then this p:sent obligacon to be void or else to remaine in full force Signed sealed & delivered in presence of

WM: DARE,   JOHN STOTT
FORTUNATUS SYDNER,   DUKE SANDERS
ANTHONY SYDNER
Recognitr in Cur Com Lancaster 12th die June 1706 et recordr
          p   JOS: TAYLOE, Clk

p.   THIS INDENTURE made ye first day of June 1706 and in the 5th yeare of the
163   reigne of or: Sovereigne Lady Anne &c.   Betweene JOSEPH BALL of the Pish: of
         St. Marys White Chapple and County of Lancastr:, Gent., of the one part and JOSEPH BALL, JUNR. the only Son of the abovesd. JOSEPH BALL, Gent., of the other part;   Wittnesseth that the said JOSEPH BALL, Gent., as well for the love and respect that he beares unto his sd. Son, JOSEPH BALL, JUNIOR as for the raiseing of the uses hereinafter exprest and for divers other good causes hath granted unto the sd. JOSEPH BALL, JUNR. all that p:cell of land containing four hundred & forty acres being all the rest residue of a tract of land of Six hundred & fifty acres late ye land of NATHANIEL CALE, two hundred acres whereof he devised by his Last Will & Testa-mt. to one of his Sisters Children called THOMAS IVES, and his heires to be laid out as by the sd. Will is exprest and the other four hundred & fifty acres more or less being the remaindr: of the sd. tract decended and came to CHARLES CALE as heire at Law to his Brother, NATHA: CALE, and by him the sd. CHARLES CALE sold unto ye aforesd. JOSEPH BALL, as by his Deeds of Lease and Release dated ye third & fourth dayes of August 1698 and authenticquely acknowledged in Lancastr: County Court relacon being thereunto had may appeare, which said Land is scituate & being upon the mouth of MARRATICOE CREEKE and soe runs up to POWELLS CREEKE in the County of Lancastr: aforesd., and was heretofore purchased by THOMAS STEPHENS of THOMAS PURFEY and late in ye occupacon of Mr. ROBERT BECKINGHAM, Mr. THOMAS WILKS & Mr. WM: MAN and now in ye tenure & occupacon of ye aforesd. JOSEPH BALL, Gent., wth: all the rights & appurtenances and other advantages to ye sd. Four hundred & fivety acres of land;   To have and to hold unto ye sd. JOSEPH BALL, JUNR. his heires & assignes for ever upon this trust & confidence neverthe less,   That ye sd. JOSEPH BALL, Gent., shall have the priviledge of tending soe much of the arable land upon

the said Plantacon as shall be hereafter cleared or that is now cleared as shall be sufficient to occupie two good able hands wth: the use of what wood timber & timber trees upon the sd. land now growing, together wth: what houseing he shall have occasion of and one Roome in the GREAT HOUSE which is now building upon the sd. Plantacon, which he the said JOSEPH BALL, Gent.

p.   shall make choice of as allsoe to keep & maintaine twenty head of neat Cattle
164   to be depastured thereon, allsoe stock of Sheep Horses & Hoggs to be main-
       tained & depastured upon the sd. Plantacon land & pr:misses for and dureing
his natural life and after his decease to and for ye use & behoofe of him the sd. JOSEPH BALL, JUNR., the only Son of the sd. JOSEPH BALL, Gent., his heires and assignes for ever and to & for noe other use or purpose whatsoever, and the sd. JOSEPH BALL, Gent., for himselfe his heires doth covenant wth: the sd. JOSEPH BALL, JUNR. in manner following, that is to say, that ye sd. JOSEPH BALL, JUNR. and his heires from henceforth shall lawfully & peaceably stand & be seized of all & singular the pr:misses hereby granted to and for the use & purposes before hereby menconed & exprest wth:out the claime or interruption of him the sd. JOSEPH BALL, Gent. or any persons claiming undr: him and for the sd. JOSEPH BALL, Gent., and his heires will att ye request of ye sd. JOSEPH BALL, JUNR. make & acknowledge not only these presents but any other Deed or Deeds requisite in Law for the conveying the pr:misses;   In Wittness whereof the parties aforesaid have to this present Indenture sett their hands & seales the day & yeare first above written
Signed sealed & delivered in p:sence of us
    JOS: TAYLOE,   JOSEPH BALL
    RANDOLPH MILLER,   JNO: CALLEHAN
    Recognitr in Cur Com Lancastr: dicimo die Julii 1706 p JOSEPH BALL
        Test   JOS: TAYLOE, Clk.   Recordr.

THIS INDENTURE made & confirmed ye 13th day of March 1705/6 Betweene WILLIAM BALL of the County of Lancastr: of ye one part and RICHD: BALL of the aforesd. County of the other part;   Wittnesseth that the sd. WM: BALL and RICHD: BALL doe now stand seized of a tract of land scituateting in ye County aforesd. which sd. land was given unto sd. WILLIAM & RICHD. BALL by the Last Will & Testamt. of their Father, Capt. WILLIAM BALL, deced., and to be equally devided betweene them.   Now to ye end yt: a devision shall be had & made betweene the sd. parties of the sd. Land thereunto belonging, it is concluded and agreed by and betweene the sd. p:ties to these presents in manner & forme following;   And first the sd. WM: BALL haveing seated on the Northermost part (which part in quality is much better then the other part whereon the sd. RICHD: BALL is seated) the sd. WM: BALL doth therefore agree that ye sd. RICHD: BALLs part shall begin att ye corner white oake standing on ye East side of the Swamp whereon the sd. WM: BALLs MILL now stands and from the sd. Oake runing the severall courses up the sd. Swamp till it comes to the mouth of the second great Branch which sd. Branch

p.   runs along ye North side of the sd. RICHD: BALLs Plantacon and thence runing
165   from the mouth of the said Branch with a course to ye South East line of the
       Nine hundred & fivety acres as will include five hundred & twenty five acres
in that part whereon the sd. RICHD: BALL is seated, which the sd. WILLIAM BALL for himselfe &c. that he the sd. RICHD: BALL his heires shall from henceforth hold & peaceably enjoy in severalty to him & to his heires for ever wth: the appurtenances thereunto belonging and that he the sd. WILLIAM BALL nor his heires shall from henceforth claim any right to the same, but that ye sd. WM: BALL & his heires be

utterly excluded and for ever debarred by these presents and the sd. RICHD: BALL for himselfe &c. that ye sd. WM: BALL his heires &c. shall from henceforth hold & peaceably enjoy in severalty to him & to his heires for ever the other part whereon his Quarter stands wth: all the appurtenances belonging and that he ye sd. RICHD: BALL nor his heires shall demand any right in ye same or any part thereof but that ye sd. RICHD: BALL and his heires shall att all times from all actions & demands thereof be utterly for ever debarred p these presents; In Wittness whereof both partys have sett their hands & seales in presence of

    JOSEPH TAYLOE,   WILLIAM BALL
    EDWIN CONWAY   RICHARD BALL
    Recognitr in Cur Com Lancastr: dicimo die Julii 1706 et recordr
         p   JOS: TAYLOE, Clk

    THIS INDENTURE made this twentieth day of Febry. one thousand seaven hundred & five six and in the fourth yeare of the reigne of or: Lady Ann by the grace of God &c., by and betwixt JOHN BOURN of WICKOCOMOCO Pish: in NORTHUMBERLAND County, Planter, and ELIZABETH his Wife of the one part and ABRAHAM BLEDSOE of the Pish; & County aforesd.

p.   Planter, of the other part; (Wittnesseth) that ye sd. JOHN BOURN and ELIZA-
166   BETH his Wife doth for the sume of Nine thousand pounds of good & mer-
      chantable tobbo: & casque in hand allready received hath granted unto the said ABRAHAM BLEDSOE his heires & assignes all the right to a certaine tract of land scituate in Xt. Church Pish. in the County of Lancastr: and formerly known or called TOMAS BALLs Plantacon and now by the name of JOHN BOURNS QUARTER, wth:all such houseing fenceing woods and appurtenances thereunto appertaining to him the said ABRAHAM BLEDSOE; To have and to hold dureing or: naturall lives & for the better assurance and sure makeing of the aforesd. land and pr:misses to ye sd. ABRAHAM BLEDSOE his heires &c., that we hereby sell unto the sd. ABRAHAM BLEDSOE and to his behoofe all manner of right & possession we have to the sd. Plantacon; In Wittness whereof wee hereunto sett or: hands and affixed or: seales the day & yeare first above written
Signed sealed & delivered in p:sence of us
    JNO: GRASSON, RICHD: SMITH,   JOHN BOURN
    JNO: BROWN   ELIZABETH BOURNE
    Recognitr in Cur Com Lancastr: 10th die Julii 1706 et recordr
         p   JOS: TAYLOE, Clk.

    THIS INDENTURE mde ye fiveteenth day of January in the fourth yeare of the reigne of or: Soveraigne Lady Anne by the grace of God &c., and in the yeare of our Lord one thousand seaven hundred & five; Betweene TOBIAS PURSELL of the County of Lancastr:, Planter, of the one part and JOHN BROWN of the sd. County, Planter, of the other part; Wittnesseth that ye sd. TOBIAS PURSELL for the sume of One hundred & sixty pounds of good and lawfull money of England to him truely paid

p.   have granted unto the said JOHN BROWN his heires & assignes the remaining
167   part of a tract of land scituate in ye Parish of Christ Church in ye County
      aforesd. att ye head of the Eastermost Branch of CURROTOMAN RIVER the whole tract of land being a Patent of Land granted formerly to Mr. WALTER HEARD beareing date ye first day of June in ye yeare of or: Lord 1666, the sd. Pattent being part of a Pattent formerly granted to WILLIAM IRONMONGER beareing date ye twelfth day of December 1663, the whole Pattent granted to Mr. WALTER HEARD aforesd.

being 350 acres bounded as in the Pattent largely doth appeare whereof was sold by
the sd. WALTER HEARD a p:cell of land lying on the South West side of a Swamp, the
quantity unknown, sold to JOHN BUNN and now in the possession of JOHN FINDLEY,
and another part thereof was sold to ROGER WILLIAMS and being now in the tenure
of JNO: HART, being in quantity one hundred acres sold by the abovesd. WM: HEARD,
the remaineing part of the sd. Pattent being the pr:misses intended to be sold was by
the sd. WM: HEARD sold & assigned over to the sd. TOBIAS PURSELL his heires &
assignes for ever by Deed of Indenture beareing date ye 10th day of Febry: 1695 and
recorded in ye sd. County Court the 3d day of May 1696, as by the Records of the sd.
Court may more fully appeare;   To have and to hold the sd. p:cell of land wth: all profitts appertaining as allsoe all the right which the said TOBIAS PURSELL now hath or
may claime of ye same hereby granted land wth: all the rights unto the sd. JOHN
BROWN his heires & assignes for ever; subject unto the Quitt Rents due to b paid; And
the said TOBIAS PURSELL for himselfe his heires the sd. granted land will for ever
warrant and defend

p.   and the sd. JOHN BROWN his heires & assignes shall possess & enjoy the same
168   wth:out interuption of the sd. TOBIAS PURSELL or any p:sons whatsoever;   In
        Wittness whereof the parties to these pr:sents have interchangeably sett their
hands & seales the day & yeare first above written
Signed sealed and delivered in p:sence of
        NICHO: (? THERCHELSEN)   TOBIAS PURSELL
        JNO: HART, SENR. PETER WOOD,
        THO: HOOPER
        Recognitr in Cur Com Lancastr: une didimo die Julii 1706 et recordr
                p   JOS: TAYLOE, Clk

        Lancaster ss.   TO ALL TO WHOME these presents shall come Greeting. Know yee
that I JANE WADE of the County of RICHMOND in the Dominion of Virginia, Wife unto
JNO: WADE, of the sd. County, Planter, have and by these presents doe appoint WM:
DARE of the aforesd. County of Lancastr: my true and lawfull Attorney in my name to
acknowledge before the Justices of the County of Lancastr: County att ye next Court
all my right of Dower to a certaine tract of land being in the County of Lancastr:
aforesd. unto Capt. WM: FOX of the sd. County of Lancastr: wch: sd. tract of land wth:
the appurtenances was confirmed unto Capt. WM: FOX his heires & assignes for ever
by my sd. Husband, JNO: WADE, RICHARD FRISTER & LETTICE his Wife and ABIGALL
WADE by Deed of Indenture of Release beareing date ye 10th day of Aprill in ye yeare
of or: Lord 1705, hereby ratifying whatsoever my sd. Attorney shall lawfully doe in
the pr:misses.   In Wittness whereof I have hereunto sett my hand and seale the 25th
day of August 1705
Signed sealed and delivered in pr:sence of
        ELIZABETH WOODWARD,   JANE WADE
        JAMES ATTCHISON
        This Letter of Attor: was proved by the Oath of JAMES ATTCHISON att Lancastr:
County ye 11th of 7br: 1706
                Test   JOS: TAYLOE, Clk, et recordr.

p.   Lancaster ss. KNOW ALL MEN by these pr:sents that I JANE WADE of the Coun-
169   ty of RICHMD. now Wife unto JOHN WADE of the sd. County, Planter, for a valu-
        able consideracon have released and for ever quitt claime unto Capt. WM: FOX
of the County of Lancastr: his heires and assignes for ever all my right of Dower unto
a certaine tract of land in ye County of Lancastr: aforesd. which sd. land wth: their

appurtenances were sold unto Capt. WM: FOX his heires & assignes for ever by my sd. Husband, JOHN WADE, RICHARD FRISTER & LETTICE his Wife and ABIGALL WADE by Indenture of Release beareing date the 10th day of Aprill in ye yeare of or: Lord 1705 soe that neither I myselfe nor my heires shall claime any right unto the same or any part thereof;   In Wittness whereof I have heretofore sett my hand & seale this 25th day of August 1705

Signed sealed & delivered in p:sence of

    ELIZABETH WOODWARD,   JANE WADE
    JAMES ATTCHISON

    Acknowledged in the County of Lancastr: the 11th day of 7br: 1706 p WM: DARE, Attorney of JANE WADE and recorded

        p   JOS: TAYLOE, Clk.

    THIS INDENTURE made ye eleventh day of Septembr: in the 5th yeare of the reigne of or: Sovereigne Lady Queen Anne 1706;   Betweene ROBERT CARTER Esqr., of Lancastr: County, Surviveing Feoffe of the TOWNE LAND of the sd. County bought & purchased by Capt. DAVID FOX, deceased, and the sd. ROBERT CARTER, the feoffes appointed for the sd Land of Capt. WM: BALL, allsoe deceased, for the use of the County as appeares by Deed of Conveyance from the sd. BALL to ye sd. feoffes beareing date ye Eleventh day of May 1692, and acknowledged in ye Court of the sd. County on the same Eleventh of May of the one part and THOMAS HOOPER of the same County of ye other part;   Wittnesseth tht ye sd. ROBERT CARTER for ye sume of one hundred and ninety two pounds of good merchantable tobbo: for each of the four Lotts to him in hand paid by the sd. THOMAS HOOPER, he the sd. ROBERT CARTER doth hereby

p.   grant unto ye sd. THOMAS HOOPER his heires & assignes for ever four Lotts of
170   Land wth:in the sd. Town now called QUEENS TOWNE, to wit, the Lotts number
     48; 49; 50; and 53: according to the Platt made of the sd. Towne and laid of into Lotts the first day of August last past by HARRY BEVERLEY, Surveyor, p:suant to an ordrL of the sd. Lancastr: Court dated the Eleventh day of July last, the said Lott number 53, containing halfe an acre & eighteen perches lying on the West North West or uper side of the Street called PRINCE STREET, being the third Lott from the Broad Street called ANNE STREET, and bounded on the West South West side by the Creeke called MADAM BALLS CREEKE, according to ye courses thereof and the other three Lotts to witt, 48; 49 and 50; lying on the East South East or lower side of the sd. PRINCE STREET being the first second & third lotts from the sd. ANNE STREET, downe towards the aforesd. Creeke and containing each of them halfe an acre according to the aforesd. Platt; as by the same more plainly appeares;   To have and to hold the said four Lotts to him the sd. THOMAS HOOPER his heires & assignes for ever in as full manner as is directed by one Act of Assembly made att a Genll. Assembly begun att WILLIAMS-BURGH the twenty third day of October 1705, intituled "An Act for Establishing Ports & Towns," he or they paying Rent for the sd. four Lotts four ounces of Flax seed & eight ounces of Hemp seed on the tenth day of October annually to ye Directors & Benchers of the sd. Town or Burgh, according to ye direction of the said Act, provided the sd. THOMAS HOOPER doe begin to build on the sd. Lotts wth:in twelve months after ye date hereof and doe proceed to finish wth:out delay one good house twenty foot square att ye least, otherwise this grant to be void and the Lotts herewth: granted lyable to the choice & purchase of any other person according to Law as fully and amply as if this grant had never been made;   In Wittness whereof both the sd. parties have hereunto sett their hands & seales to two of these Indenures both of this tenor & date

Signed sealed & delivered in p:sence of
    WM: FOX,   ROBERT CARTER
    JAMES HAINES
    JOS: HEALE,   SHARSHALL GRASTY
    Memd. That Livery & Seizin was this day given by the wth:in named ROBERT CAR-
TER unto the wth:in mentioned THOMAS HOOPER of every of the aforesd. four Lotts by
the delivery of Turf & Twigg upon every of the sd. Lotts by the sd. CARTER unto the sd.
HOOPER
In p:sence of WM: FOX,   JOS: HEALE
    JAMES HAYNES,   SHARSHALL GRASTY
    Recognitr in Cur Com Lancastr: uno dicimo die 7bris: 1706 p ROERT CARTER et
recordr   p   JOS: TAYLOE, Clk

p.   WHEREAS ROBERT CARTER of Lancastr: County, Esqr., Surviving Feofee of the
171   TOWNE LAND of the sd. County now called QUEENS TOWNE by a paire of Inden-
        tures bareing date wth: these p:sents hath granted unto THOMAS HOOPER four
Lotts of land lying wth:in the sd. Towne number 53; 48; 49 and 50; (the Lotts described
as in the foregoing Deed); This Indenture made ye Eleventh day of September 1706 between the said THOMAS HOOPER and the sd. ROBERT CARTER therefore wittnesseth that
ye sd. THOMAS HOOPER for the sume of one hundred and ninety two pounds of sound
merchantable tobacco for each of the sd. four Lotts to him paid by the said ROBERT
CARTER his heires and assignes for ever the aforesd. four Lotts number 48; 49; 50
and 53; lying in QUEENS TOWNE as aforesd., To have and to hold in as full manner as is
directed in an Act of Assembly begun att WILLIAMSBURGH the 23d day of Octobr:
1705, paying the Rents for the sd. four Lotts four ounces of Flax seed & eight ounces
of Hemp seed annually to the Directors & Benchers of the sd. Towne; In Wittness
whereof both parties have interchangeably sett their hands & seales
Signed sealed & delivered in p:sence of
    WM: FOX, JOSEPH HEALE,   THO: HOOPER
    JAMES HAYNES,   SHARSHALL GRASTY

p.   Septembr: ye 11th 1706
172   Memord. That Livery and Seizin was this day given by ye wth:in named
    THOMAS HOOPER unto ROBERT CARTER of every of the aforesd. four Lotts by
delivery of Turff & Twigg upon every of the said Lotts by the sd. HOOPER to the sd.
CARTER in the p:sence of us
    WM: FOX, JOSEPH HEALE
    JAMES HAYNES,   SHARSHALL GRASTY
    Recognitr in Cur Com Lancastr: 11th die 7bris: 1706 et recordr
        p.   JOS: TAYLOE, Clk

    THIS INDENTURE made the Eleventh day of September 1706 Betweene ROBERT
CARTER, Esqr. of Lanastr: County, Surviving feofee of the TOWNE LAND of the sd.
County, bought by Capt. DAVID FOX, deceased, and the sd. ROBERT CARTER of Capt. WM:
BALL allsoe deceased, for the use of the sd. County beareing dte ye eleventh day of
May 1692 and acknowledged in the Court of the sd. County on the same Eleventh of
May of the one part and JOHN TURBERVILE of the other part; Wittnesseth tht the sd.
ROBERT CARTER for the sume of One hundred ninety two pounds of tobacco hath
granted unto the sd. JOHN TURBERVILE his heires & assignes for ever one Lott or
halfe acre of land wth:in the Towne now called QUEENS TOWNE, the sd. Lott being
numbered 38 and bounded by the Street called GEORGE STREET on the uper side
thereof being the fourth Lott on the said Street from the Great Street called ANNE

STREET downe towards the Creeke called MADAM BALLS CREEKE; To hae and to hold in
as ample manner as is directed by Act made att a Genll. Assembly begun att
WILLIAMSBURGH the twenty third day of Octobr: one thousand seaven hundred &
five paying rent for the sd. Lott of one ounce of Flax seed and two ounces of Hemp
seed on the tenth day of Octobr: annually and the sd. JOHN TURBERVILE to begin to
build on the sd. Lott wth:in twelve months after the date hereof and doe finish wth:-
out delay one good house twenty foot square att the least or otherwise this grant to be
void and the Lott lyable to ye choice of any other persons according to Law

p.   as if this grant had never been made.   In Wittness whereof the partys to these
173   p:sents have hereunto interchangeably sett their hands & seales
          Signed sealed and delivered in p:sence of
          A. SWAN, JOS: HEALE,   ROBERT CARTER
          THO: HOOPER, SHARSHALL GRASTY
     Septr. ye 11th 1706. Memord. That Livery and Seizin of the wth:in Lott was given
by ROBERT CARTER unto JOHN TURBERVILE by delivery of Turff & Twigg upon the sd.
Lott by sd. CARTER unto ye sd. TURBERVILE in p:sence of
          A. SWAN,   JOS: HEALE
          THO: HOOPER,   SHARSHALL GRASTY
     Recognitr in Cur Com Lancastr: 11th die 7bris: 1706 et recordr
               p   JOS: TAYLOE, Clk

          THIS INDENTURE made the Eleventh day of September in the yeare one thou-
sand seven hundred and six,   Betweene ROBERT CARTER, Esqr., of Lancastr: County,
the surviving Feofee of the TOWNE LAND of the sd. County and HENRY FLEET of the sd.
County of the other part;   Wittnesseth tht the sd. ROBERT CARTER for the sume of two
hundred pounds of good merchantable tobbo: doth sell unto the sd. HENRY FLEET his
heires & assignes for ever one Lott of halfe acre of land wth:in the Towne now called
QUEENS TOWNE No. 20, according to the Platt laid of into Lotts by HARRY BEVERLEY,
Surveyor, being the fifth Lott from the Broad Street called ANNE STREET, downe towards the Creeke called MADAM BALLS CREEKE as by the sd. Platt appeares;   To have
and to hold the sd. Lott to him the sd. HENRY FLEET his heires & assignes for ever in as
full manner as is directed by Act of Assembly made at the Genll. Assembly begun at
WILLIAMSBURGH the twenty third day of October 1705

p.   paying the annual rent of one ounce of Flax seed and two ounces of Hemp seed
174   on the 12th day of Octobr: annually provided that the sd. HENRY FLEET doe
          build on the sd. Lott wth:in twelve months one good house twenty foot square
at least otherwise this grant to be void and the Lott lyable to the purchase of any
other p:son;   In Wittness whereof the parties to these p:sents have interchangeably
sett their hands & seales
Signed sealed and delivered in p:sence of us
          ROWD. LAWSON, EPA: LAWSON,   ROBERT CARTER
          THO: HOOPER, SHARSHALL GRASTY
     Memd. Septembr: the 11th: That Seizin and delivery was this day given by ROBERT
CARTER unto HENRY FLEET by delivery of Turff and Twigg upon the sd. Lott in p:sence
of us ROWD: LAWSON, EPA: LAWSON
          THO: HOOPER, SHARSHALL GRASTY
     Recognitr in Cur Com Lancastr: 11th die 7bris: 1706 et recordr
               p   JOS: TAYLOE, Clk.

THIS INDENTURE made the Twelfth day of September one thousand seven hundred and six; Betweene ROBERT CARTER, Esqr., of Lancastr: County, surviving feofee of the TOWNE LAND of the sd. County of the one part and HANCOCK LEE of the other part; Wittnesseth that the sd. ROBERT CARTER for the sum of one hundred and ninety two pounds of tobbo: hath granted unto the sd. HANCOCK LEE his heires and assignes for ever one Lott or halfe acre of land wth:in the sd. TOWNE now called QUEENS TOWNE the sd. Lott being numbered Seventy, and bounded by the Street called CULPEPER STREET on the uper side thereof being the corner Lott on the sd. Street from the Great Street called ANNE STREET on the North North East or uper side of the sd. ANNE STREET as by the sd. Platt more plainly appeares; To have and to hold to im the sd. HANCOCK LEE his heires and assignes for ever

p.   paying one ounce of Flax seed and two ounces of Hemp seed on the tenth day
175   of Octobr: annually provided that the sd. HANCOCK LEE doe build on the sd. Lott
        wth:in twelve months one good house twenty foot square at the least otherwise
this grant to be void and the Lott herein granted lyable to purchase of any other
p:sons; In Wittness whereof the parties to these p:sents have sett their hands & seales
Signed sealed & delivered in p:sence of
        JAMES BALL,   SHARSHALL GRASTY,   ROBERT CARTER
        THO: HOOPER
        Memord. Septr. the 12th 1706. That Livery and Seizin was this day delivered by
ROBERT CARTER to HANCOCK LEE by delivery of Turff and Twigg on the sd. Lott by the
sd. CARTER to the sd. LEE in p:sence of us
        JAMES BALL,   SHARSHALL GRASTY
        THO: HOOPER
        Recognitr in Cur Com Lancastr: 12th die Septembr: 1706 et recordr
                p   JOS: TAYLOE, Clk.

THIS INDENTURE made the eleventh day of September one thousand seven hundred and six; Betweene ROBERT CARTER, Esqr., of Lancastr: County, Surviving feoffee of the Towne of ye sd. County of the one part and HANCOCK LEE of NORTH-UMBERLAND County of the other part; Wittnesseth that the sd. ROBERT CARTER for the sume of One hundred and ninety two pounds of good sound merchantable tobacco in hand paid by the sd. HANCOCK LEE, the sd. ROBERT CARTER hath sold unto the sd. HANCOCK LEE his heires and assignes for ever one Lott or halfe acre of land wth:in the sd. Towne now called QUEENS TOWNE number Forty Seven, according to the Platt thereof

p.   the sd. Lott lying on the lower side of the Street called PRINCES STREET being
176   the corner Lott on the Broad Street called ANNE STREET on the North North East
        or uper side of the sd. ANNE STREET; To have and to hold the said Lott to him
the sd. HANCOCK LEE his heires and assignes for ever in as full manner as is directed
by the Genll. Assembly at WILLIAMSBURGH the 23d day of Octobr: 1705, paying Rent
for the sd. Lott of one ounce of Flax seed and two ounces of Hemp seed on the 10th day
of Octobr: annually, provided the sd. HANCOCK LEE do begin and finish one good house
twenty foot square at the least otherwise this grant to be lyable to the purchase of
any other p:sons; In Wittness whereof the parties have interchangeably sett their
hands and seales
Signed sealed and delivered in p:sence of
        RICHARD BAYLEY,   BEN: HERNE,   ROBERT CARTER
        SHARSHALL GRASTY
        Memord. Septr. ye 12th 1706. That Livery and Seizin was this day given by ROBERT

CARTER unto HANCOCK LEE by delivery of Turff and Twigg upon the sd. Land in
p:sence of WM. LISTER
            RICHARD BAYLEY,   JOHN BRYAN

    THIS INDENTURE made the twelfth day of September one thousand seven hun-
dred and six;   Betweene ROBERT CARTER, Esqr., of Lancastr; County, Surviving feoffee
of the TOWNE LAND of the sd. County of the one part and THO: CARTER of the sd. County
of the other part;   Wittnesseth that the sd. ROBERT CARTER for the sume of One hundred ninety two pounds of good sound merchantable tobacco hath granted unto the
sd. THO: CARTER his heires and assignes for ever one Lott or halfe acre of land wth:in
the sd. Towne now called QUEENS TOWNE, number Eighty Eight

p.   the sd. Lott lying betweene the Street called DUKE STREET & the Street called
177   FAIRFAX STREET, being the second Lott from ANNE STREET in the N. N. E. or
       uper side from sd. ANNE STREET as by the sd. Platt more plainly appeares,   To
have and to hold the sd. Lott to him the sd. THO: CARTER his heires & assignes for ever
he or they paying the Rent for the sd. Lott of one ounce of Flax seed and two ounces
of Hemp seed on the 10th day of Octobr: annually to the Directors & Benchers of the
said Towne, provided that the sd. THO: CARTER begins to build and finish wth:out delay
a house twenty foot square at the least otherwise this grant to be void and lyable to
the purchase of any other p:son;   In Wittness whereof the parties to these p:sents
have sett their hands & seales
Signed sealed and delivered in p:sence of
       HANCOCK LEE, THO: HOOPER,   ROBERT CARTER
       SHARSHALL GRASTY
    Memord. Septr. ye 12th 1706. That Livery and Seizin was this day given by ROBERT
CARTER unto THO: CARTER by the delivering of Turff and Twigg upon the sd. Lott in
p:sence of HANCOCK LEE,
            THO: HOOPER, SHARSHALL GRASTY
    Recognitr in Cur Com Lancastr: duo dicimo die 7br: 1706 et recordr
            p   JOS: TAYLOE, Clk.

    THIS INDENTURE made the eleventh dy of September one thousand seven hun-
dred and six;   Betweene ROBERT CARTER, Esqr., of Lancastr: County, surviving feofee
of the TOWNE LAND of the sd. County of the one part and ALEXANDER SWAN of the sd.
County of the other part;   Wittnesseth that the sd. ROBERT CARTER for the sume of One
hundred and ninety two pounds of good sound merchantable tobacco hath granted
unto the sd. ALEXANDER SWAN his heires and assignes for ever, one Lott or halfe acre
of land wth:in the sd. Towne now called QUEENS TOWNE number Thirty Five

p   the Lott or halfe acre of land lying on the lower side of the Street called
178   GEORGE STREET being the fifth Lott from the Broad Street called ANNE STREET
       downe towards the Creeke called MADAM BALLS CREEKE;   To have and to hold to
him the sd. ALEXANDER SWAN his heirs and assignes for ever he or they paying the
Rent of one ounce of Flax seed and two ounces of Hemp seed to the Directors or Benchers of the said Towne for the use of the sd. Towne on the 10th day of Octobr:
annually provided that the sd. ALEXANDER SWAN doe begin to build and doe finish
wth:out delay one good house twenty foot square at the least otherwise this grant to
be void and the land granted lyable to the choice of any other p:son;   In Wittness
whereof the parties to these p:sents have sett their hands and seales

Signed sealed and delivered in p:sence of
    JOHN TURBERVILE,   ROBERT CARTER
    JOSEPH HEALE, SHARSHALL GRASTY
    Memord. 7br: ye 11th 1706. That Seizin and Livery was this day given by ROBERT CARTER unto ALEXANDER SWANN by Turffe & Twigg upon the wth:in Lott in p:sence of us JOHN TURBERVILE,
    JOSEPH HEALE, SHARSHALL GRASTY
    Recognitr: in Cur Com Lancastr: 12th die 7bris: 1706 et recodr
              p   JOS: TAYLOE, Clk

THIS INDENTURE made the Eleventh day of September one thousand seven hun-dred and six; Betweene ROBERT CARTER, Esqr., of Lancastr: County, Surviving feoffee of the TOWNE LAND of the sd. County, of one part and RICHARD BAYLEY of GLOSTER County of the other part; Wittnesseth tht the sd. ROBERT CARTER for the sume of two hundred pounds of good sound merchantable tobacco hath

p.   sold unto the sd. RICHARD BAYLEY his heires and assignes for ever one Lott
179   or halfe acre of land wth:in the sd. Towne No. 54, lying on the upper side of the Street called PRINCE STREET being the second Lott from the Broad Street called ANNE STREET downe towards the Creeke called MADAM BALLS CREEKE; To have and to hold to him the sd. RICHARD BAYLEY his heires or assignes for ever, he or they paying the Rent for the sd. Lott of one ounce of Flax seed and two ounces of Hemp seed on the 10th day of Octobr: annually provided that the sd. RICHARD BAYLEY build on the sd. Lott wth:in twelve months one good house twenty foot square at the least and finish wth:out delay otherwise this grant to be void and the Lott herein granted lyable to the purchase of any other p:son. In Wittness whereof the parties to these p:sents have sett their hands and seales
Signed sealed & delivered in p:sence of
    WM: FOX, JAMES HAYNES,   ROBERT CARTER
    JOSEPH HEALE, THO: HOOPER
    Memord. Septr. the 11th 1706. That Livery and Seizin was this day given by ROBERT CARTER unto RICHARD BALEY by the delivery of Turff and Twigg upon the sd. Lott in p:sence of
    WM: FOX, JAMES HAYNES
    JOSEPH HEALE, THO: HOOPER
    Recognitr in Cur Com Lancastr: 12th die 7bris: 1706 et recordr
             p   JOS: TAYLOE, Clk.

THIS INDENTURE made the Eleventh day of September one thousand seven hundred and six; Betweene ROBERT CARTER, Esqr., of Lancastr: County, surviving feoffee of the TOWNE LAND of the sd. County of the one part and WM: LISTER of the sd. County of the other part; Wittnesseth tht the sd. ROBERT CARTER for the sume of three hundred eighty four pounds of good sound merchantable tobacco hath

p   granted unto the sd. WM: LISTER his heires and assignes for ever two Lotts of
180   land wth:in the sd. Towne now called QUEENS TOWNE, number Thirty six and Forty Two, according to the Platt threof, one of the sd. Lotts, to wit, number Thirty Six, lying on the lower side of the Street called GEORGE STREET being the lower Lott of the sd Street, and bounded by the Creeke called MADAM BALLS CREEKE contai-ning Forty five square perches; the other Lott, to wit, number Forty Two, lying on the great Street called ANNE STREET on the N. N. E. side thereof being a corner Lott on the upper side of the sd. GEORGE STREET and ANNE STREET containing halfe an acre as by

the said Platt more plainly appeares, To have and to hold the sd. two Lotts by the sd.
WM: LISTER his heires and assignes for ever, he or they paying rent for the sd. Lotts
two ounces of Flax seed and four ounces of Hemp seed on the 10th day of Octobr:
annually for the use of the said Burg, provided that the sd. WM: LISER doe begin to
build and proceed to finish one good house twenty foot square at the least, otherwise
this grant lyable to the choice and purchase of any other p:son. In Wittness whereof
the parties to these p:sents have sett their hands and seales
Signed sealed and delivered in ye p:sence of
     HANCOCK LEE, RICHARD BALEY,   ROBERT CARTER
     JOHN BRYAN
    Memord. Septr. the 12th 1706. That Livery and Seizin was this day given by
ROBERT CARTER unto WM: LISTER by the delivering of Turff and Twigg upon the sd.
Lott in the p:sence of HANCOCK LEE,
     RICHARD BALEY, JOHN BRYAN
    Recognitr: in Cur Com Lancastr: 12th die 7bris: 1706 et recordr
        p   JOS: TAYLOE, Clk

    KNOW ALL MEN by these p:sents that I HENRY SALKELD, Merchant, of the
County of Lancastr: and Collony of Virginia for divers good causes have made THOMAS
WHITE of the County & Collony aforesd. to be my lawful Attorney for me to demand
and receive from all manner of persons all such sums of money and tobaccoe as are
to me

p   in any wise due let it be either by Bond, Account or otherwise and allsoe
181   giveing my sd. Attorney all my full power to prosecute in my name in any
     Court of Judication in this Collony of Virginia both in Common Law and Equity
for the better recovering of the same and upon recovery to deliver acquittances or
other sufficient discharges in my name as if I were then p:sonally p:sent and I doe by
these p:sents authorize and impower my sd. Attorney to receive all manner of goods &
merchandise directed to me by any Ship or Vessell whatsoever either in the Collony
of Virginia or in the Province of MARYLAND, and performe all lawfull acts about the
pr:misses as shall be needfull in as ample a manner as I my selfe might or could doe
were I p:sonally p:sent. as Wittness my hand and seale this twenty first day of August
one thousand seven hundred and six
     JOHN WILLCOCKES,   HENRY SALKELD
     RICHARD WORRALL
    Proved ye 11th Septr: ano 1706 et recordr.
        p   JOS: TAYLOE, Clk.

    THIS INDENTURE made the twelfth day of September in the fifth yeare of the
reigne of or: Sovereigne Lady Ann &c., and in the yeare of or: Lord one thousand
seven hundred and six; Betweene JOHN HALL of County of Lancastr:, Inholder, of the
one part and WM: BALL of the sd. Coty., Gent., of other part; Wittnesseth tht the sd.
JOHN HALL for the sume of fifty pounds Sterling money of England have granted
unto the sd. WM: BALL his heires and assignes, the full and just quantity of One hun-
ded and fivety acres of land being in the Coty. of Lancastr: and Parish of White Chapp-
pell and bounded as followeth, vizt., Beginning at the head of a small Creeke or
Branch of GRIMES his CREEKE, thence North Westerly to a corner tree neer

p.   the EAGLES NEST, thence West South West eighty one poles, thence South one
182   seventy seven degees East fifty poles to GRIMES his CREEKE, thence downe
     alongst the sd. Creeke its severall courses to the place where it first begun,

which sd. land is part of a Patent of Three hundred acres of land first granted to
THOMAS HARWOOD which sd. Pattent bears date the fourteenth day of November one
thousand six hundred fourty & nine, and by the sd. HARWOOD sold and assigned to
JOHN SHARP and by and by seveall assignmts. sold and conveyed downe to the sd.
JOHN HALL as by the sd. Conveyances relacon being had may more fully appeare;   To
have and to hold the sd. tract of land wth: appurtenances belonging as allsoe all the
rights which sd. JOHN HALL now hath or may claim unto the sd. WM: BALL his heires
or assignes henceforth for ever, subject nevertheless unto the Quitt Rents which
shall grow due and that the sd. WM: BALL his heires and assignes quietly hold & enjoy the same wth:out the trouble of him the sd. JOHN HALL or any p:sons whatsoever;
In Wittness whereof the parties mentioned in this p:sent Indenture hath hereunto
sett their hands and seales the day and yeare first abovementioned
Signed sealed and delivered in p:sence of us
        JAMES BALL,   JOSEPH BALL, JUNR.   JOHN HALL
        JOSEPH HEALE
    Memord.   That on the day and yeare wth:in mentioned the wth:in mentioned JOHN
HALL entred into the wth:in mentioned pr:misses & thereof delivered quiet and
peaceable possession of the wth:in mentioned land and pr:misses to the with:in mentioned WM: BALL by

p   .delivering him the Ring of the Great Doore of the Cheif Mansion House of the
183   sd. pr:misses and putting him in the peaceable possession thereof in the name
        and token of Livery and Seizin of the wth:in mentioned pr:misses in the
p:sence of us whose names are hereto subscribed
        JAMES BALL,   JOSEPH BALL, JUNR.,
        JOSEPH HEALE
    Recognitr in Cur Com Lancastr: duo dicimo die Septembris 1706 et recordr
                p   JOS: TAYLOE, Clk.

    THIS INDENTURE made this eighth day of February Anno Dom: 1697 and in the
fourth yeare of the Reigne of or: Sovereigne Lord & Lady, William and Mary, by the
grace of God &c.,   Betweene ROBERT NEASUM of the Coty: of Lancastr: in RAPPA-
HANOCK RIVER in Virginia, Planer, Son and heire of WILLIAM NEASUM, late of the sd.
Coty., deced., of the one part and MATHIAS GILES of the same Coty, Planter, of the
other part;   Wittnesseth that the sd. ROBERT NEASUM for a valuable consideracon by
these p:sents hath granted unto the sd. MATHIAS GILES his heires and assignes all
that tract of land whereon the sd. MATHIAS GILES now liveth scituate in the Pish: of
Wite Chappell and Coty. aforesd. wth: all houses orchards fences which said tract of
land is part of a Pattent of Five hundred and fifty acres granted unto the sd. WM: NEA-
SUM and others by Pattent bearing date the 29th day of January 1649; as by the sd.
Pattent more fully and at large appeares and is bounded as followeth; vizt., Beginning
at a corner red Oakeof THOMAS WILDGOS now belonging to THOMAS PHILLIPS, thence
running East six degrees South 71 poles to a corner Pine standing in Mr. WILLIAM
MERRIMANs Line, thence along MERRIMANs line North a quarter of a point East 112
poles to a corner Pine of sd. MERRIMANs and Mr. ROBERT NEASUMs, thence along
NEASUMs line W. S. W. 110 poles to a Cedar Post being a corner post of THOMAS WILD-
GOS, now belonging to THOMAS PHILLIPS, thence along PHILLIPS Line of marked
trees S. S. E. 68 poles to the corner red Oake where it first began;   To have and to hold
the sd. Plantacon and pr:misses and every part thereof unto the sd. MATHIAS GILES
his heires and assignes for ever in as large and ample manner as are exprest in the
Pattent of the sd. Land and by the Rents and Services therein mentioned to be due ,
And the sd. ROBERT NEASUM doth for himselfe promise to warrant and defend the

aforesd. Plantacon unto the sd. MATHIAS GILES his heires and

p.   assignes for ever against every p:son whatsoever that shall at any time here-
184   after make any claime and allsoe that the sd. ROBERT NEASUM shall acknowledge this pr:sent Indenture in the Coty: Court of Lancastr: according to Law
and that FRANCES NEASUM, his now Wife, shall by her selfe or Attorney acknowledge in the sd. Court her right of Dower in the pr:misses;   In Wittness whereof, the
sd. ROBERT NEASUM to this Indenture have hereunto putt his hand and seale the day
and yeare first above mentioned
Signed sealed and delivered in p:sence of
    JAMES WOOD,   ROBERT NEASUM
    JOHN HARRIS
    Recognitr: in Cur Com Lancastr: duo decimo die Aprillis 1693 et record decimo
septimo die sequen   JOHN STRETCHLEY

    KNOW ALL MEN by these pr:sents that I MATHIAS GILES doe assigne all my
right of this wth:in mentioned Deed to THOMAS CHITWOOD to him and his heires from
me my heires or assignes for ever, as Wittness my hand this 13th day of July 1698
                        MATHIAS GILES
                        MARGRT. GILES
    Recognitr in Cur Com Lancastr: 14th die Septr: 1698 p MATH: GILES et MARGTT.
Uxor. et record 16th die   p   JOS: TAYLOE, Clk.
    Acknowledged in the County Court of Lancastr: the 9th day of Octobr: 1702 p THO:
CHITWOOD   Test   JOS: TAYLOE, Clk
    Acknowledged p MATHIAS GILES and his Wife to JNO: REEVES Septr. the 11th 1706 et
recordr   p.   JOS. TAYLOE, Clk

p.   TO ALL TO WHOME these p:sents shall come Greeting. Whereas there is a
185   Marriage shortly to be solemnized by and betweene HUGH LADNER of the Pish:
    of St. Marys White Chappel in the Coty: of Lancastr:, Gent., & SUSANNA PAINE
of the sd. Coty., and Pish; Widow, Know ye therefore that I SUSANNA PAINE for a
valuable consideracon in hand reced., of the sd. HUGH LADNER have sold and doe by
these p:sents give unto the sd. HUGH LADNER his heires & assignes for ever foure
Negroes (vizt) two men named James and Will and two women named Marreah and
Bess, (togeather) wth: all and every their future encrease, the sd. Negroes now being
in the actuall possession of the sd. SUSANNA PAINE; To have and to hold the aforesd.
Negroes unto HUGH LADNER his heires and assignes for ever as allsoe all the
encrease of the sd. Marreah and Bess, male and female, to his the sd. HUGH LADNER
his heires and assignes for evermore wth:out the lawfull hindrance of the sd.
SUSANNA PAINE my heires or any other p:sons claiming undr: me.   In Wittness
whereof I have hereunto sett my hand and seale this 13th day of November 1706
Signed sealed and delivered in p:sence of us
    THO: MARTIN,   SUSANNA PAYNE
    PATRICK MACKRONE

    TO ALL TO WHOME thse p:sents shall come Greeting. Whereas there is by the
grace of God a Marriage intended and shortly to be had betweene WM: MERIDITH of
the Coty. of Lancastr:, Planter, and MARY LAWRENCE, Widow, of the sd. County; Know
ye therefore that in consideracon of the naturall love & affection I have unto her the
sd. MARY LAWRENCE, as for divers other good consideracons doe give unto the sd.
MARY LAWRENCE one halfe of my p:sonall Estate that I now have or shall die possest
of to be disposed of by her the sd. MARY as she shall see fitt, provided nevertheless

that if the sd. MARY shall die before the sd. WILLIAM MERIDETH, then the sd. Estate shall be equally divided amongst the minor Children of her the sd. MARY begotten of her body by WM: LAWRENCE, deced., and to no other use whatsoever, and further it is agreed betweene the sd. WM: MERIDITH and the sd. MARY LAWRENCE tht she shall be seized of the whole p the delivery of one piece of Silver being part of the pr:misses commonly known by the name of RYALTIES SEVEN PENCE HALFE PENNY in token of the whole;   In Wittness whereof I have hereunto sett my hand and seale this eleventh day of November 1706

Sealed and delivered in p:sence of
    JOS: TAYLOE,
    JNO; RANKIN

WILLIAM ✝ MERRIDITH

    Recognitr in Cur Com Lancastr: 14th die 9bris: Ano Dom: 1706 et recordr
        p   JOS: TAYLOE, Clk

p.   THIS INDENTURE made the Eleventh day of Novemer Ano Dom: 1706, and in
186   the fifth yeare of or: Sovereigne Lady Anne &c.   Betweene MARY LAWRENCE of the Coty: of Lancastr: and Pish: of St. Marys White Chappell of the one part and JOSEPH TAYLOE of the Pish: and Coty: aforesd. of the other part;   Wittnesseth that the sd. MARY LAWRENCE for the sume of five shillings Sterling to her paid doth discharge the sd. JOSEPH TAYLOE his heires and assignes for ever and hath granted unto him the sd. JOSEPH TAYLOE and his assignes Fifty acres of land belonging to the Plantacon whereon the said MARY LAWRENCE now liveth together wth: all houses woods timber with its appurtenances unto him the sd. JOSEPH TAYLOE and his assignes for the terme of ninety nine yeares or for and dureing the naturall life of WM: MERRIDITH of the Pish: and Coty: aforesd: To have and to hold the aforesd. Fifty acres of land and pr:misses wth: the appurtenances, one third part of the Orchard only excepted and reserved for the use of FRANCIS WRIGHT his heires or assignes for and dureing the terme of ninety nine yeares or during the naturall life of him the sd. WM: MERRIDITH which shall first happen, with the confidence nevertheless that the sd. MARY LAWRENCE shall have & enjoy the aforesaid Land and pr:misses wth: the appurtenances dureing her naturall life wth:out controules (except as before excepted) any thing in this Deed to the contrary notwithstanding,   And after to revert to the heires of the body of the said MARY LAWRENCE begotten by her late Husband, FRANCIS WRIGHT, according as her Will in Writeing or Deed of Gift she the said MARY LAWRENCE shall see fitt to dispose of the same;   In Wittness whereof to this p:sent Indenure I have hereunto sett my hand and affixed my seale the day and yeare first above written

Sealed and delivered in p:sence of us
    JNO: RANKIN,
    FRANCISCO FRIZELL

MARY *M* LAWRENCE

    Recognitr in Cur Com Lancastr: 14th die 9bris: Ano Dom 1706 et recordr.
        p   JOS: TAYLOE, Clk.

    KNOW ALL MEN by these pr:sents that whereas there is by Gods grace a Marriage to be solemnized betweene the within named WM: MERRIDITH and the wth:in named MARY LAWRENCE;   Therefore for the sume of five shillings Sterling to me paid I doe hereby discharge him the sd. WM: MERRIDITH his heires & assignes and have granted and assigned over unto the sd. WM: MERRIDITH dureing the terme of his naturall life all my right of the wth:in Indentures according to the meaning of the articles and exception therein contained from me my heires or Administratrs: for ever;   To have and to hold to him the sd. WM: MERRIDITH dureing the terme aforesd. subject nevertheless to the Quitt Rents to be yearely paid to the Lord of the Fee or Fees

of his Manor of Greenwich in free and common soccage;   In Wittness whereof I have
sett my hand this Eleventh day of November 1706
Sealed and delivered in p:sence of
    JNO: RANKIN,   JOS: TAYLOE
    FRANCISCOE FRIZELL
   Recognitr in Cur Com Lancastr: 14th die 9bris: 1706
          p   JOS: TAYLOE, et recordr

p.   KNOW ALL MEN by these pr:sents that I JAMES HAYNES of the Coty. of PRIN-
187   CESS ANN doe make and appoint my true & well beloved Friend, GEORGE
FLOWER of the Coty: of Lancastr: to be my true & lawfull Attorney for me to sue
for and recover all debts due unto the sd. HAYNES and likewise for to pay all debts due
from me as far as my sd. Attorney hath effects in his hands and likewise to ratifie all
that my sd. Attorney shall doe;   In Wittness whereof I have hereunto sett my hand
and fixt my seale this 10th dy of August 1706
Signed sealed and delivered in p:sence of
    JOHN *Ch* BROWN,   JAMES HAYNES
    THOMAS ᴣ SIMMONS

KNOW ALL MEN by these p:sents that I ROBERT HALL, Merchant, for divers
consideracons have made & doe appoint my well beloved Friend, Capt. THO: PINCKARD
of Lancastr: Coty: & Mr. JOHN STEPTOE of NORTHUMBERLAND Coty., in the Collony of
Virginia, Gent., to be my true and lawfull Attorneys joyntly and severally for me to
demand sue for and receive from all manner of p:sons whatsoever dwelling wth:in
the Collony of Virginia all sumes of money tobaccoe or any other goods wares or
merchandizes oweing to me; giveing and hereby granting to my sd. Attorneys and
either of them my full power to doe all such things in the Law as shall be necessary
for the recovering of all such sumes of money or merchandizes and acquittances or
other discharges from me to deliver and generally to performe all & singular my
affaires in Virginia as fully as I might or could doe were I p:sonally p:sent, confirming and allowing all my sd. Attorneys shall lawfully doe or cause to be done about
the pr:misses;   In Wittness whereof I have hereunto sett my hand and seale this
twenty third day of August 1705
Signed sealed and delivered in p:sence of us
    ROBERT SCHOLFIELD,   ROBERT HALL
    THOMAS HATHAWAY

p.   BY THIS PUBLIC INSTRUMENT or Letter of Attorney be it evident to all men
188   that before me, JNO: HUMPHRY, Notary Public duly sworn dwelling in BEL-
FAST & of the wittnesses hereundr: subscribing p:sonally appeared HENRY
CHADS, ROBT: ANDREWS, JNO: McMUN, JNO: GREG, ROBT: WILSON & JNO: ECCLES in
behalfe of themselves and partners, Owners of the Ship "CHARLES of BELFAST" and
did appoint and by these pr:sents in their stead & place putt GABRIEL HOLMS of
ELIZABETH RIVER in Virginia their true and lawfull Attorney to their use to call to
Account Mr. CARTER of RAPPAHANNOCK & Major BUSH of their and each of their
transactions for these Constituants p:suant to a Lettr: of Attorney from JNO: MOOR its
superacargo upon the sd. Ship, "CHARLES"   and to take the effects Bills and Notes out
of their hands & to ask sue for recover & receive all such debts quantitites of tobaccoe
or other things as stand due to these Constituants by any p:sons in Virginia whatsoever and upon payment made acquittances deliver & in generall performe by himselfe or any p:son undr: him every act & thing in the Law for recovery as fully to all
intents as the Constituants might doe if p:sonally p:sent, ratifying whatsoever the sd.

Attorney shall lawfully doe by vertue of these p:sents; As Wittness their hands and seales this third day of Febry: Ano Dom: one thousand seven hundred and five 1705/6 Signed sealed and dd. in p:sence of us

JNO: GREEN   HEN: CHADS
HUGH HENRY   ROBT: ANDREWS
JNO: BOYD   JNO: ECCLES
JNO: HUMPHRY. Notr: Publ.   JNO: McMUN
                                                  ROBERT WILSON
                                                  JNO: GREG

Probatr: Lettr: de Attor: in Cur Com Lancastr: dicimo tertio die 9bris Ano Dom: 1706 et record 16th die p   JOS: TAYLOE, Clk

THIS INDENTURE made the 14th dy of September in the yeare of or: Lord God one thousand seven hundred and six; Betweene EDWARD TOMLIN of the Pish: of St. Marys White Chapple and Coty: of Lancastr: of the one part and NICHOLAS MARTIN of the Pish: of Xt. Churh in Coty: of Lancastr: of the other part; Wittnesseth that the sd. EDWARD TOMLIN for the sume of five shills: Sterling money of England & one Mare of the value of twelve hundred pounds of tobbo: and casque, ath granted to farm letten unto NICHOLAS MARTIN his heires & assignes all that his messuage or farm house now or late in the tenure & occupacon of him the sd. EDWARD TOMLIN whereon THOMAS SANDERS now liveth scituate in the Pish: of St. Marys White Chapple in the Coty: aforesd. wth: the appurtenances houses barns orchards woods timber to the sd. land belonging dureing the full terme of eleven whole yeares commencing from the twenty and fifth day of December next ensueing the date hereof; To have and to hold the said tenemts. or farm house

p.   and other the demised pr:misses unto the sd. NICHO: MARTIN his heires &
189   assignes for the full and whole terme of Eleven yeares as aforesd., paying to
        the sd. EDWARD TOMLIN his heires or Administratrs: on the twenty fifth day of December every yeare dureing the terme aforesd., one eare of Indian Corne in token of acknowledgment; And if it shall happen that the sd. yearly rent shall be unpaid by the space of two months next over the aforesd. twenty fifth day of December in which the same ought to be paid being lawfully demanded, from thence forth it shall be lawfull for the sd. EDWARD TOMLIN his heires or Administratrs: to reenter and enjoy as in his or their former Estate & from thence utterly to expell and putt out, And it is further agreed betweene the sd. parties that the sd. NICHOLAS MARTIN his Exrs. or assignes at the expiracon of the sd. terme shall redeliver to the sd. EDWARD TOMLIN possession of the sd. Land & pr:misses in tenantable repaire. In Wittness whereof the party first above named hath hereunto sett his hand and seale the day and yeare first above written
Sealed and delivered in p:sence of us
        JOS: TAYLOE,   EDWARD ⌐T⌐ TOMLIN
        JNO: HALL, DRAKE DRUMMOND
        Recognitr: in Cur Com Lancastr: ye 12th die 9bris: 1706 et recordr
                p   JOS: TAYLOE, Clk

THIS INDENTURE made the thirteenth day of November in the fifth yeare of the reigne of or: Sovereigne Lady Anne &c., Ano Dom: one thousand seven hundred and six; Between THOMAS TAYLOR of the Pish: of GREAT WICOCOMOCO in the County of NORTHUMBERLAND, Planter, and ELIZABETH his Wife, one of the Daughters of WM: THERRIOTT, late of St. Marys White Chapple and Coty: of Lancastr: aforesd., Widow, of the one part and ELLEN HEALE of the Pish: of St. Marys White Chapple and Coty: of

Lancastr: aforesd., Widow, of the other part;   Wittnesseth that THO: TAYLOR and ELIZA-BETH his Wife for the just sume of One hundred pounds of good and lawfull money of England doe fully sell unto the sd. ELLEN HEALE her heires & assignes the full and just quantity of Five hundred acres of land being in the aforesd. Coty: of Lancastr: & Pish:

p
190
of St. Marys White Chapple & bounded as followeth, (vizt) Beginning at a cor-ner Stake of Capt. RICHD: BALLs standing on a Point of THERRIOTTs head lines thence South East fifty pole to a Branch of FOXES MILL SWAMP, thence down the sd. Branch the severall courses thereof to a corner Ash standing neere the mouth of a Branch by the Run, being alsoe in THERRIOTTs head line, thence downe the sd. Branch & FOXES MILL SWAMP South ten degrees East ninety pole, thence West South West thirty two pole, thence South South West twenty pole, thence South West thirty seven pole to a corner white Oake standing by the side of the Maine Swamp, thence North forty four degrees West three hundred & eighty pole to the first mentioned Stake where it firt began, which sd. Land is part of a p:cell of Eight hundred and fifty acres of land given in copartnership to ANNE THERRIOTT & ELIZABETH THERRIOTT, party to these p:sents by WM: THERRIOTT aforesd., the naturall Father of the sd. ANNE & ELIZABETH by Deed of Gift bearing date the Eleventh day of Febry: 1688/9 & authentiqually acknowledged in Lancastr: Coty: and is upon the Records in the sd. Coty: of which sd. Five hundred acres is the one moiety of the sd. Eight hundred & fifty acres given to the sd. ELIZABETH, party to these p:sents as aforesd., and the other part of the sd. five hundred acres being part of a tract of land belonging to the aforesd. THOMAS TAYLOR adjoyning upon the first mention'd part of the aforesd. five hundred;   To have and to hold the aforesd. five hundred acres of land with all profitts and appurtenances belonging unto the sd. ELEN HEALE her heires and assignes from henceforth & for ever subject unto the Quitt Rents which become due and peaceably and quietly to hold and enjoy the same wth:out the trouble of us the sd. THO: & ELIZA-BETH our assignes or any other p:son

p.
191
In Wittness whereof the parties above mentioned have hereunto sett their hands & fixed their seales the day and yeare first above mentioned
Signed sealed and delivered in p:sence of
JOS: TAYLOE, DAN: McCARTY,   THOMAS TAYLOR
RICHD: BUSHROD   ELIZABETH TAYLOR
Recognitr in Cur Com Lancastr: 13th die 9bris: 1706 et recordr
          p   JOS: TAYLOE, Clk.

THIS INDENTURE made the fourteenth day of Novembr: one thousand seven hundred and six;   Betweene ROBERT CARTER, Esqr., of Lancastr: Coty: surviving feoffee of ye TOWNE LAND of the sd. Coty: of the one part and WM: DARE of the same Coty: of the other part;   Wittnesseth that the said ROBERT CARTER for the sume of One hundred eighty eight pounds of good sound merchantable tobaccoe hath granted unto the sd. WM: DARE his heires one Lott of land lying wth:in the sd. Towne now called QUEENS TOWNE, No. Sixty Seven, according to the Platt thereof, the sd. Lott lying on the Creeke called MADAM BALLS CREEKE at the head of the sd. Creeke & on the N. N. E. side of the Lane called BALLS LANE being the Lott next the Creeke as by ye sd. Platt more plainly appeares;   To have and to hold the sd. Lott to him the sd. WM: DARE in as full manner as is directed by Act of Assembly made at a Genll. Assembly begun at WMS: BURGH the 23d day of Octobr: 1705, intituled "An Act for Establishing Ports & Townes" he paying for the sd. Lott one ounce of Flax seed and two ounces of Hemp seed annually to the Directors and Benchers of the sd. Towne, Provided that the sd. (blank) do begin twelve months afer the date hereof and finish wth:out delay one good House twenty foot square at the least, otherwise this grant to be void and the Lott lyable to the purchase of any other person according to Law as fully

p.   as is this grant had never been made.   In Wittness whereof the parties to this
192   Indenture have interchangably sett their hands & seales
        Signed sealed & delivered in p:sence of
        WM: FOX,   EDWIN CONWAY,   ROBERT CARTER
        RICHD: BALL
      Memord. November the 14th 1706.   That Livery Seizin of possession was this day given by the wth:in named ROBERT CARTER unto the wth:in named WM: DARE by the delivery of Turff & Twigg on the sd. land in the p:sene of us
        JOSEPH HEALE,
        JO: BALL, JUNR.,   RICHD: BALL
      Recognitr in Cur Com Lancastr: 14th die 9bris: 1706 p ROBERT CARTER et recordr
              p   JOS: TAYLOE, Clk

      THIS INDENTURE made the fourteenth day of Novembr: one thousand seven hundred and six;   Betweene ROBERT CARTER, Esqr. of Lancastr: Coty., Surviving Feoffee of the TOWNE LAND of the sd. Coty., of the first part and WM: HOWARD of the other part;   Wittnesseth that the sd. ROBERT CARTER for the sume of One hundred eighty eight pounds of good merchantable tobbo: hath granted unto the sd. WM: HOWARD his heires & assignes one Lott or halfe acre of land wth:in the sd. Towne now called QUEENS TOWNE No. Thirteen, bounded by the Street called KING STREET on the lower side thereof being the first lott on the sd. Street from the Great Street called ANNE STREET downe towards the Creeke called MADAM BALLS CREEKE;   To have and to hold the sd. Lott paying Rent of one ounce of Flax seed and two ounces of Hemp seed on the 10th day of Octobr: annually, provided that the sd. WM: HOWARD doe begin to build on the sd. Lott wth:in twelve months one house twenty foot square at the least otherwise this grant to be void and lyable to the purchase of any other p:son;   In Wittness whereof the parties have sett their hands and seales

p.   Signed sealed and delivered in p:sence of
        WM: BALL,   WM: KIGHT,   ROBERT CARTER
        SHARSHALL GRASTY
      Memord. Novembr: the 14th 1706.   That Seizin and possession was given of the wth:-in Lott by delivering of possession of the Dwelling House built on the sd. Lott by the sd. HOWARD upon the incouragemt. of an Order of Court before the date of this Deed, in the p:sence of us
        WM: BALL,   JOS: BALL, JUNR.
        EDWIN CONWAY,   JOSEPH HEALE
      Recognitr in Cur Com Lancastr: 14th die 9bris: 1706 p ROBERT CARTER et recordr
              p   JOS: TAYLOE, Clk.

      THIS INDENTURE made the fourteenth day of Novembr: one thousand seven hundred and six;   Betweene ROBERT CARTER, Esqr. of Lancastr: Coty. Surviving Feoffee of the TOWNE LAND of the sd. Coty., of the first part and WM: KIGHT of the other part;   Wittnesseth that the sd. ROBERT CARTER for the sume of one hundred eighty eight pounds of tobbo: to him paid hath granted unto the sd. WM: KIGHT his heires & assignes for ever one halfe acre of land wth:in the sd. Towne now called QUEENS TOWNE, the sd. Lott being numbered Seventy Four, and bounded by ye Street called FAIRFAX STREET on the lower side thereof being the Lott on the sd. Street from

the upper side of the Great Street called ANNE STREET; To have and to hold the sd. Lott or halfe acre of land to him the sd. WM: KIGHT his heires & assignes for ever, he or they paying rent for the sd. Lott one ounce of Flax seed and two ounces of Hemp seed on the tenth day of Octorbr: annually to the Directors or Benchers of the sd. Towne, provided if the sd. WM: KIGHT doe begin to build on the sd. Lott wth:in twelve months one good house twenty foot square at the least otherwise this grant to be void & the Lott granted lyable to the purchase of any other p:son according to Law; In Wittness whereof ye sd. parties have sett their hands & seales
Signed sealed and delivered in the p:sence of
    WM: FOX, WM: DARE,   ROBERT CARTER
    JNO: CARNEGIE

p.   Memord. Novembr: the 14th 1706. That Livery & Seizen was this day given by
194   ROBERT CARTER unto WM: KIGHT by the delivery of Turff & Twigg upon the sd. Lott by the sd. CARTER to the sd. KIGHT in p:sence of us
    JOSEPH HEALE, WM: DARE
    EDWIN CONWAY
    Recognitr in Cur Com Lancastr: quarto dicimo die 9bris: 1706 p ROBERT CARTER et
recordr   p   JOS: TAYLOE, Clk.

THIS INDENTURE made the thirteenth day of Novembr: one thousand seven hundred and six; Betweene ROBERT CARTER, Esqr. of Lancastr: County, Surviving Feoffee of the TOWNE LAND of the sd. Coty. of the one part and JOSEPH BALL, JUNR. of the other part; Wittnesseth that the sd. ROBERT CARTER in consideracon of the sume of one hundred and eighty eight pounds of tobbo: to him paid hath granted unto the sd. JOSEPH BALL, JUNR. his heires & assignes for ever one Lott or halfe acre of land wth:in the sd. Towne now called QUEENS TOWNE, the sd. Lott or halfe acre of land being No. Fourty One, bounded by the Street called GEORGE STREET on the upper side being the first Lott on the sd. Street, from the Great Street called ANNE STREET downe towards the Creeke called MADAM BALLS CREEKE, as by the sd. Platt appeares; To have and to hold the sd. Lott to him the sd. JOSEPH BALL, JUNR. his heires & assignes for ever; he or they paying the Rent for the said Lott one ounce of Flax seed and two ounces of Hemp seed on the 10th day of Octobr: annually, provided the sd. JOSEPH BALL, JUNR. doe begin to build on the sd. Lott wth:in twelve months one good House twenty foot square at the least otherwise this grant to be void and lyable to the purchase of any other p:son; In Wittness whereof the parties to these p:sents have hereunto sett their hands & seales
Signed sealed & delivered in the p:sence of
    JOS: TAYLOE, JOS: HEALE,   ROBERT CARTER
    THO: HOOPER

p.   Memord. That Livery & Seizin was this day given by ROBERT CARTER unto
195   JOSEPH BALL, JUNR. by the delivery of Turff and Twigg upon the sd. Lott by the sd. CARTER to the sd. BALL, Novembr: the 14th 1706 in p:sence of us
    RICHD: BALL, JOSEPH HEALE,
    WM: DARE
    Recognitr in Cur Com Lancastr: quarto dicimo die 9bris: 1706 p ROBERT CARTER et
recordr: p   JOS: TAYLOE, Clk

THIS INDENTURE made the fourteenth day of Novembr: one thousand seven hundred and six; Betweene ROBERT CARTER, Esqr., of Lancastr: Coty., Surviving Feoffee of the TOWNE LAND of the sd. Coty. of the one part and JOSEPH HEALE of the other part; Wittnesseth that the sd. ROBERT CARTER for the sume of One hundred and eighty eight pounds of good sound merchantable tobbo: to him paid hath sold unto the said JOSEPH HEALE his heires and assignes for ever one Lott of land containing halfe an acre wth:in the Towne now called QUEENS TOWNE, No. Fifty One, according to the Platt thereof, the sd. Lott lying on the lower side of the Street called PRINCESS STREET being the fourth Lott on the sd. Street from the Great Street called ANNE STREET downe towards the Creeke called MADAM BALLS CREEKE as by the sd. Platt appeares; To have & to hold the sd. Lott to him the sd. JOSEPH HEALE his heires & assignes he or they paying rent for the sd. Lott one ounce of Flax seed and two ounces of Hemp seed on the 10th day of Octobr: annually to the Directors or Benchers of the sd. Towne for the use of the sd. Burgh; Provided that the sd. JOSEPH HEALE doe being to build on the sd. Lott wth:in twelve months after the date hereof and doe proceed to finish one good House twenty foot square at the least, otherwise this granted to be void and the Lott lyable to the choice of any other p:son as fully as if this grant had never been made; In Wittness whereof the partys to these p:sents have sett their hands and seales

Signed sealed and delivered in p:sence of
  RICHD: BALL, ROBERT GIBSON,   ROBERT CARTER
  WM: KIGHT

p.   Memord. That Livery & Seizin was this day given by ROBERT CARTER unto
196   JOSEPH HEALE by delivery of Turff and Twiff upon the sd. Lott by the sd. CARTER to the sd. HEALE in p:sence of
  EDWIN CONWAY,
  WM: DARE, WM: KIGHT
  Recognitr in Cur Com Lancastr: 14th die 9bris: 1706 et recordr
          p   JOS: TAYLOE, Clk

THIS INDENTURE made the Thirteenth day of Novembr: in the fifth yeare of the reign of or: Sovereigne Lady Queen Ann one thousand seven hundred & six, Betweene ROBERT CARTER, Esqr. of Lancastr: Coty., Surviving Feoffee of the TOWNE LAND of the sd. Coty. of the one part and JOHN CARNEGIE of NORTHUMBERLAND Coty. of the other part; Wittnesseth that the sd. ROBERT CARTER for the sume of One hundred eighty eight pounds of good sound merchantable tobbo: to him paid hath sold unto the sd. JNO: CARNEGIE his heires and assignes one Lott or halfe acre of land wth:in the sd. Towne, now called QUEENS TOWNE, No. Twenty Five, according to the Platt thereof, the sd. Lott being on the N. N. E. or upper side of the Street called ANNE STREET & on upper side of KING STREET being a coner to the sd. two Streets as by the said Platt more plainly appeares, To have and to hold the sd. Lott to him the sd. JNO: CARNEGIE his heires and assignes for ever; he or they paying rent for the sd. Lott one ounce of Flax seed and two ounces of Hemp seed on the 10th day of Octobr: annually to the Directors or Benchers of the sd. Towne, Provided that the sd. JNO: CARNEGIE doe begin to build on the sd. Lott and doe proceed to finish wth:in twelve months one good House twenty foot square at the least otherwise this grant to be void & the Lott herein granted lyable to the purchase of any other p:son; In Wittness whereof the parties to these p:sents have sett their hands & seales

Signed sealed and delivered in p:sence of
  RICHD: BALL,   EDWIN CONWAY,   ROBERT CARTER
  SHARSHALL GRASTY
  Memord. Novembr: 13th 1706. That Livery & Seizen was given by ROBERT CARTER to the wth:in named JNO: CARNEGIE

p.   by the delivering of Turff and Twigg on the sd. Lott in p:sence of us
197   EDWIN CONWAY
      WM: BALL,   SHARSHALL GRASTY
      Recognitr in Cur Com Lancastr: 14th die 9bris: 1706 et recordr
                p   JOS: TAYLOE, Clk

      THIS INDENTURE made the Fourteenth day of Novembr: one thousand seven
hundred and six;   Betweene ROBERT CARTER, Esqr., of Lancastr: County, Surviving
Feoffee of the TOWNE LAND of ye sd. County of one part and JOSEPH BALL of ye same
Coty. of the other part;   Wittnesseth that the sd. CARTER for the sume of one hundred
eighty eight pounds of good sound merchantable tobbo: hath sold unto the sd. JOSEPH
BALL his heires and assignes for ever one Lott or halfe acre of Land wth:in the sd.
Towne, now called QUEENS TOWNE,   No. Nineteen, according to the Platt thereof made,
the sd. Lott lying on the upper side of KING STREET being the first Lott upon MADAM
BALLS BREEKE next to the sd. KING STREET as by the sd. Platt more plainly appeares;
To have and to hold the sd. Lott to him the sd. JOSEPH BALL his heires nd assignes for
ever, he or they paying the rent for the sd. Lott one ounce of Flax seed and two
ounces of Hemp seed to the Directors or Benchers of the sd. Towne on the 10th day of
Octobr: annually, Provided that the sd. JOSEPH BALL doe begin to build on the sd. Lott
and doe proceed to finish wth:in twelve months after the date hereof one good House
twenty foot square at the least otherwise this grant to be void and lyable to the purchase of any other p:son.   In Wittness whereof the parties to these p:sents have sett
their hands and seales
Signed sealed & delivered in p:sence of
      WM: FOX,   ROBERT CARTER
      EDWIN CONWAY, RICHD: BALL
   Memord. Novembr: ye 14th 1706. That Livery & possession was this day given by
ROBERT CARTER unto the wth:in named JOSEPH BALL by the delivery of Turff and
Twigg on the sd. Land in the p:sence of us
      WM: DARE,
      EDWIN CONWAY, JOSEPH HEALE
      Recognitr: in Cur Com Lancastr: 14th die 9bris: 1706 et recordr
                p   JOS: TAYLOE, Clk.

p.   THIS INDENTURE made the Fourteenth day of Novembr: in the fifth yeare of
198   the reigne of or: Sovereigne Lady Queen Anne Annoq: Dom: one thousand
        seven hundred and six;   Betweene ROBERT CARTER, Esqr., of Lancastr: Coty.
Suviving Feoffee of the TOWNE LAND of the sd. Coty., and purchased by Capt. DAVID
FOX, deceased, and the sd. ROBERT CARTER the Feoffees appointed for the sd. Land of
Capt. WILLIAM BALls, alsoe deceased, for the use of the sd. Coty as appeares by Deed
of Conveyance from the sd. WILLIAM BALL to the sd. Feoffees bearing date the
Eleventh day of May 1692, and acknowledged in the Court of the Coty: on the same
Eleventh of May of the one part and ROBERT GIBSON of the other part;   Wittnesseth
that the sd. ROBERT CARTER for and in consideracon of the sume of one hundred and
eighty eight pounds of good sound merchantable tobacco to him in hand paid, the
receipt whereof he the sd. ROBERT CARTER, doth acknowledge, and doth acquit and
discharge the sd. ROBERT GIBSON from the same, hath granted bargained and sold and
doth by these pr:sents grant bargain and sell unto the said ROBERT GIBSON his heires
and assignes for ever one Lott or halfe acre of land wth:in the Towne now called
QUEENS TOWNE, according to the Platt thereof made and laid of into Lotts the first day
of August last by HARRY BEVERLEY, Surveyr:, pursuant to an Order of Lancastr: Court
made the Eleventh day of July last, the sd. Lott or halfe acre being No. Three, and

bounded by the Street called MALBROUGH STREET on the upper side thereof being the fourth Lott on the sd. Street from the Great Street called ANNE STREET downe towards the Creeke called MADAM BALLS CREEKE as by the sd. Platt more plainly appeares; To have and to hold the sd. Lott or halfe acre of land to him the sd. ROBERT GIBSON his heires and assignes for ever in as full and ample manner as is directed by one Act of Assembly made at a Genll. Assembly begun at WMS:BURGH the 23d day of October 1705 intituled, "An Act for Establishing Ports & Towns," he or they paying rent for the sd. Lott one ounce of Flax seed and two ounces of Hemp seed on the 10th day of Octobr: annualll to the Directors or Benchers of the sd. Towne or Burg according to the directions of the sd. Act; Provided that the sd. ROBERT GIBSON doe begin to build on the sd. Lott wth:in twelve months after the date hereof and doe proceed to finish wth:out delay one good House twenty foot square at the lease, otherwise this grant to be void and the Lott herein granted lyable to the choice and purchase of any other person according to the Law as fully and amply as if this Grant had never been made; In Wittness whereof the partys to these p:sents have interchangeably sett their hands and seales to two of these Indentures of the same tenor and date
Signed sealed and delivered in p:sence of
WM: BALL,   ROBERT CARTER
SHARSHALL GRASTY, WM: KIGHT

Memord. November 14th 1706. That Livery & Seizen was this day given by the wth:in named ROBERT CARTER unto the wth;in named ROBERT GIBSON of ye wth:in mentioned Lott of Land by the delivery of Turff and Twigg upon the sd. Lott by the sd. CARTER to ye sd. GIBSON in p:sence of us
RICHD: BALL,
EDWIN CONWAY, WM: KIGHT
Recognitr in Cur Com Lancastr: 14th die 9bris: 1706 et recordr
p   JOS: TAYLOE, Clk

p.   THIS INDENTURE made the Thirteenth day of Novembr: Annoq Dom: one thou-
199   sand seven hundred and six; Between ROBERT CARTER, Esqr. of Lancastr: Coty.
         Surviving Feoffee of the TOWNE LAND of the sd. Coty. of the one part and Collo:
WM: TAYLOE of RICHMOND Coty. of the other part; Wittnesseth that the sd. ROBERT CARTER for the sume of One hundred eighty eight pounds of good sound merchantable tobbo: hath sold unto the sd. WM: TAYLOE his heires and assignes for ever one Lott or halfe acre of land in the sd. Towne now called QUEENS TOWNE, No. Fifty Five, according to the Platt thereof made by HARRY BEVERLY, Surveyr: the sd. Lott lying on the S. S. W. side of the Street called ANNE STREET and on the upper side of PRINCES STREET being a corner Lott to the sd. two Streets as by the sd. Platt more plainly appeares; To have and to hold the sd. Lott to him the sd. WM: TAYLOE his heires and assignes for ever; he or they paying rent for the sd. Lott one ounce of Flax seed and two ounces of Hemp seed on the 10th day of Octobr: annually to the Directors or Benchers of the sd. Burg, Provided that the sd. WM: TAYLOE doe begin to build on the sd. Lott wth:in twelve months of the date hereof and proceed to finish wth:out delay one good House twenty feet square at the least, otherwise this Grant to be void & the Lott herein granted lyable to the purchase of any person according to Law; In Wittness whereof the parties have sett their hands and seales
Signed sealed & delivered in p:sence of
HANCOCK LEE,   ROBERT CARTER
JOSEPH BALL, THO: PINKARD

Memord. That Livery & seizen was this day given by the above named ROBERT CARTER of the wth:in mentioned Land unto the wth:in named WM: TAYLOE by delivery of Turff and Twigg on the sd. land in p:sence of

JOSEPH HEALE,
WM. DAIR,   WM: KIGHT
Recognitr in Cur Com Lancaster 14th die 9bris: 1706 et recordr
        p   JOS: TAYLOE, Clk.

THIS INDENTURE made the fourteenth day of Novembr: Annoq Dom: one thousand seven hundred and six; Betweene ROBERT CARTER, Esqr., of Lancastr: Coty., Surviving Feoffee of the TOWNE LAND of the sd. Coty of the one part and JNO: HARRIS of the other part;   Wittnesseth that the said

p.   ROBERT CARTER in consideracon of the sume of One hundred and eighty eight
200   pounds of good sound merchantable tobbo: to him paid hath sold unto the sd.
JNO: HARRIS his heires and assigne for ever one Lott of Land in the sd. Towne now called QUEENS TOWNE, containing Thirty one square perches according to the Platt thereof made the first day of August last by HARRY BEVERLEY, Surveyor, the sd. Lott being No. Thirty Seven, and bounded by the Street called GEORGE STREET on the upper side thereof & the meanders of the Creeke called MADAM BALLS CREEKE being the fifth Lott on the sd. Street from the Great Street called ANNE STREET downe towards the sd. Creeke as by the Platt more plainly appeares; To have and to hold to him the sd. JNO: HARRIS his heires and assignes for ever, he or they paying rent for the sd. Lott one ounce of Flax seed and two ounces of Hemp seed on the 10th day of Octobr: annually to the Directors or Benchers of the sd. Towne for the use of the sd. Burg, Provided tht the sd. JNO: HARRIS begin to build wth:in twelve months and doe proceed wth:out delay one good House twenty foot square at the least otherwise the Lott herein granted lyable to the choice and purchase of any other p:son; In Wittness whereof the parties to these p:sents have sett their hands and seals
Signed sealed and delivered in p:sence of
    WM: FOX.   ROBERT CARTER
    WM: DAIR,   WM: KIGHT
   Memord. That Livery & seizen was this day given by the wth:in named ROBERT CARTER unto the wth:in named JNO: HARRIS of the wth:in menconed Lott of land by the delivery of Turff and Twigg upon the sd. Lott by the said CARTER to the said HARRIS in the p:sence of us
    RICHD: BALL,
    EDWIN CONWAY,   JOS: BALL, JUNR.
   Recognitr: in Cur Com Lancastr: 14th die 9bris: 1706 p ROBERT CARTER et recordr
        p   JOS: TAYLOE, Clk

THIS INDENTURE made the Thirteenth day of Novembr: Annoq Dom: one thousand seven hundred and six: Between ROBERT CARTER, Esqr., of Lancastr: Coty., Surviving Feoffee of the TOWNE LAND of the sd. Coty., of the one part and ELLEN HEALE of the same Coty. of the other part; Wittnesseth that the sd. ROBERT CARTER in consideracon of the sume of One hundred and eighty eight pounds of good sound merchantable tobbo: hath sold unto the sd. ELLEN HEALE her heires or assignes for ever one Lott or half acre of Land wth:in the sd. Towne, now called QUEENS

p.   TOWNE, No. Two, according to the Platt thereof, the sd. Lott being the second
201   Lott upon MALBOROUGH STREET from MADAM BALLS CREEKE by the sd. Platt
    more plainly appeares; To have and to hold to her the sd. ELLEN HEALE her heires & assignes for ever she paying rent of one ounce of Flax seed and two ounces of Hemp seed on the 10th day of Octobr: annually to the Directors or Benchers of the

sd. Towne, Provided that the sd. ELLEN HEALE doe wth:in six months build on the sd. Lott and proceed to finish wth:out delay one good House twenty feet square at the least otherwise this grant to e void & the Lott lyable to the purchase of any other person; In Wittness whereof the sd. parties to these p:sents have sett their hands and seales

Signed sealed & delivered in p:sence of

    JOSEPH HEALE,   ROBERT CARTER

    THO: HOOPER, SHARSHALL GRASTY

   Memord. Novemb: 13th 1706. That Livery & Seizen was tis day given by ROBERT CARTER to ELLEN HEALE of the wth:in menconed Lott of land by the delivery of Turff & Twigg upon the sd. Lott by the sd. CARTER to the sd. HEALE in p:sence of us

    SHARSHALL GRASTY

    THO: HOOPER, JOSEPH HEALE

   Recognitr in Cur Com Lancastr: 13th die 9bris: 1706 p ROBERT CARTER et recordr

         p   JOS: TAYLOE, Clk

    THIS INDENTURE made the Fourteenth day of Novembr: in the yeare one thousand seven hundred & six; Betweene ROBERT CARTER, Esqr., of Lancastr: County, Surviving Feoffee of the TOWNE LAND of the sd. Coty., of the one part and WM: GIBSON of the other part; Wittnesseth that the said ROBERT CARTER for the sume of One hundred eighty eight pounds of good sound merchantable tobbo: hath sold unto the sd. WM: GIBSON his heires and assignes for ever, one Lott or halfe acre of land wth:in the sd. Towne, now called QUEENS TOWNE, according to th Platt thereof made, the sd. Lott or halfe acre of land being No. Fourteene, & bounded by the Street called KING STREET on the lower side thereof being the second Lott on the sd. Street from the Great Street called ANNE STREET downe towards the Creeke called MADAM BALLS CREEKE

p.   To have and to hold the sd. Lott or halfe acre of land to him the sd. WM: GIBSON

202   his heires and assignes for ever; he or they paying the rent of one ounce of Flax seed and two ounces of Hemp seed on the 10th day of Octobr: annually to the Directors or Benchers of the sd. Towne for the use of the sd. Burg, Provided that the sd. WM: GIBSON do begin to build on the sd. Lott wth:in twelve months after the date hereof and doe proceed to finish one good House twenty foot square at the least, otherwise this grant to be void and the Lott herein granted lyable to the purchase of any other p:son according to Law. In Wittness whereof the sd. partys have sett their hands and seales

Signed sealed and delivered in p:sence of

    WM: BALL,   ROBERT CARTER

    SHARSHALL GRASTY, WM: KIGHT

   Memord. Novembr: ye 14th 1706. That Livery & Seizen was this day given by ROBERT CARTER unto WM: GIBSON of the wth:in menconed Lott of Land by delivery of Turff and Twigg upon the sd. Lott by the sd. CARTER to the sd. GIBSON in p:sence of us

    RICHD; BALL,

    EDWIN CONWAY, WM: KIGHT

   Recognitr in Cur Com Lancastr: 14th die 9bris: 1706 et recordr

         p   JOS: TAYLOE, Clk

    THIS INDENTURE made the Fourteenth day of Novembr: Annoq Dom: one thousand seven hundred and six; Betweene ROBERT CARTER, Esqr. of Lancastr: Coty., Surviving Feoffee of the TOWNE LAND of the sd. Coty., of one part and EDWIN CONWAY of the sd. Coty. of Lancastr: of the other part; Wittnesseth tht the said ROBERT CARTER for the sume of One hundred and eighty eight pounds of good merchantable tobbo:

hath sold unto the sd. EDWIN CONWAY his heires and assignes for ever one Lott or halfe acre of land wth:in the sd. Towne now called QUEENS TOWNE No. Eighty Three, according to the Platt thereof, the sd. Lott lying and being betweene DUKE STREET & FAIRFAX STREET opposite to the entrance of BALLS STREET, being the fourth Lott from the Broad Street called ANNE STREET, as by the sd. Platt more plainly appeares;   To have and to hold the sd. Lott or halfe acre of land to him the sd. EDWIN CONWAY his heires and assignes for ever; he or they paying rent for the sd. Lott one ounce of Flax seeds and two ounces of Hemp seeds on the 10th day of Octobr: annually to the Directors or Benchers of the sd. Towne for the use of the sd. Burgh, provided that the sd. EDWIN CONWAY do begin to build on the sd. Lott wth:in twelve months after the date hereof & doe proceed to finish one

p.   good House twenty foot square at the least, otherwise this grnt to be void and
203   the Lott herein granted lyable to the choice and purchase of any other p:son
       as fully as if this grant had never been made;   In Wittness whereof the parties
to these p:sents have sett their hands & seales
Signed sealed & delivered in p:sence of
     WM: FOX,   ROBERT CARTER
     WM: DAIR,   RICHD: BALL
   Memord. Novemb: the 14th 1706. That Livery & Seizen was this day given by the wth:in named ROBERT CARTER unto EDWIN CONWAY of the wth:in menconed Lott of land by the delivery of Turff & Twigg upon the sd. Lott by ye sd. CARTER to the sd. CONWAY in p:sence of
     WM: KIGHT,   RICHD: BALL,
     WM: DAIR,   JO: BALL, JUNR.
     Recognitr in Cur Com: Lancastr: 14th die 9bris: 1706 p ROBERT CARTER et recordr
          p   JOS: TAYLOE, Clk

   THIS INDENTURE made the Fourteenth day of Novembr: Annoq Dom: one thousand seven hundred and six; Betweene ROBERT CARTER, Esqr., of Lancastr: Coty., Surviving Feoffee of the sd. TOWNE LAND of the sd. Coty. of the one part and RICHD: BALL of the same Coty. of the other part; Wittnesseth that the sd. ROBERT CARTER for sume of One hundred and eighty eight pounds of good sound merchantable tobbo: hath sold unto the sd. RICHD: BALL his heires & assignes for ever one Lott or halfe acre of land wth:in the sd. Towne now called QUEENS TOWNE, No. Sixty Six, the sd. Lott or halfe acre lying on the Creeke called MADAM BALLS CREEKE at the head of the sd. Creeke and on the S. S. W. side of the Cane called BALLS CANE, being the Lott next the Creeke as by the sd. Platt more at large will appeare, to him the sd. RICHD: BALL his heires & assignes for ever, he or they paying rent for the sd. Lott one ounce of Flax seeds and two ounces of Hemp seed on the 10th day of Octobr: annually to the Directors or Benchers of the sd. Town for the use of the sd Burgh, Provided that the sd. RICHD: BALL doe proceed to build on the sd. Lott wth:in twelve months from the date hereof & proceed to finish wth:out delay one good house twenty foot squre at the least, otherwise this grant to be void and the Lott herein granted lyable to the choice & purchase

p.   of any other p:son according to Law. In Wittness whereof the parties to these
204   p:sents have sett their hands and seales
       Signed sealed and delivered in p:sence of
       EDWIN CONWAY,   ROBERT CARTER
       WM: DAIR,   WM: FOX
   Memord. Novembr: ye 14th 1706. That Livery & Seizen was given by the wth:in named ROBERT CARTER of the wth:in land unto the wth:in named RICHD. BALL by the

delivering of Turff and Twigg on the sd. Land in p:sence of us
>   WM: DAIR,
>   JO: BALL, JUNR.,   EDWIN CONWAY
>   Recognitr in Cur Com Lancastr: quarto dicimo die 9bris: 1706 p ROBERT CARTER et
> recordr   p   JOS: TAYLOE, Clk.

THIS INDENTURE made the Fourteenth day of Novembr: Annoq Dom: one thousand seven hundred and six;   Betweene ROBERT CARTER, Esqr. of Lancastr; County, Surviving Feoffee of the TOWNE LAND of the sd. Coty., of the one part & JOHN HEALE of the sd. Coty. of the other part;   Wittnesseth tht the sd. ROBERT CARTER for the sume of One hundred and eighty eight pounds of good sound merchantable tobo: hath granted unto the sd. JNO: HEALE his heires and assignes for ever, one Lott or halfe acre of land wth:in the Towne now called QUEENS TOWNE, No. 18,   according to the Platt thereof, the sd. Lott lying on the lower side of KING STREET being the Lott on the side of MADAM BALLS CREEKE being the first Lott next the sd. Creeke as by the sd. Platt more plainly appeares,   To have & to hold the sd. Lott to him the sd. JOHN HEALE his heires & assignes for ever; he or they paying rent for the sd. Lott one ounce of Flax seed and two ounces of Hemp seed on the 10th day of Octobr: annually to the Directors or Benchers of the sd. Towne for the use of the sd. Burgh; Provided that the sd, JOHN HEALE doe begin to build wth:out delay a good House twenty foot square at the least wth:in twelve months after the date hereof otherwise this grant to be void & the Lott herein granted lyable to the choice of any other p:son according to Law.   In Wittness whereof the parties to these p:sents have sett their hands & seales
Signed sealed & delivered in p:sence of
>   WM; BALL,   ROBERT CARTER
>   EDWIN CONWAY,   SHARSHALL GRASTY
>   Memord. Novembr: 14th 1706.   That Livery and seisen was this day given by
> ROBERT CARTER of the wth:in menconed land unto the with:in named JOHN HEALE

p   by delivery of Turff and Twigg upon the sd. Land in p:sence of us
205   WM: DAIR,
>   JO: BALL, JUNR., EDWIN CONWAY
>   Recognitr in Cur Com Lancastr: 14th die 9bris: 1706 et recordr
>   p   JOS: TAYLOE, Clk

THIS INDENTURE made the Thirteenth day of Novembr: one thousand seven hundred and six;   Between ROBERT CARTER, Esqr., of Lancastr: Coty, Surviving Feoffee of the TOWNE LAN of the sd. Coty., of the one part and DANLL. McCARTY of WESTMORELAND Coty. of the other part;   Wittnesseth that the sd. ROBERT CARTER for sume of One hundred and eighty eight pounds of good sound merchantable tobbo: hath sold unto DANLL: McCARTY his heires and assignes for ever one Lott or halfe acre of land wth:in the sd. Towne now called QUEENS TOWN No. Five,   according to the Platt made and laid of into Lotts, the sd. Lott lying on the E. S. E. side of the Street called MARLBROUGH STREET being the second Lott from the Broad Street called ANNE STREET towards the Creeke as by the sd. Platt more plainly appeares,   To have and to hold the sd. Lott or halfe acre of land to the sd. DANLL. McCARTY his heires & assignes for ever he or they paying rent for the sd. Lott one ounce of Flax seed and two ounces of Hemp seed on the 10th day of Octobr: annually to the Directors or Benchers of the sd. Towne for the use of the sd. Towne, Provided that the sd. DANLL. McCARTY doe begin to build on the sd. Lott wth:in twelve months after the date of these p:sents and finish wth:out delay one good House twenty foot square at the least, otherwise this grant to be void & the Lott lyable to the choice & purchase of any other p:son as if this grant had never

been made. In Wittness whereof the parties to these p:sents have sett their hands and seales
Signed sealed & delivered in p:sence of
    RICHD; BALL   ROBERT CARTER
    EDWIN CONWAY, SHARSHALL GRASTY
   Memord. Novembr: ye 13th 1706. That Livery & possession was this day given by ROBERT CARTER of the wth:in menconed land to DANLL. McCARTY by the delivering of Turff & Twigg on the sd. Land in the p:sence of us
    RICHD; BALL,
    EDWIN CONWAY, SHARSHALL GRASTY

p.   THIS INDENTURE made the thirteenth day of Novembr: Annoq: Dom: one thou-
206   sand seven hundred and six; Between ROBERT CARTER, Esqr. of Lancastr: Coty.
Surviving Feoffee of the TOWNE LAND of the sd. Coty., of one part and JOSEPH TAYLOE of the same Coty. of the other part; Wittnesseth that ROBERT CARTER for the sume of One hundred and eighty eight pounds of good sound merchantable tobbo: hath sold unto JOSEPH TAYLOE his heirs & assignes for ever one Lott or halfe acre of land wth:in the Towne now called QUEENS TOWNE No. Thirty according to the Platt thereof made, the sd. Lott lying on the N. N. E. side of the Street called ANNE STREET and on the corner side of GEORGE STREET being a corner lott to the sd. two Streets as by the sd. Platt appeares. To have and to hold the Lott or halfe acre of land to JOS: TAYLOE his heires & assignes for ever, he or they paying rent for the sd. Lott one ounce of Flax seed and two ounces of Hemp seed on the 10th day of Octobr: annually to the Directors or Benches of the sd. Towne for the use of the sd. Towne, Provided that JOSEPH TAYLOE doe begin to build on the sd. Lott wth:in twelve months and doe pro-ceed to finish wth:out delay one good House twenty foot square at least, otherwise this grant to be void & the Lott herein granted lyable to the choice and purchase of any other p:son in as full manner as if this grant had never been made; In Wittness whereof the parties to these p:sents have sett their hands and seales
Signed sealed & delivered in p:sence of
    HANCOCK LEE,   ROBERT CARTER
    JOSEPH HEALE, THO: PINCKARD
   Memord. Novembr: ye 13th 1706. That Livery & possession was this day given by ROBERT CARTER unto ye wth:in JO: TAYLOE by the delivering of Turff and Twigg on the sd. land in p:sence of
    WM: DAIR,
    JOSEPH HEALE, WM: KIGHT
   Recognitr in Cur Com Lancastr. 14th die 9bris: 1706 et recordr
      p.   JOS: TAYLOE, Clk.

   (Lancaster County Deeds &c. No. 9, 1701-1715, will be continued in another book begin-ning in the middle of page 206.)

ACTS of ASSEMBLY. Water Mills 33, For Establishing Towns, 92-98, 104-114.

ADAMS. John 12.

AGRINBY. Edward 16.

ALDERSON. John 84, 85; Lydia 84, Richard 45, 47, 48, 85, 86.

ALLERTON. Isaac (Colo.) 31; William 30, 79. Willoughby 31.

ANCKETILL. Charles 40.

ANDERSON. Ann 50, 51, 62, 63; Henry 5, 51, 63, (William (Carpenter) 50, 63, 80.

ANDREWS. Robert 102, 103.

ANGELL. Uriah 77.

ANGOON. John 54.

ANISS. Walter 59.

ARBUTHNOTT. David (Mercht.) 76.

ARMISTEAD. William 77.

ARNOLD. Grace 4, John (deced) 4.

ATTCHISON. James 55, 56, 92.

ATTKINS. Mark 79.

ATTWOOD. Edward 80, 84.

BABE. John 41, 42, 49.

BAILEY/BAYLEY. Arthur 75; John (deced) 15, 77-79; Richard 95-98; William 71.

BALL. Elizabeth 39; Hannah 35, 58; James 9, 10, 95, 99; Joseph (Colo.) 9, 81; Joseph 59, 60, 88, 89, 108; Joseph Junr. 88, 89, 99, 105, 110, 112, 113, Joseph Senr. 76; Richard 12, 32, 33, 65, 89, 90, 105-110, 112, 112; Richard (Capt.) 104; Thomas 90; William 32, 33, 35, 58, 59, 71, 89, 90, 98, 105, 108, 109, 113; William (Capt., deced) 89, 92-98.

BANKS. Thomas (Cooper) 50, 54.

BARE. William 53, 54.

BARKER. Thomas 20; Thomas Junr. 32, 33.

BARR. John 19.

BEACHER. John 14.

BECKINGHAM. Robert 88.

BELFIELD. Joseph 5, 21, 24, 80-82.

BENDALL. John 71; William (deced) 71.

BENNET. Richard Esqr. 10, 11.

BERKELEY. Sr. William 6, 7, 47.

BERRY. John 1, (deced-20), 59; Sarah 20.

BERTRAND. Charles 13; Chalote 60; John 25.

BEVERLEY. Harry (Surveyor) 92-98.

BEVIS. Richard 50, 54.

BLACKMAN. Mr. (Lieut) 55.

BLACKWELL. John 7.

BLANCH. Thomas 57.

BLEDSOE. Abraham 90.

BLEWFORD. Richard 11.

BOND. Thomas 73.

BOURN. Elizabeth 90; John 90.

BOYD. John 103.

BRADLEY. Henry 10; John 64, 65, Robert 10.

BRASON. John 77.

BRASTER. Thomas 71.

BRENT. George 17, 19, 74, 84; Hugh 7, 74, 75; Hugh Junr. 74, 75.

BRISTOW. Robert 77.

BROMELEY. Margaret 37-39, 48, 49; Mich: 80; Samuel 37-39, 48, 49.

BROUGHTON. Thoams 53, 54.

BROWN. Benjamin 31, 32, 72; John 59, 78, 90, 91, 102; William 8.

BRYAN. Elizabeth 35; John 37, 96, 98.

BUCKLEY. Thomas 16, 17.

BUCKSTON/BUXSTON. John 63, 64, 83, 84.

BUDD. John (a Brewer) 43, 44.

BUNN. John 91.

BURFORD. John 78.

BURGIS. Richard (of Bristoll) 9.

BURMAN. Robert 30.

BURRIDGE. John (Mercht.) 79.

BURROUGHS. Thomas 36.

BUSH. Abraham 19, 73, 74, 82-84; George 73, 74; Jane 42, 82-84, John 13, 31, 32, 64, 73, 74, 82-84; Margaret 63, 64; Nace 31, 32.

BUSHROD. Richard 104.

BUTTLER. Nicholas 25, 26.

BUXTON. John 31, 32, 64, 83, 84; Mercy. 31.

CALE. Charles 88; Nathaniel 88.

CALLIHAN. John 34, 87. 88.

CAMELL. James 44; William 13.

CARNEGIE. John 4, 5, 13, 107, 108.

CARPENTER. Field of 59; John 45, 85; Line of 47, 86; Thomas 20, 66, 67.

CARROLL. Charles 30; John 37.

CARTER. Catherine 28; Edward 27, 28, 34; Henery 3, 13, 22, 27, 28, 66; John 27, 28; John (Lt. Colo.) 39; Peter 13, 66; Robert (Colo.) 8, 9, 19, 21, 39, 40-42, 49, 75, 92-98, 104-114. Thomas 3, 6, 13, 16, 22, 27-29, 33, 34, 66, 96; Thomas (deced) 27, 28; William 37.

CARTYS. Henry 59.

CARY. John 43, 44.

CATHMEAD. Francis 77.

CHADS. Henry 102, 103.

CHATTWIN. Thomas 45, 73, 84, 85.

CHETWOOD. Thomas 26, 27, 100.

CHEWNING. Ann 1, 32, 34, 35, 63, George 31.

CHICHESTER. Richard 14-16, 79, 80.

CHILTON. E. 30, 31; George 12, 27, 65; Joan 40; John 12; John Senr. 39, 40; Tom: 62; William 18.
CHINN. Rawleigh 60.
CHRISTOPHER. Robert 19.
CLAPHAM. William 6, 39; William Junr. 6.
CLARKSON. Thomas 52, 70.
CLAYBOURNE. William 6, 11.
COATES. Thomas 76.
CODD. Anna 30, 31; Berkeley. 31. St. Leger 29-31.
COLE. Mr. 11.
COLLETT. Daniell 73.
COLLINS. Mr. (Cheife Mate) 55.
COLLINGS. Katharine 62.
COMBS. John 55.
COMELINE. James 9, 32, 33.
CONDON. Piere 43.
CONE. John Junr. 45.
CONWAY. Edwin 17, 24, 25, (deced.-30), 47, 90, 105-114; Mr. 72.
COOKE. Elizabeth 21; John 21. Richard (Carpenters Mate) 53, 54; Thomas (Notary Public) 13.
COOPER. Thomas (Capt.) 13.
CORBIN. Gawin Esqr. 15, 52. Thomas (Mercht.) 50.
CORRELL. Abraham 49, 67, 68; Teague 49.
CORRONETT. Peter 54.
COTTEN. Thomas 19.
COTTERELL. William 37.
COUNTIES: Essex 71; Middlesex 5, 40, 41; Northumberland 23, 40, 41, 67, 72, 90, 95, 102, 103, 107; Princes Ann 26, 72, 80, 84, 102; Richmond 19, 25, 26, 29-31, 34, 45, 55, 70, 74, 80, 87, 88, 91, 92. Stafford 19, 74, 84; Westmoreland 31, 40, 113.
COX. Mary 36; Thomas 36.
CRAIG. Gabriell 22.
CRAWFORD. John 22.
CREEKS: Abbyes 59; Claphams 46, 47; Conaways 30; Grimes 98; Hutching his Creek 68; Indian 74; Machmaps Branch 41; Machih: Point 27; Madam Balls 92-97; Marshalls 1; Mine Branch 63; Moraticoe 34, 41, 55, 66, 67, 69, 70, 83, 85, 87, 88; Mount Tierall 60; Nansunsia Branch 41; Nantepeyson 36, 37; Parting 51; Peavine 63; Powells 37, 88; Reedy Branch 37; Slaughters 23; Tabbs 49, 67.
CROMWELL. Contraction of 9.
CROSSE. David (Mercht.) 61.
CUDLIP. Richard 50-54.
CULLIN. Elizabeth 70; Katherine 70; Sarah 70.
CULPEPER. Lady Margtt. 19, 40, 73, 83.
CURTIS. John 40-42.

DALE. Edward (Majr., deced) 28, 39.
DARE. John 55; Mr. 75; William 36, 56, 57, 60, 69, 70, 75, 88, 92, 104-106, 110, 112-114.
DAVENPORT. Fortunatus 53, 87, 88; William 50, 51, 62.
DAVIS. Corderoy 51; Elizabeth (Lawson) 23; John 28; John (Mate of ye Ketch) 43, 44; Nathaniel 21; Robert 23; Thomas 54.
DAWKINS. William 77.
DENHAM. Elenor 58; Martha 58; Robert 57-59.
de PERRUE. Peters 54.
DEVERALL. Jeremiah 14.
DICKESON. Henry 13, 14.
DICKIE. David 77.
DICKSON. John 45.
DOWNEMAN. Rawleigh 77.
DRAPER. William (Blacksmith) 11, 12, 25, 26, 32.
DRUMMOND. Drake 103.
DUDLESTON. Susana 14.
DUGGAN. John 18.
DUKESHALL. Joseph 15, 71.
DUNBABIN. Thomas 53.
DUNN. William Junr. 22.

ECCLES. John 102, 103.
EDGAR. John (deced) 73; Thomas 72, 73.
EDMONDS. Elyas 30.
EDWARDS. John 4.
ELDRIDGE. John (Lieut) 55.
ELLIS. Edward 80.
ELMORE. Peter 74.
ENGLAND: Bristoll 9, 13, 51, 66, 74; Cork 43; County of Middlesex 2; Dorsett 40; Kingdom of 33; Liverpoole 8, 24, 33, 34, 66, 72, 73, 76; London 2, 8, 9, 10, 30, 50, 52, 55, 75-80; Londonderry 21; Lyme 79; Waterford 43; Weymouth 76; White Haven 8, 75, 79.
ESKRIDGE. George 79.

FAIREMAN. John 59.
FAIRFAX. Catherine 19, 40, 73, 83; Thomas Lord 19, 40, 73, 83.
FANTLEROY. Moore 11.
FARR. Judith 71.
FINCH. Elizabeth 85; George 45, 60; George Senr. 85, 86.
FINDLEY. John 91.
FITZHUGH. William 17, 19, 74, (Colo.) 82, 84; William Junr. 74, 84.
FLEET. Henry (Capt.) 21, 62, 94; Henry Junr. 62.
FLIN. Edward 28, 29.

FLINT. Martha 58, 61; Richard 1, 2, 58, 61, 63, 69, 70.

FLOWER. George 37, 102; John 37.

FLOYD. John (deced) 12, 65; William 12.

FORBES. George 7, 9.

FOULER. James 8.

FOX. David (Capt., deced) 92-98; Samuell 11, 12, (Capt.) 25, 55; Mill of 60; William (Capt.) 55, 56, 69, 70, 93, 97, 105, 106, 108, 110, 112.

FRISTER. Lettice (Wade) 55-57, 92; Richard 55-57, 92.

FRIZELL. Franciscoe 15, 71, 72, 101, 102; Mary 71.

GARRETT. Richard 24.

GARTON. William 35, 36.

GATES. James 25.

GAYNER. James 72.

GENDRON. Mark 7-9, 36, 37; Mary 36, 37.

GEORGE. Grace 4; Grace (Dau. of Grace) 4; Mary 3, 4; Nicholas 3, 4, 10.

GESTER. Anthony (Capt.) 78, 79.

GIBSON. Edward 22, 37, 49, 68; John 57; Robert 21, 23, 80-82, 107-109; William 111.

GILES. Margtt: 100; Matthias 4, 16, 33.

GLASSCOCKS. John 54.

GOODRIAR. Robert 33.

GOODRIDGE. William 45, 84-86.

GOODWIN. John 50, (Mercht) 75, 78, 79; Nicholas (Mercht.) 79.

GOOKINS. Daniell (Capt.) 7, 11.

GOSLIN. Samuell 3, 20.

GOURDOUNE. William 30.

GRASSON. John 37, 90.

GRASTY. Sharshall 92-97, 107-109, 111, 113, 114.

GRAVES. Thomas 3, (Capt.) 10, 40, 77.

GREEN. John 103.

GREG. Land of 17, 23, 102, 103.

GRIFFIN. Madam 52.

GRIGGS. Ann (Scholfield) 23; Line of 23; Michaell 23.

GRIMLY. Old Field 31.

GROVE. Bryan 18, 49, 68; Robert 40.

GRYMES. Charles 59, Old Field 63; Patrick 83.

GUESS. Johnathan 15.

GWYE. John 22.

HACKETT. Thomas (Capt.) 1.

HAINES. James 75, 78.

HALL. Jane 51; John 51, 71, 84, 98, 99, 103; Robert 75-80, (Mercht.) 102; William (Publique House) 43, 44.

HALTRIDGE. James 22.

HANKS. William 25; William Senr. 26.

HARDING. Thomas 77.

HARRIS. John 36, 59, 100, 110.

HARRISON. Edward (Cl Cur) 83; Joseph 20.

HART. John 91; John Senr. 91.

HARTWELL. Henry (Cl.) 46.

HARVEY. Isaac 76.

HARWARD. George 17.

HARWOOD. George 21; Thomas 51, 99.

HATHAWAY. Thoams 102.

HAY. Timothy 80.

HAYES. Edward 84; John 84.

HAYNES. Edward 58; James 36, 93, 97, 102; Martha 57, 58; Thomas 43.

HAYNIE. Anthony 72; Richard 57.

HAYWARD. Hugh 45, 46.

HAYWOOD. Charles 40.

HEAD. John (Comdr.) 7.

HEALE. Ellen 103, 104, 110, 111; John 113; Joseph 93, 94, 97, 99, 105-107, 110, 111, 114; Nicholas 4.

HEARD. Martha 36; Walter 90, 91; William 36, 91.

HENRY. Hugh 103.

HERNE. Ben: 95.

HEWARD. William 29.

HICKSON. Anthony 79.

HIDE. John (Capt.) 80.

HIGGINSON. Charles 22.

HILL. James 24, 25, 70; Job 73; John 13; Joseph 50; Robert 16.

HINDE. John 7; Thomas 24, 25.

HOLLAND. Joseph 4.

HOLMS. Gabriel 102.

HONE. Theophilus 60.

HOOPER. Thoams 9, 92, 94-97, 106, 111.

HOPKINS. Philip 44; Robert 61, 62.

HORTON. Tobias 49, 68, 74.

HOWARD. Martha 44; William 44, 63, 64, 74, 82, 83, 105.

HUFF. Robert 67, 68.

HUGHES. Robert 70, 71.

HUMPHREY. John (Notary Public) 102, 103.

HUNTER. William 72.

HUTCHINS/HUTCHINGS. Ellinor 12; John 12, 17, 65.

INNIS. James (Clk. Prop. Off.) 41.

INNYS. Jeremy 65.

IRELAND. Belfast 21, 22, 103; Beaumaurice 8; Dublin 7; Kingdom of 22.

IRONMONGER. William 90.

IVES. Thomas 88.

JACKSON. Andrew 5, 75, 76.

JAMES. Jeremy 13; Richard 11; Walter 68.

JAMES CITTY 10.
JEFFREY. Edward 25, 26, 60; Herbert 46,
  (Governor-83).
JENKINS. Abigall 73; Henery 73.
JOHNSON. Mary 60.
JONES. John 30; Robert 19.

KELLY. Amy 20; Charles 62; Jane 62;
  John 20, 49; William 55-57.
KENNAN. James 73.
KILLGORE. Peter 38.
KING. Charles 13; James 7, 9.
KINLEY. Hugh (deced) 39.
KIRK. Christopher 13, 35, 65, 66, 68;
  Christopher Junr. 35, 66; Elizabeth 66;
  James 13, 65, 68; Thomas 35, 68.
KIGHT. William 105-107, 109-111, 114.
KIRKMAN. Fra: 7.
KNIGHT. Ann 67, 68; Leonard 67, 68.

LADNER. Ann 32, 33; Hugh 32, 33, 74, 100;
  Susanna 100.
LANCASTER. John 24, 25.
LAWNE. John 20.
LAWRENCE. Mary 29, 100, 101; Sarah 29;
  William 68, 101; William (deced) 57.
LAWRIE. John 1, 2, (Ship Carpenter) 28, 29,
  51, 62.
LAWSON. Elizabeth 23; Epaphroditus (deced)
  6, 23, 94; Henry 78; Mr. 17; Robert Junr. 79;
  Rowland 75, 78, 94; Rowland Senr. 22;
  William 66.
LAX. William 13, 16.
LEE. Charles 17; Elizabeth (Medstaid) 23;
  Hancock 39, 79, 95, 96, 98, 109, 110, 114;
  Richard 30, (Colo. -31).
LEWIS. John 31.
LIGGATT. William (Comdr.) 8.
LISTER. William 13, 39, 65, 75, 76, 78, 79,
  96-98.
LOE. Martha 59; Thomas 20, 59, 62, 70.
LOMAX. Elizabeth 49; John 41, 42.
LORD. William 40.
LOVE (Capt.) 55.
LOYD. George 80; John 81.
LUCKHAM. John 35, 64, 65; Line of 63.
LUDWELL. Phillip (Clerk) 7, 47;
  Thomas (Secretary) 7.

McCARTY. Daniell 17, 24, 61, 69, 104, 113.
McMILLAN. John 73.
McCLUER. James 22.
McMUN. John 102, 103.

MacADAMS. Patrick 75, 76.
MACKENNY. John 53, 54.

MACKEY. Thomas (Mercht) 45, 46.
MACKRELL. James 43.
MACKRONE. Patrick 100.
MAKENIE. Francis 21.
MADISON. Land of 17.
MAIN. John 22.
MALLIS. John 51.
MALSCET. John 54.
MAN. Elizabeth 72; William 32, 33, 88.
MARSHALL. Thomas (deced) 1, 44.
MARTIN. Nicholas 103; Thomas 16, 37,
  100.
MARYLAND. Cecile Co. 44; Kent Co. 29-31;
  Somerset Co. 73.
MASON. George 45, 46; Thomas 27.
MASTERS. Abraham 54.
MATHEW. John 45, 48, 85, 86;
  Jonath: 50; Samuell (Governor -6).
MEDSTAID. Elizabeth 23; Thomas 23.
MEEKS. Mary 86,.
MERIDITH. John 30; Mary 100, 101;
  William (Marriage -100, 101).
MERRALL. Thomas 3, 10.
MERRYMAN. William 27, 99.
MERRIS. John 49.
MILLER. John 64, 72; Randolph 72, 89;
  William 64.
MILLING. Arch: 22.
MILLNER. William 35.
MILLS: Balls 32; Foxes 32, 72;
  Moraticoe 67.
MINGE. James (Clerk -43).
MINNS. Jacob Junr. 43.
MITCHELL. William 3, 4.
MONK. Thomas (Carpenter) 53, 54.
MOON. Abraham (deced) 40, 41, 55, 58, 69;
  Elizabeth 40-42; Robert 33, 34.
MOORE. Fran: 9; Hanah 15, 71, 72;
  Patrick 22; William 3, 15, 71, 72.
MORRIS. John (deced) 37; Line of 68.
MORSE. Francis 27.
MOTT. John 12, 44, 45, 65, 84, 85;
  John Junr. 35; Line of 59.
MOULD. Lawrence 23.
MULLIS. Abigall 18; Elizabeth (Wife of
  John) 17, 18, 29; Elizabeth (Dau. of John)
  18; George 17, 18; John 17, 18, 29, 72;
  John (Son of John) 17, 18; Mary 18;
  Richard 17, 18; Stephen 17, 18.
MYARS. Mathew 59.

NEASUM. Frances 100; Robert 99, 100;
  William (deced) 99.
NEWMAN. John 71.
NICHOLS. Zachariah 25, 26.

PACKQUET. Jeremy (Naturalizacon of) 42, 43.
PAINE. Susanna 58, 100.
PARRISH. North Farnham 70.
PASSATT. Richard 77.
PEIRCE. Benjamin 54.
PEMBERTON. John (Mercht) 76.
PENSAX. Samuell 30, 31.
PENSILVANIA 14; Philadelphia 43.
PERRY. Micajah & Compa. 75, 80.
PETER. Thomas (Mercht.) 61.
PETTY. Katharine 20; Thomas 19, 20
PHILLIPS. James 20, 34; John 11, 13, 34;
  Thomas 26, 27, 99; Thomas (Father of Tho-
  mas) 27; Tobias 49.
PILL. John 45.
PINKARD. John 20; Thomas 77, (Capt.) 102,
  108.
PLACES. Winsmoores Cove 1; Court House 1,
  Corotoman 3, 13, 47; Gum Swamp 49;
  Jamaico 52, 55; Rappahannock 102; Spring
  Cove 51; Guinny 55; Millstone Point 57; Car-
  ter's Mill 21; Fleets Bay 12, 36, 65, 67, Rappa:
  Forrest 17; Torkill Neck 36, ye Gulfe 37, 49;
  Tylers Neck 15; Potomack 21; Little Wicocomoco
  21; Wattery Swamp 24; Vine Neck 31; Hoggs
  Hedd Neck 31, 63, New Plantacon Neck 31;
  Morrattico 32; Faire Wethers Neck 3; Deep Bottom
  Bridge 37; Margaries 39; Nominie 40; Mettotos-
  son Swamp 41; Mount Noddy Swamp 48; Nante-
  poyson Path 49; Plantation Neck Swamp 63; New
  Plantation Neck Swamp 63; Morraticoe Mill Swamp
  73; Pocokences Cove 74; Thatchers Mill Damm 68;
  Eagles Nest 98; Foxes Mill Seamp 104; Great
  Wicocomoco 103.
POLLARD. Martha 11; Robert (Secretary) 6, 7, 10,
  11, 25, 71.
POPE. Thomas 13.
POWE. Lewis 80.
PRICE. Elinor 61.
PRITCHARD. Mrs. 48; Robert 16.
PUCKLE. James (Notary Public) 3, 9, 10.
PURFEY. Thomas 88.
PURSELL. Tobias 90, 91.
PURVIS. George (Mariner) 9, 10; John 2, 3.
PYLE. Anthony Senr. 43.
PYNES. John 34, 35.

QUEENS TOWNE. 92-98, 104-114.

RANKIN. John 51, 101, 102.
READ. William 79.
REEVES. John 100.
REYNOLDS. Peter 13.
RHOODES. John 61.
RICHARDSON. John 44.
RICHISON. John 80.

RINE. Martha 74.
RIVERS: Corotoman 4, 7, 11, 12, 30-32, 39,
  46, 47, 57, 65, 90; Elizabeth 102;
  James 52; Morratico 45, 47, 64; Rappa-
  hannock 5-7, 9, 11, 12, 14, 22, 59, 61, 99;
  Sassafras 44; Washington 12, 25.
ROACH. John 13.
ROBERTSON. John 15, 33, 81, 82;
  William 9.
ROBINSON. Elizabeth 35; Giles 35, 38;
  Isaac 35; John 77; Thomas 77;
  William 22, 35, 38, 39, 48.
ROGERS. Noah 51, 71.
ROSE. Matthias 4.
ROSS. Ruben 16.
ROWDEN. Isaac 19.
ROWLEY. Line of 73.

SALKELD. Henry (Mercht.) 98.
SAMPSON. Grace(George) 4; Thomas 4.
SANDERS/SAUNDERS. Duke 63, 64, 88;
  Edward 72.
SCHOLFEILD. Ann (deced) 23; Elinor
  (deced) 23; Judith 24; Robert 15, 17, 23,
  24, 38, 102; Robert Junr. 17.
SCOT. Hugh 22.
SCOTTLAND. Dumfries 73.
SEMHOUSE. Peter 80.
SENR. Robert 77.
SEWALL. Nicholas 30.
SHAPLEIGH. Phillip 21.
SHARP. John 1, 41, 61, 62, 69, 70, 83,
  99; John (deced) 56, 69, 70; Margaret
  Widow 70.
SHAW. John 37, 38, 49, 50, 52;
  Rebecca 37, 38.
SHELLTON. John 34.
SHIPS & VESSELLS: America of London 7;
  Africa 79; Charles of Belfast 102; Feild
  Frigitt 78; Glocester 80; Keel Boat 59;
  Ketch of Waterford 43, 44; Expectacon
  Ketch of Maryland 44; Corbin 50; Nor-
  wich 55; ye Earl Gally 55; Seaflower Car-
  goe 80; William of Belfast 3; John &
  Susanna 13, 14; Providence 8, 9; Shal-
  lope ye Vine of Rappa: 15.
SHORT. Elizabeth 67, 68; William 67, 68.
SIMMONS. Jon: 67; Thomas 102;
  William 60, 61.
SIMPSON. John 87.
SMITH. Nicholas 14, 74; Richard 90;
  Robert 14; William 43, 76.
SMITHER. George 42, 43.
SMOOT. William 13.
SPENCER. Elizabeth 32; George 32.
STANFORD. Vincent 6, 7, 11.